PRACTICING LEADERSHIP

Principles and Applications

SECOND EDITION

ARTHUR SHRIBERG
Xavier University

DAVID SHRIBERG
Northeastern University

CAROL LLOYD
Lloyd Communications

JOHN WILEY & SONS, Inc.
New York • Chichester • Weinheim
Brisbane • Singapore • Toronto

Acquisitions Editor   Jeff Marshall
Associate Editor   Cindy Rhoads
Marketing Manager   Charity Robey
Senior Production Editor   Norine M. Pigliucci
Senior Designer   Kevin Murphy
Production Management Services   Charlotte Hyland

This book was set in New Caledonia by Pine Tree Composition, Inc., and printed and bound by Courier Westford. The cover was printed by Phoenix Color Corp.

This book is printed on acid-free paper. ∞

Library of Congress Cataloging in Publication Data:
Shriberg, Arthur.
     Practicing leadership : principles and applications / Arthur Shriberg, David Shriberg, Carol Lloyd.—2nd ed.
          p. cm.
     Rev. ed. of: Practicing leadership / Arthur Shriberg . . . [et al.].
     Includes bibliographical references and index.
     ISBN 0-471-39283-9 (pbk. : alk. paper)
     1. Leadership. I. Shriberg, David. II. Lloyd, Carol (Carol A.) III. Practicing leadership. IV. Title.

HD57.7 .P7 2001
658.4′092—dc21

                                                                                          2001017835

Printed in the United States of America

10   9   8   7   6   5   4   3   2

ABOUT THE AUTHORS

Arthur Shriberg is the Downing Professor of Management at Xavier University and a well-known leadership and management consultant. He has degrees from Columbia University (Ed.D.), Boston University (M.A.), Xavier University (MBA), and the Wharton School at the University of Pennsylvania (B.A.). He has served as Vice President and/or Dean at four universities. He has assisted over fifty companies with various organizational challenges.

David Shriberg received his B.S. from Cornell University, his M.S. from Northeastern University, and is working on his Ph.D. at Northeastern. Mr. Shriberg is a school psychologist, writer, and diversity trainer in the greater Boston area.

Carol Lloyd is a professional writer and syndicated columnist who has been published in several well-known magazines, newspapers, and journals.

Gordon Barnhart, creator of the Heroes' Journey Model found in Chapter 9, is a management consultant who has worked with numerous *Fortune* 500 companies.

Amy Burke, a professional writer, has a B.A. from the University of Illinois, an M.A. from Georgetown University, and is a Ph.D. candidate at Brandeis University.

Megan Clough has a B.A. from Bates College and an M.S. from Miami University of Ohio. She currently resides in Hampden, Maine, and is a management consultant for Global Lead Management Consulting

E. Paul Colella received his Bachelor's, Master's, and Doctorate degrees from Fordham University. He is a Professor of Philosophy and the Director of University Scholars program at Xavier University. He is also an accomplished musician.

Stephen R. Covey is the founder and chairman of the Covey Leadership Center. His book, 7 *Habits of Highly Successful People,* has sold over 2 million copies.

Anne Harbison is cofounder and President of Leadership & Learning Solutions, LLS, a performance consulting firm based in Medford, Massachusetts. She consults and writes on issues of adult development and workplace learning.

Timothy Kloppenborg received his Bachelor's, Master's, and Doctorate degrees from the University of Cincinnati. He is an Associate Professor of Management at Xavier University and a consultant in project management, quality and teaming.

James M. Kouzes and **Barry Z. Posner** are the authors of the critically acclaimed *Credibility* and many other well-known management and leadership books.

Stephen Mullin is a reserve officer in the U.S. Marines. He is rising in the ranks of Fifth-Third Bank, where he has served as a Trust Officer and Director of Training.

John E. Pepper, after serving in a variety of roles including President and Chief Executive Officer, recently returned to the role of Chairman of the Board of Procter & Gamble.

Judy L. Rogers is a well-known educator and Director of Graduate Services in Student Personnel Administration at Miami University (Ohio).

Steven Ruedisili, Esq. has taught law at the University of Zambia in Africa and at Marquette University. He is currently a management consultant with the Gallup Organization in Boston, Massachusetts.

Mary Lynn Williamson recently joined private industries after serving as Senior Student Affairs Officer at several universities, including Arkansas State University and Henderson State University.

ACKNOWLEDGMENTS

The initial text and the second edition have been a collaborative effort including a great many dedicated people. David Shriberg, my son and co-author, was the primary writer of several chapters and profiles and helped coordinate all aspects of the project. He wrote most of the Leadership Moments, Create Your Own Theory, and Questions for Discussion and Review. A longtime colleague, Carol Lloyd gave continuity to the text by editing many of the chapters and writing several profiles. Much of the creativity in the exercises is the result of Mary Lynn Williamson's insight and skill.

Judy Rogers, Ann Harbison, Amy Burke, Paul Collela, Steve Ruedisili, Megan Clough, and Steve Mullin all took primary responsibility for the content of chapters in their areas of expertise, while Tim Kloppenborg and Gordon Barnhart helped write parts of chapters in this edition. We are particularly grateful to Lou Kruger, Professor at Northeastern University, John E. Pepper, Chairman of the Board of Procter & Gamble, and well-known leadership authors James Kouzes, Barry Posner, and Stephen Covey for their original contributions to this text.

Researchers for this edition include Katia Zhestkova, Eddie Bitzer, Nikkil Kockhar, Libby Nash, and Joyce Cerejo. Assistance was also given by Marjorie Shriberg, Rebecca Shriberg, Michael Shriberg, Steven Shriberg, Ena Vazquez-Nuttall, Mauricio Munoz, and many of my students who wrote reviews of the first edition. Valuable typing assistance was given by Shirlee James and Donna Waymire.

We also appreciate the work of the staff at Wiley, including Jeff Marshall, Jessica Garcia, Charlotte Hyland, Jeff Marshall, Norine Pigliucci, and Kevin Murphy and the reviewers, including Dennis Slevin, University of Pittsburgh; Bill Bolton, Washington University; Richard Boyatsis, Case Western Reserve University; Paula Hill, Southern Methodist University; William Howe, University of Richmond; Dan Costly, New Mexico State University; Dayle Smith, University of San Francisco; Charles Sterrett, Frostburg State University; Joseph Koppel, University of San Francisco; Jeffrey Miles, University of Illinois at Urbana-Champaign; Michael Whitty, Santa Clara University; Bill Greenwood, Shepherd College.

Art Shriberg

TABLE OF CONTENTS

CHAPTER 7   MILITARY SCIENCE: THE ART OF COMMAND
Stephen Mullin

Section III Leadership Theory: Present and Future

CHAPTER 8   PRACTICING LEADERSHIP
IN A MULTICULTURAL SOCIETY   *Anne Harbison,*
Steven Reudisili, Arthur Shriberg

INDEX   241

For Appendix II, Appendix III, and the References, please visit the Wiley Web site at www.wiley.com/college/shriberg. Appendix II gives brief overviews of popular books that are readily available and reinforce concepts found in the subject matter of each chapter. A list of the works discussed follows.

APPENDIX II   LEADERSHIP BY THE BOOK: SUMMARIES OF POPULAR LEADERSHIP WORKS

Chapter 1: Stephen R. Covey, *Principle-Centered Leadership;* John W. Gardner, *On Leadership;* Peter Senge, *The Fifth Discipline: The Art and Practice of the Learning Organization*
Chapter 2: Dean Tjosvold and Mary M. Tjosvold, *Psychology for Leaders: Using Motivation, Conflict, and Power to Manage More Effectively;* Abraham H. Maslow, *Maslow on Management*
Chapter 3: Lee G. Bolman and Terrence E. Deal, *Reframing Organizations: Artistry, Choice and Leadership*
Chapter 4: Jay A. Conger and Rabindra N. Kanungo, *Charismatic Leadership in Organizations*
Chapter 5: James M. Kouzes and Barry Z. Posner; *Credibility*
Chapter 6: Mark Landy and Sid Milkis, *Presidential Greatness*
Chapter 7: Joe D. Batten, *Tough-Minded Leadership*
Chapter 8: George F. Simons, Carmen Vazquez, and Philip R. Harris, *Transcultural Leadership: Empowering the Diverse Workforce*
Chapter 9: Bert Nanus, *Visionary Leadership*
Chapter 10: Warren Bennis, *Managing the Dream: Reflections on Leadership and Change;* Ken Blanchard and Sheldon Bowles, *Gung Ho!* Peter Block, *Stewardship;* Mas De Pree, *Leading Without Power: Finding Hope in Serving Community;* Robert K. Greenleaf, *The Power of Servant Leadership;* Charles C. Manz and Henry P. Sims, Jr., *Superleadership: Leading Others to Lead Themselves*
Chapter 11: James A. Belasco and Ralph C. Stayer, *Flight of the Buffalo*

CHAPTER 1

Getting Started

LEADERSHIP MOMENT

It is the first day of class and the professor has written the following question on the board: "Who is a leader?" The class is then divided into groups of four, with instructions that they talk about their ideal leaders and identify their common denominators.

Johannes is first. He says, "This is easy. Leaders are people who can direct others—like Napoleon or Patton. They don't let other people tell them what to do and they are people that everyone respects because if you cross them..."

"I agree that leaders are people that others respect," says Peter, "but I think the mark of a great leader is someone who works not for glory but for the betterment of others, like Mother Teresa or Gandhi or Nelson Mandela—or even Jesus Christ. Leaders do it for other people—if you're only in it for glory, you're not really a leader."

"I think you both are forgetting about the little guy," says Maya. "Sure, Napoleon and Mandela are leaders who changed the world, but what about people who aren't heads of armies or heads of state? I think leadership is found in everyday acts, like the Columbine teacher [Dave Sanders] who died trying to save his students or the single mom who works three jobs to send her children to college. Those are the real leaders."

"Looks like it's up to you to make sense of it all," says Johannes.

1. *What would you do?*
2. *Which leaders might you add to this list?*
3. *Are all of the group's ideas about leadership valid? Why or why not?*
4. *Are there any common denominators among these differing ideas on leadership?*

As we begin the new millennium, everyone is talking, writing, theorizing about, and searching for leadership. We have only to look at the abundance of literature, popular videos, seminars, and formal courses to see how the notion of leadership captivates us. Leadership development is now considered an increasingly important part of a college education as evidenced by the burgeoning number of graduate and undergraduate leadership courses and the new centers and schools for leadership established at numerous colleges.

However, our fascination with leadership is nothing new. Long before the psychologists and management scientists of the twentieth century worked at defining and measuring leadership, Plato, Machiavelli (see Appendix I for more detail on preindustrial influences on leadership), and Shakespeare offered images of leadership cast in the context of their times. And yet there is no common agreement on leadership's meaning. James McGregor Burns (1979) captured the elusiveness of the concept when he noted, "Leadership is one of the most observed and least understood phenomena on earth."

Whatever it is, we need it, desperately. We yearn for a great leader who, we imagine, can foresee what we must know and do to negotiate the constant change and ambiguity facing us in the twenty-first century. We bemoan the absence of great leaders who can give us rock-solid answers in these uncertain times.

Because it is generally agreed that leadership is vital for our survival as a society, we should hasten to prepare people to be leaders. It is in this context—the call for twenty-first-century leadership—that we set about writing this book.

WHY THIS BOOK?

Why add to the already towering pile of books on the subject? We offer a fusion of several different ways to examine leadership in a decidedly unconventional leadership text. Although we include some of the traditional perspectives on the subject, we have tried to build into the text a more comprehensive approach.

Not simply a collection of theories, this book considers the ideas most useful to building a personal approach to practicing leadership. Nor is this book a skills approach. Don't look to this text as *The Five Minute Leader*. We will certainly incorporate information about the implications of many disciplines for practicing leadership, but it's *not* a how-to book.

Finally, this book is not about finding the ideal model. We haven't found the "perfect leader" whom we can all simply study and emulate. We don't think there is such a person. However, we have included "snapshots" of people practicing leadership in a variety of settings and cultural contexts. Here are four such snapshots of leaders for the ages—Miep Gies, who, risking her own life every day, provided aid to the family of Anne Frank during World War II; King Hussein of Jordan, the man who courageously befriended both Israel and Palestine in the name of peace; Martin Luther, whose acts of leadership and conviction led to the formation of modern Protestantism; and Nelson Mandela, an imprisoned hero whose moral leadership was pivotal to the end of apartheid in South Africa. Facing vastly different challenges, these leaders combined moral force and dogged determinism to accomplish their end goals. Their lives and choices, along with those of other individuals profiled in this textbook, serve as models as each of us seeks to create our own leadership path.

MIEP GIES: HIDER, HELPER

In the Prologue to *Anne Frank Remembered, The Story of the Woman Who Helped to Hide the Frank Family*, Miep Gies wrote:

> I am not a hero. I stand at the end of the long, long line of good Dutch people who did what I did or more—much more—during those dark and terrible times years ago, but always like yesterday in the hearts of those who bear witness. Never a day goes by that I do not think of what happened then.
>
> More than twenty thousand Dutch people helped to hide Jews and others in need of hiding during those years. I willingly did what I could to help. My husband did as well. It was not enough.

Just over five feet tall, this blue-eyed blonde was a sickly child in Vienna when WWI began. Sent to the Netherlands in a humanitarian program for hungry Austrian children, Gies was informally adopted by a large and loving Dutch family. Eventually she came to consider herself a Dutch national. In her early adolescence she kept a diary, much like her future friend Anne Frank was to do.

In Amsterdam, Gies started working for Travies and Co., makers of products for the homemaker. She became friends with the president, a shy man named Otto Frank. Gradually she and her fiancé became good friends with the entire Frank family.

Gies was given increasing responsibility in the small company, and eventually she became a trusted advisor to Otto. She and her husband, Jan, were among the very few to know the whereabouts of the Franks and the four others hidden above the business address in Amsterdam. Daily she visited the residents of the "Annex," as Anne called it in her diary. She saw to every detail of their lives, growing exhausted with the strain of trying to feed eight people on stolen ration cards for five, a situation made more frantic by the poor conditions in occupied Holland.

She and Jan also sheltered another Jewish person in their own house for months at a time, although she never told the Franks of this fact, fearing that it would worry them. Jan also took part in the underground resistance.

Despite their careful efforts, the German Secret Service discovered the secret annex, and on August 4, 1945, Miep watched them take away her friends. She was able to save the diary that became a classic tale of courage. Miep notes that she had to be persuaded to write *Anne Frank Remembered:*

> I had to think of the place that Anne Frank holds in history and what her story has come to mean for the many millions of people who have been touched by it. I'm told that every night when the sun goes down, somewhere in the world the curtain is going up on the stage play made from Anne's diary.... Her voice has reached the far edges of the earth.

Gies and her husband hoped for an eventual return of the Franks—in fact, she even went on foot to the Gestapo in a bold attempt to bribe officials for their freedom. She kept the business going despite horrible conditions—no food, no coal, little hope. Many times she bicycled out to the country, evading German guards, to beg for food from farmers. She somehow managed to keep the company alive, knowing once again that others depended on her.

After the Germans surrendered, Otto Frank came home from Auschwitz; the rest of the Frank family did not. Miep relinquished the leadership of the business to him. She had been an effective leader in an extremely difficult period, but she knew it was time to step down.

Otto Frank lived with Jan and Miep, coming to consider them family, for seven years until he moved to be near his mother in Switzerland. For long months after the war ended, Mr. Frank, Miep, and Jan waited to hear about Anne and her sister who had been sent to a work camp at Bergen-Belsen. Finally, a letter from the camp nurse confirmed the worst: both girls had died from typhus. Anne had died only a few weeks before the camp was liberated.

It was only then that Miep turned to Anne's diary. Having left it untouched for over a year, she gave the papers to Mr. Frank, saying, "Here is your daughter Anne's legacy to you."

Miep withdrew totally from the business, feeling that taking care of three men at home—Jan, Otto Frank, and another family friend—was her full-time job.

She has since turned her attention to keeping Anne's memory alive. Working with the Anne Frank Foundation, Miep Gies has traveled throughout the world, telling the story of a young girl whose humanity could not be silenced. Characteristically, she shrugs off praise for her role in the drama:

> My story is the story of very ordinary people during extraordinarily terrible times. Times the like of which I hope with all my heart will never, never come again. It is for all of us ordinary people all over the world to see to it that they do not.

KING HUSSEIN: A MONARCH TURNS INTERNATIONAL PEACEMAKER

Being a head of state in the treacherous terrain of the Middle East is a significant challenge for even the most savvy of leaders. Jordan's King Hussein, however, did not have the luxury of time or experience before assuming leadership of his nation. Born on November 14, 1935, he was only 16 when he witnessed the assassination of his grandfather King Abdullah—then King of Jordan—in Jerusalem. The young Hussein's life was saved when a bullet headed for his chest was deflected by a medal he was wearing. He was named King at age 17 and formally ascended the throne on his eighteenth birthday. Few at this time expected that this young King would hold his throne, let alone become by the time of his death in 1999 the longest-ruling head of state in the world.

Not that Hussein did not have challenges to his rule. Acting decisively, before his twenty-first birthday this distinctive 5-foot-4-inch leader had already ousted the British army commander he had inherited and fended off an attempted military coup. Over the next 43 years, he survived 17 known assassination attempts, a disastrous war with Israel in 1967 in which Jordan lost much territory (including all of its holdings in Jerusalem), a civil war with the Palestinians in which he sent Yassir

Arafat into exile, and a shaky balancing act during the Persian Gulf War between his Western and Middle Eastern allies.

Never a typical king, Hussein ruled with a firm hand yet demonstrated an extraordinary capacity for forgiveness. Those who plotted to assassinate him were arrested, but not executed, rare in the "eye-for-an-eye" ethos of much of the Middle East. An avid ham radio enthusiast, he was known throughout the world as the friendly voice of "JY1." He also was known to pilot his royal jet and could frequently be seen racing around Aqaba on his motorcycle, queen in tow. Toward the end of his life, he was an active Internet participant, always seeking to connect with the world.

If his legacy were simply consolidating his authority while a teenager and building Jordan up to its current extremely influential role in the Middle East, that alone would be the story of an extraordinary leader. However, what transformed King Hussein into a leader for the ages was his ability to become a living symbol of hope for peace in the Middle East. During his rule, his most damaging military defeat was at the hands of Yitzhak Rabin and the Israelis and his most significant internal threat took place when Yassir Arafat led Palestinians who had been displaced from Israel in a war against Hussein. Few people in the world were more entitled to as personal a grudge with both Rabin and Arafat, yet Hussein was able to move beyond this and by the end of his life he counted both as friends.

When Hussein's plane landed in Jordan for the last time, two days before his death, Arafat was there to greet him with a kiss on his forehead. Far from a token gesture, the greeting was a tribute to a man who worked tirelessly for peace in the Middle East, a man credited by President Clinton with saving the groundbreaking Oslo Peace Accords and who twice left his sickbed at the Mayo Clinic to go to the Wye River meetings of 1998 to push its participants toward peace.

So also did Hussein make peace with Yitzhak Rabin and Israel. In a scene that once seemed impossible, Hussein rushed to the side of the parents of Israeli children who had been killed by a crazed Jordanian soldier and apologized. Having formally made peace with Israel in 1994, he formed a strong friendship with its then-president, the former military general Yitzhak Rabin. In a moving tribute at Rabin's funeral in 1995, Hussein eulogized,

> I had never thought that the moment would come like this when I would grieve the loss of a brother, a colleague, and a friend—a man—a soldier—who met us on the opposite side of the divide. You lived as a soldier, you died as a soldier for peace. I commit before you, before my people in Jordan, before the world, myself, to continue to do our utmost to ensure that we leave a similar legacy.

MARTIN LUTHER: A HAMMER FOR RELIGIOUS EXPRESSION

Whereas some leaders enter the world stage quietly, achieving international acclaim toward the end of their careers, others arrive with all the subtlety of a lightning bolt. Such was the story of Martin Luther, who, by nailing his famous 95 *Theses* to the doors of the Wittenberg Castle Church on October 31, 1517, sparked a religious debate that continues to this day.

"During the Reformation, the Church feared that Martin Luther would hit like an atomic bomb and drive a wedge that would permanently divide West Europe's Christianities," said *Time* magazine senior religion writer David Van Biema in a November 1, 1999, article. And the church's fears were legitimate, for, greatly aided by the recent invention of the printing press, Luther's "heretical" words were printed in several editions within months and spread like wildfire across Europe, inspiring others to challenge the hegemonic church.

The church initially ignored Luther, but after his writings became more widespread, a papal bull was issued against him, which Luther burned. This bull ordered Luther to recant his writings, which he refused to do. Instead, he wrote a letter to Pope Leo X in which he apologized personally to the Pope but continued to denounce what he viewed as the false doctrine and corruption of the church. Despite his growing popular support, Luther was subsequently excommunicated from the church and barred from the Empire by Emperor Charles V. However, Luther was squired to safety by friends and continued to write, even after he was ordered to stop publishing. In the meantime, Protestantism continued to spread across Europe. The genie had emerged from the bottle, based in large part on the courage and writings of one man.

Nearly 500 years later, despite real divisions between modern-day Lutherans and the Vatican, a 1999 event took place that surely would have surprised Martin Luther: the Catholic and Lutheran churches formally made peace.

NELSON MANDELA: ENDURING TO TRIUMPH

The saga sounds more like a myth than a historical event: after spending 27 years behind bars for protesting South Africa's oppression of blacks and people of color, Nelson Mandela became the first popularly elected president of South Africa in the nation's first all-race election.

His autobiography, *Long Walk to Freedom*, chronicles his birth to a royal family in the Transkei section of South Africa, his decision to renounce his right to succeed his father as chief of the Tembu in order to study law, and his gradual awakening to the realities of the political situation in his country. Mandela became convinced of the need to join forces with the other people of color—the "coloreds" and the Indians—who were also discriminated against by the government. Deeply influenced by Mahatma Gandhi's teachings and by his example in South Africa, Mandela espoused nonviolence for years, until he determined that armed hostility would be the only way to overcome the oppressor. He set about to help plan armed resistance to the government.

Mandela had complied with countless bans against participating in any meeting or group event. Finally, after the 1960 massacre of thousands of unarmed people protesting the pass laws (which limited travel by blacks and insisted that they submit to checks of their passes), he became a fugitive. He lived underground for 18 months, donning a variety of disguises to avoid being caught. He was disguised as a chauffeur when security police arrested him in 1962. Two years later, Mandela was found guilty of sabotage against the government. He was eventually taken to desolate Robben Island to begin his long imprisonment.

In his trial, Mandela summarized the purpose of his wrongdoings:

> I would say that the whole life of any thinking African in this country drives him continuously to a conflict between his conscience on the one hand and the law on the other. This is not a conflict peculiar to this country. The conflict arises for men of conscience, for men who think and who feel deeply in every country. . . . The law as it is applied, the law as it has been developed over a long period of history, and especially the law as it is written and designed by the Nationalist government is a law which, in our views, is immoral, unjust, and intolerable. Our consciences dictate that we must protest against it, that we must oppose it and that we must attempt to alter it... men, I think, are not capable of doing nothing, of saying nothing, of not reacting to injustice, of not protesting against oppression, of not striving for the good society and the good life in the ways they see it.

Never losing hope that both he and his people would eventually be free, Mandela somehow survived his time in prison and continued to communicate with the still-banned African National Congress (ANC). When South African President F.W. de Klerk announced to Parliament a series of sweeping reforms that signaled the death knell of apartheid, he also announced that the ANC was no longer banned and that political prisoners would be freed.

On February 11, 1990, Mandela walked out of prison to a tumultuous welcome. He delivered his first remarks after the long silence: "Friends, comrades and fellow South Africans. I greet you all in the name of peace, democracy and freedom for all! I stand here before you not as a prophet but as a humble servant of you, the people. Your tireless and heroic sacrifices have made it possible for me to be here today. I therefore place the remaining years of my life in your hands."

He wrote in his autobiography, "I wanted first of all to tell the people that I was not a messiah, but an ordinary man who had become a leader because of extraordinary circumstances. I wanted immediately to thank the people all over the world who had campaigned for my release. . . . It was vital for me to show my people and the government that I was unbroken and unbowed, and that the struggle was not over for me but beginning anew in a different form. I affirmed that I was 'a loyal and disciplined member of the African National Congress.' I encouraged the people to return to the barricades, to intensify the struggle, and we would walk the last mile together."

In the next few days he reiterated the dream of a nonracial, united and democratic South Africa based on one-person, one-vote rule, expressing no hatred for whites but instead outrage at the system that turned blacks and whites against each other.

He was under enormous pressure after his release. Knowing that the government wanted nothing more than to see him appear foolish and fallible, Mandela nevertheless had to begin negotiations about the future of the country.

Time and time again, he sought to assure the whites that they were also South Africans and that this was their land, too. "I would not mince words about the horrors of apartheid, but I said, over and over, that we should forget the past and concentrate on building a better future for all."

He set about what he explains is his mission: "One of preaching reconciliation, of binding the wounds of the country, of engendering trust and confidence....At every opportunity I said all South Africans must now unite and join hands and say we are one country, one nation, one people, marching together into the future."

In *Days of Grace*, Arthur Ashe Jr. expressed many people's marvel about Mandela:

> To have spent twenty-seven years in jail for political reasons, to have been deprived of the whole mighty center of one's life, and then to emerge apparently without a trace of bitterness, alert and ready to lead one's country forward, may be the most extraordinary individual human achievement that I have witnessed in my lifetime. I marvel that he could come out of jail free of bitterness and yet uncompromising in his basic political beliefs; I marvel at his ability to combine an impeccable character, to which virtually everyone attests, with the political wisdom of a Solomon. In jail, I am told his white guards came to have such respect for him that in some ways he was their warden and they the prisoners, more prisoners of apartheid.

OUR METHODS FOR FRAMING LEADERSHIP

As powerful as the lessons are from the lives and decisions of these four men and women, our goal is not for our readers to become the next Nelson Mandela or Miep Gies. Nor do we expect our readers to adopt the personal leadership styles of the authors of this text. Rather, our approach to leadership mirrors our belief about learning: just as we see no universally accepted theory of leadership, just as the information age has cast doubt on the image of the leader as omnipotent hero, we do not pretend to have all the answers about leadership. Students of leadership are experts in their own right. Readers bring with them unique backgrounds, experiences, and perceptions that are important to the discussion of leadership. We see learning about leadership as melding the ideas and experiences of our readers with our ideas as authors of this text, as well as with the ideas of the scholars whose works we present. In this way, learning becomes a relational activity, a dialogue. We seek to engage readers in examining the material, their own perspectives, and those of current leaders to make sense of this phenomenon called leadership.

We have included several pedagogical features that underscore our belief that knowledge is socially constructed and that leadership is a journey. We will give you frequent reminders of where you are on the journey, where common roadblocks can be found, and much commentary about the passing scene. Be prepared for delays in your journey, however, since a large part of the trip is under construction.

Here are some other guidelines for your trip:

- We have attempted to integrate the implications of diversity and international-ism throughout the text and we have created a new chapter entitled "Practicing Leadership in a Multicultural Society."

- Along with a variety of lenses with which to view the scenery, we don't hesitate to pose questions—questions without one clear answer. We want to engage you in the process.

- And speaking of process, the way in which we developed this text illustrates our notion of practicing leadership. The authors are a mix of managers, administrators, and professors from several disciplines and practitioners in a variety of settings.

- At the start of each chapter, we use Leadership Moments to demonstrate how individuals face leadership challenges every day.

- The text does not necessarily have to be read sequentially. Different instructors may want to highlight different aspects, depending on the backgrounds of students and their own teaching strengths.

- You will learn about current leaders—including some that are well known and some that are not—and we will describe their contributions to leadership. Their stories are intended to bring to life how these leaders' closely held assumptions about leadership directly shape their behavior.

- In each chapter we offer two or more Leadership Profiles of leaders who demonstrate the characteristics discussed in the chapter. Leadership Skills for the Twenty-first Century boxes highlight skills and principles illustrated in the chapter. The Create Your Own Theory section prompts readers to personalize the main message of the chapter and consider it for their own emerging theory. We complete each chapter with a Summary, Key Terms, Questions for Discussion and Review, and either links to self-assessment tools found on the Internet and/or a closing exercise(s).

- Finally, in the closing chapters, we encourage readers to refine their own theories about leadership as well as their action plans for practicing leadership. Leaders and collaborators in the twenty-first century must be able to reflect on what they believe and why, make sense of situations from multiple perspectives, and form sound conclusions about actions to take based on those interpretations.

- We give the instructor added cases, tools, references, and activities, as well as Teaching Notes and multiple-choice and essay test questions in our *Instructors' Guide* on our Web site.

OUR ASSUMPTIONS

We are convinced that we must begin thinking about leadership in new ways in the twenty-first century. Our approach is built on seven basic premises:

1. *Where we are in our understanding of leadership is a function of where we once were.*
   We must learn from our past attempts to understand leadership. Most texts trace leadership back to only the middle of the twentieth century, but this one returns to Plato and considers the evolution of leadership. Historical approaches

to leadership allow us to examine their hold on our perceptions, weigh their merits, and if necessary, demystify them so we can advance our thinking about what leadership is and is not.

2. *There is no one formula for leadership.*

   This is true, even though many bestsellers such as *The Leadership Challenge* by Kouzes and Posner and *7 Habits of Highly Successful People* by Covey, among a plethora of others, suggest helpful techniques. Practicing leadership involves a multidimensional integration of theory, process, and practice. What is effective in one situation may not be useful in another. Leadership comes in many shapes and forms.

3. *Leadership is not differentiated by setting.*

   Most current leadership texts are written primarily for specific markets such as education, management, the military, and nursing. We assert that *Practicing Leadership* applies in all settings—this multidisciplinary text speaks to the concept rather than to a particular setting. We draw from many disciplines in our theoretical discussions and our examples. This book is written not only for those who aspire to organizational or political leadership, but also for anyone who wishes to make a difference by exerting leadership for a valued cause.

4. *Our understanding of leadership requires the vantage point of multiple perspectives.*

   During the twentieth century, leadership came under intense scrutiny as a subject of study, largely because the Industrial Revolution led to large organizations—and large organizations need people to run them. Researchers set about finding out just what kind of leadership was required to make these new enterprises effective.

   The body of research accumulated from this effort over the past 90 years has molded much of what we think about leadership. These perspectives, now labeled the *industrial paradigm of leadership,* are often presented as the "best way" to perceive and practice leadership.

   We propose, instead, that as valuable as it has been, the industrial paradigm is only one way of viewing leadership. It is definitely not the only way to do so.

5. *Studying leadership across a range of human differences is the only way to approach the subject in the twenty-first century.*

   The study of human differences—those of race, gender, age, ethnicity, religion, and lifestyle, among other factors—affects nearly every discussion about leadership. Leadership in this new millennium is inextricably linked to the spectrum of human differences. Period. Therefore, although we are excited about our new chapter on "Practicing Leadership in a Multicultural Society," we have also incorporated this knowledge throughout the book. We have tried to make a credible start in this ongoing process, but there is much more to do.

6. *Leadership can best be understood through metaphors and described indirectly through paradigms.*

   Since no single, straightforward definition or view of leadership captures its essence, our approach to studying leadership is gathered from a variety of disciplines. In Rost's groundbreaking book, *Leadership for the Twenty-first Century,* the hundreds of definitions he cites show how difficult an entity leadership is to pin down. We follow his example and find that leadership is better understood when we don't come straight at it.

7. *Leadership is a verb.*

We are committed to the notion that training to *be* a leader is a misguided, though pervasive, form of leadership development. The view that great men and women are the sole practitioners of leadership—what some have dubbed the "John Wayne" view of leadership—is deeply embedded in Western culture.

The information age has begun to show the difficulties with this image of the leader as the lonely-at-the-top, all-knowing hero. In every context, a flood of information makes it impossible for one person to go solo. We need each other's eyes, ears, and insights to better gauge the situation and the necessary actions for exerting leadership.

In the new paradigms of leadership, leaders and *collaborators* (a term we prefer to followers) together "practice leadership." Leadership is the process by which people work together to achieve mutual goals. We focus, accordingly, on the roles of collaborators, as well as on those who practice leadership. Both are vital to twenty-first century leadership and we must develop the skills to do both well.

A central point of this book is that although each of the disciplines we discuss has contributed to our understanding of leadership, none can stand alone as the defining set of assumptions. By viewing leadership through multiple lenses, we come closer to understanding it and become more skilled in practicing it in different contexts.

This point can be illustrated by the Indian tale of the six blind men and the elephant. The first man felt the elephant's trunk and announced that the animal was a snake. The second, feeling a leg, said it was a tree. Grabbing a tusk, the third asserted the animal was a spear; a fourth patted the elephant's side and claimed it was a wall. Holding onto the tail, the fifth man said it was much more like a rope, while the sixth, having seized the elephant's ear, pronounced it closer to a fan.

Although each man's perspective held some truth, we can see that none on its own captured the reality of the elephant. Only by combining these views do we begin to understand this phenomenon called elephant.

Each person, depending on his or her position in relation to the "elephant," can contribute some important information to the task of describing an elephant; however, each can only "see" the animal from a narrow vantage point. Each has only a partial perception. These restricted views would lead each person to reach very different conclusions about the nature of an elephant and its possible use in their lives.

Thomas Kuhn (1970) describes the utility of paradigms in much the same way. We use paradigms as tools to make sense of nature, as a means to create knowledge. "To be accepted as a paradigm, a theory must seem better than its competitors [at describing reality], but it need not, and in fact never does explain all of the facts with which it is confronted" (Kuhn, 1970, pp. 17–18).

A paradigm that is widely accepted becomes a foundation for research and practice; consequently, it shapes what we "see" and also what we study and how we study it.

An example is Louis Pasteur's introduction of the rabies vaccine. The vaccine represented a paradigm shift in medicine. Prior to that time, bloodletting was the favored approach to cleanse the body of its evil invaders. Pasteur's discovery completely reversed this set of assumptions by showing the value of actually introducing a virus into the body to spur the development of antibodies.

Yet, as Kuhn tells us, no paradigm can explain all the facts that confront it. We see certain things about the world because of this new perspective, but are unable to perceive others. In this way, competing paradigms coexist and some eventually fade away. Newer ones come onto the scene and more fully describe the reality of the moment.

In the same way, the stories about leadership in this text should be viewed with the understanding that there are no universal truths about leadership. Our purpose in offering multiple stories of leadership for critique and evaluation is to help you become your own leadership theorist. It is vital that you retain the images of leadership that hold the most power for you, for these images shape your behavior and eventually become part of how you "practice leadership." The way you practice leadership is a direct result of how you imagine it.

A PREVIEW OF THE JOURNEY

The road to leadership is a personal journey with multiple pathways, and there are a number of pathways you might take in reading this book. Some may choose to read the traditional way, from this chapter directly to the finish. Others, with more of a historical bent, may wish to start with Appendix I—"How We Got Here: Pre-Modern Thoughts on Leadership," which provides a historical context for our current dialogue on leadership. This book provides multiple chapters on the contributions of different disciplines—such as psychology, communications, and military science, to name a few—to our understanding of leadership. Readers with a particular interest in the disciplines represented in this textbook may well choose to begin with their own discipline. Regardless of approach, our goal is to help you further develop your own view of leadership and to provide information and guidance for choosing your own leadership pathway.

Read from start to finish, this text progresses as follows. In this section we have discussed our view of leadership in relationship to other definitions and approaches. Section II of this text, "The Disciplinary Roots of Leadership," discusses some of the major contributions to leadership theory made in the fields of psychology; management, total quality, and teambuilding; communication; anthropology; political science; and military science. Readers are encouraged to review each discipline to decide its usefulness to their own theory. Section III, "Leadership Theory: The Present and the Future," discusses contemporary theories and approaches, giving specific applications for each. This section includes "Practicing Leadership in a Multicultural Society" and "Modern Leadership Theories." The final section, "Practicing Leadership: It's Your Turn," includes "Leadership for the Twenty-first Century," which discusses modern leadership theories, and "It's Your Turn," which encourages readers to create their own total approach to leadership. Appendix I,

"How We Got Here: Pre-Modern Thoughts on Leadership," considers ancient and modern philosophers who created the roots of modern leadership theories. Different leaders are influenced by different philosophies and our final two appendices provide the reader with resources to use when selecting further reading. Appendix II, "Leadership by the Book," summarizes a variety of classic and contemporary leadership books. Appendix III, "Leader's Bookshelf," provides a comprehensive bibliography of current and classic leadership texts.

Good luck on your journey!

CREATE YOUR OWN THEORY

At the start of this chapter, we put you in the position of mediating with three individuals who had differing ideas about leadership and who best embodied it. As is clear by now, we believe that no one "correct" model of leadership exists. Each of us must form our own conceptualization of what leadership means to us. With this in mind, let's return to the opening Leadership Moment. Which of the three students do you agree with most? Do you agree with more than one student? None of these students? Why or why not?

Throughout this text, we prompt you to examine the information presented through your own personal leadership lens. A brief exercise helps to begin this process. On the following lines, write five adjectives that describe your "ideal leader":

1. _____

2. _____

3. _____

4. _____

5. _____

CHAPTER 2

Psychology

LEADERSHIP MOMENT

Wally Walker was once the rising star of Winkler's Widgets, Inc. Nobody else in the company could understand as well as Wally could the workings of a particularly complex widget, the Widgetmaster 2000. Always coming up with ideas for ways of improving the Widgetmaster 2000, he was the acknowledged expert, sought out whenever anyone had any questions related to this product. Unfortunately for Wally, upper management decided six months ago to discontinue Widgetmaster 2000 production and reassigned Wally to a different department. Since this change, Wally has changed noticeably. Although intellectually more than capable of handling his new duties, Wally isn't thrilled about the new product and realizes that dozens of other employees know more about it than he does. He says he no longer feels needed at work and, as a result, he has started to come in later and leave earlier.

Upper management has started to notice this change. As Wally's immediate supervisor, you have been instructed by your boss that unless that "lazy Wally" starts to turn things around, he will be fired.

1. *What would you do?*
2. *Do you think it is possible for grown adults like Wally to adapt to such a dramatic work change? Why or why not?*
3. *What assumptions has your boss made about Wally's abilities?*
4. *What steps might you take to motivate Wally to pursue his new job with his old vigor?*

W hen one examines the great leaders of today and yesterday, one cannot help but be awed by the sheer range of backgrounds from which these leaders emerge. Consider the U.S. presidents. Some, like Thomas Jefferson, were of "noble" birth and had a meteoric rise to prominence. Others, such as Abraham Lincoln and Bill Clinton, came from extremely humble beginnings and slowly fought their way to the top.

It is also astonishing to examine the ability of leaders to inspire those who follow them. How did Moses convince the ancient Hebrews to rise up, rebel against incredible odds, and follow him to the Red Sea? How did FDR (see Leadership Profile in

Chapter 6) inspire hope in millions of Americans faced with the worst depression in history and an upcoming world war?

An examination of psychology does not provide all the answers to these questions (only you can do that), but in this chapter we will look at two central components of the intersection of psychology and leadership—personality and motivation. We address the age-old question of whether great leaders are born or made (the answer may surprise you) and consider some of the many theories about motivating others.

PERSONALITY

Psychology is the study of human behavior. Human behavior is of course a broad area, the scope of which is well beyond that of this text. What then are the most salient aspects of human behavior that apply to leadership? Certainly, one important aspect of human behavior is how it forms what we call individual personalities. We'll define **personality** as how people affect others and understand themselves. Personality traits are important aspects to consider in terms of leaders and followers. In terms of leadership skills, five traits have been recognized by Luthans (1995, p. 114) as major affectors of task performance:

1. Extroversion—Are you sociable, talkative, and assertive?
2. Agreeableness—Are you good-natured, cooperative, and trusting?
3. Conscientiousness—Are you responsible, dependable, persistent, and achievement oriented?
4. Emotional stability—Viewed from a negative standpoint, are you tense, insecure, and/or nervous?
5. Openness to experience—Are you imaginative, artistically sensitive, and intellectual?

Theories on Personality Development

In Appendix I, we discuss some of the great thinkers such as Plato and Aquinas in terms of their perspective on what contributes to a great leader. Only within the past 150 years, however, has there been significant research that examines personality development over the course of the entire life span. Driven by Darwin's theory of evolution, early personality theorists such as Freud were generally biologists and physicians who sought to understand personality development through the study of physiology. One of the earliest questions theorists addressed was one that is still debated today: Are great men (in the nineteenth century, these discussions were about men only) born, or are they made?

Are Leaders Born or Are They Made?

In 1869, Sir Francis Galton was among the first to assert that those qualities that make great leaders are biologically inherited. This is a notion that continues to be hotly disputed in psychology—primarily through what is known as the **nature/**

nurture debate. The "nature" side of this equation is that individual personality is based largely on genetics. One either has the biological material to be a leader or one does not. The "nurture" position of this debate, by contrast, believes that whether or not somebody becomes a leader is based less on physiology than on real-life experience. Thus, in a case where two individuals are born with similar physiology (such as identical twins), one twin may develop into a great leader while the other may not, depending on life circumstances.

On the "nature" side, some, like Galton and others, would assert that some individuals are simply "natural leaders." History is littered with the exploits of these men and women, and they are commonly depicted in television shows and movies. Although the fundamental characteristics ascribed to these types of leaders vary, typically the characteristics of great leaders were thought to include:

- Intelligence, including judgment and verbal ability
- A record of achievement in school and athletics
- Emotional stability and maturity
- Strong achievement drive, persistence, and dependability
- People skills and social flexibility
- Drive to find status and socioeconomic position

Perhaps you can add a few more characteristics to this list.

But were these traits present at birth? Those who have spent time around infants can attest to the fact that, from very early ages, one can often see stark differences between the personalities of young children, even children from the same family. Some babies are easily soothed, for example, while others seem to cry and cry. Clearly, children are born with different personalities, and it is reasonable to assume that some personalities are more conducive to developing leadership than others.

Sigmund Freud did not write about personality development in terms of leadership, but he became the most widely known personality theorist and a major articulator of a viewpoint that leaned more heavily toward the "nature" side. A biologist by training, Freud postulated that one's personality was formed based on one's ability during childhood to adapt to a world filled with conflict. Children were viewed as passive recipients of stimulation and maladaptive personality development was attributed to bad mothering. Thus, from this perspective, one's core personality is formed very early on and is created via one's physiological responses to external stimulation. Because the source of personality is so deeply rooted in physiology and early childhood experiences, the classic Freudian framework views treatment as a long process that may require the analyst to assume parental roles in order to recreate the scene of developmental roadblocks.

At the other end—the "nurture" end—of the continuum are those who follow in the tradition of John Locke, who viewed the infant's mind as a ***tabula rasa*** (blank slate), amenable to all sorts of influences depending on the environment in which one is raised. Among the leading proponents in the United States of the "nurture" perspective were John Watson (see Leadership Profile) and, later, B. F. Skinner. Skinner, who will be discussed in greater detail later in this chapter, began by studying reinforcement mechanisms in animals. He discovered that when he rewarded animals for certain behaviors, those behaviors increased. A human application of this process can be observed in families where children are required to perform chores in order to receive their allowance. Through the work of Watson, Skinner, and many others, the notion of biological determinism began to be challenged. The argument was that children's (and to a certain extent adults') personalities were not fixed in infancy, but rather reflected the experiences they encountered throughout their lives. Thus, a child of an alcoholic may not necessarily grow up to abuse alcohol as an adult if raised in an environment where alcohol is not present.

JOHN BROADUS WATSON: "FATHER OF BEHAVIORISM," ADVERTISING PIONEER

Born to a family of meager means in Greenville, South Carolina, John B. Watson rose to become the preeminent psychologist of the United States (and an influential figure in advertising) in the first half of the twentieth century. Along the way, he founded a movement—behaviorism—that continues to enjoy considerable influence in psychology today.

Working in the shadow of Freud, who placed great emphasis on introspection and events that take place and have meaning primarily within the realm of the mind, Watson was first and foremost interested in that which can be observed. Defining psychology as the "science of behavior," he pushed for the field to become more "scientific" in nature as he formed and chaired the first department of psychology in the country.

According to Watson, we are all born with three basic emotional reactions— fear, rage, and love. He felt that environmental events determine the time and the extent to which these emotions are expressed and that science could be applied to condition certain responses in certain situations. He demonstrated his point in his most famous experiment—the Little Albert experiment—in which he conditioned a young boy to be fearful of rabbits after scaring the child each time a rabbit was presented. Through this and other experiments, he argued that human emotions, such as fear, are not due to biology or neurosis or unresolved feelings of wanting to sleep with one's parent or any other ideas put forth by Freud and his followers, but rather to actual experience. In essence, Watson was saying that if he were given a young child, he could turn that child into anything one desired given the right manipulation of the child's experiences.

It is not surprising that Watson, forced out of academia due to a sex scandal with one of his graduate students (whom he later married), found an easy application of his ideas in the world of advertising. Credited by some as the first to bring research into advertising, Watson pioneered the notion of understanding one's customers and their needs before attempting to sell any products to that customer. Prior to this time, most of advertising consisted of what we would now consider bland and entirely rational descriptions of products. Watson was in the vanguard of moving advertising from appealing to reason to a more emotion-based approach.

Watson also advocated capitalizing on children's emotions, but perhaps not as you might think. In fact, Watson used his research on children to advance an approach to childrearing that might appear extreme to some today, but was extremely influential in the early twentieth century. Watson summarized his beliefs on childrearing as follows: "Never hug and kiss them, never let them sit on your lap. If you must, kiss them once on the forehead when they say good night. Shake hands with them in the morning. Give them a pat on the head if they have made an extraordinarily good job of a difficult task. Try it out. In a week's time you will find how easy it is to be perfectly objective with your child and at the same time kindly. You will be utterly ashamed of the mawkish, sentimental way you have been handling it." To Watson, attending to crying children serves only to reinforce the crying. What children learn from this exchange when parents comfort them is, "If I want my parents' comfort, all I have to do is cry."

Fortunately, the days of scaring young children with rabbits are long gone, yet modified versions of Watson's behaviorism continues to have tremendous influence within current psychology. Today's behaviorism continues the legacy of focusing on the here and now and on that which is observable and measurable. It also maintains the belief that individuals can learn to control their emotions through a series of concrete steps, with particular emphasis on rewarding the positive versus punishing or ignoring the negative. Just as young children can be trained to fear rabbits, so also can individuals of all ages be trained to change their behaviors and conquer their fears.

It is now very rare to find an individual who believes in a strictly "nature" or a strictly "nurture" perspective. This is due to a number of factors, most notably studies of monozygotic (identical) twins and of children who have been raised in adoptive or foster homes. Accumulating evidence supports the position that both physiology and environmental influences play important roles in human development. For example, in comparing prevalence rates of certain diseases in monozygotic (identical) versus dizygotic (fraternal) twins, a very common finding is that there are higher concordance (meaning both twins have the trait) rates in monozygotic twins, providing evidence for the "nature" perspective since monozygotic twins are genetically identical. However, if monozygotic twins are identical, should not it be the case that if one monozygotic twin has a personality trait the other one would as well? As anyone who has met identical twins knows, their personalities, while often similar, are also often quite different in key ways—which supports the "nurture" side of personality development.

So it is that human behavior is a combination of biological and environmental influences. However, even though there is wide consensus that both nature and nurture play a role in personality development, that does not mean that where one falls on the nature/nurture continuum is unimportant. Consider the case of something that virtually all of us have experienced at one point or another in life—depression. If you were a physician treating depression, how would you conceptualize this illness? If you lean more toward the "nature" end of the nature/nurture continuum, you might view the depression as essentially biological in origin and perhaps would prescribe an antidepressant such as Prozac as treatment. On the other hand, if you subscribe to more of a "nurture" perspective, you might feel that therapy based on discussing real-life experiences that may have led to the onset of the depression would be the more effective route. In many cases, the best option might be a combination of these approaches.

But we don't need to be Sigmund Freud or B.F. Skinner to determine what drives personality to make an impact on others. We make these assessments every day when we come to conclusions about the personalities of those around us. These assessments are reflected in our attitudes, perceptions, and attributions.

Attitudes Successful leadership demands an understanding of attitudes and their manifestations in an organization. For our purposes, we'll define **attitude** as a series of beliefs and feelings held by people about specific situations, ideas, or other people. As shown in Table 2–1, three main aspects of attitudes include affect, the emotional content of a situation; behavior, specific actions taken in response to or in anticipation of a situation; and cognitions, an individual's thoughts or perceptions of a situation.

In general, it is believed that people try to maintain a balance between these three components as they form attitudes. In some situations, the three components come into conflict and a skilled leader will consider feelings as well as behaviors in the attempt to promote positive attitudes.

Perception and Attribution We pay attention to people and objects in such a way that gives them meaning to us. That idiosyncratic aspect of perception can mean that two people can form two different impressions of the same evidence, as the classic illusion in Figure 2–1 shows.

TABLE 2–1   The Components of Attitudes

Components	Definition	Example
Affective	Favorable or unfavorable feelings	The workers' feelings about the new regulations
Behavior	Human actions	The workers' performance
Cognitive	Beliefs, knowledge, understanding	The workers' beliefs about performance standards and supervision

Figure 2–1   The Old Woman/Young Woman Illusion

Figure 2–1 (which did you see first, an old woman or a young woman?) shows how our perceptions of people are affected by a number of elements, including the characteristics of the person we perceive, such as physical appearance, clothing, and verbal and nonverbal communication, as well as the ascribed attributes, including status, occupation, and personal characteristics.

Social perceptions have much to do with our impressions of people who are different from ourselves. Upon meeting a person with a disability, for instance, we may react by speaking too loudly, asking questions of others instead of speaking directly to the person, or not knowing what to say for fear of saying the wrong thing. Similarly, our first impressions of people whose accent is different from our own or whose height, or clothing, or even vehicle is not like ours may be erroneous (would you expect a nun to drive a pickup?).

Our perceptions can be inaccurate for three main reasons: **stereotyping, selective perception,** and **perceptual defense.** We might negatively **stereotype** the person with an Italian accent by inferring connections to organized crime, or the person with a disability by assuming he or she is unable to respond to conversation. A stereotype can also be positive, as hearing a Scandinavian's accent and assuming the person must be a good skier. Frequent workplace stereotyping occurs with differences in age and gender.

Selective perception occurs when we hear or see only what we want to see or hear. Teenagers have marvelous powers of selective perception when they screen out parental requests. We select on the basis of our own experiences, needs, and orientations.

The third way to block perceptions is through *perceptual defense*. Typically, perceptual defense takes place when we distort or deny something that is too difficult to acknowledge.

Yet it is not only how we perceive people and events that affects our response to them; *attribution,* or the reasons we ascribe for our behavior, plays an important role. We interpret an event and then try to uncover its cause. Much depends on our view of ourselves and the world and seeing ourselves on a continuum as having a great deal of control over events or as being powerless.

LEADERSHIP SKILLS FOR THE TWENTY-FIRST CENTURY

LEADER AS LEARNER

Contrary to popular perception, leaders are not people who are always certain of themselves and their direction. Rather, leaders are people who are open-minded learners. What's more, they are not afraid to let others see them in this light. In fact, creating an environment in which learning and its natural byproduct, mistakes, are okay can be a potent tool to unite a group and inspire creativity, risk-taking, and effort.

Today those who practice leadership must be open to learning about their colleagues and followers. That includes their differences in personality and work styles, their lifestyle as it affects their effort, and the interplay of such factors as age, race, religion, sexual orientation, and gender. No one can be expected to grasp all the implications of such a wide range of differences, so leaders especially must show they are willing and able to learn. But interpersonal skills in understanding group members do not stop with the leader. The leader must promote such understanding among group members themselves, so they can empower each other and call forth and recognize each other's contributions.

Section Summary

Our unique personalities affect our ability to lead. Whereas once it was believed that all leadership traits were inherited, modern psychological research supports a perspective that includes both biological and environmental contributors to personality development. We are born with certain dispositions toward leadership that can be aided, stunted, or otherwise altered by the experiences we have during the course of our lifetime. Every day, our personality affects our ability to lead through our perception and attitudes toward other people and situations.

GENE CHELBERG: DISABLED AND PROUD

Gene Chelberg never started out to be a leader in the disability community. He remembers, in fact, that his whole purpose in going to college at the 40,000-student Twin Cities campus of the University of Minnesota was to get lost in the crowd: "I was trying to figure out who I was, from the inside out. My entire life before that had been telling me who I was from the outside in—Gene, the blind kid."

Now the project director of Disabled Student Services at the University of Minnesota, Chelberg says that he probably wouldn't have been so conscious of the need to find his identity had he not been born with blindness. The value of disability—in Gene's case its fueling of the search for personal identity—is becoming central to current thought in disability issues.

"To a large extent, we are taught that disability is inherently negative," Chelberg says. "Now we're trying to look at our disability in a new light as something that has added to our lives. It's not all of who we are, but it's a central piece of it."

Chelberg's life modeled the leadership steps he now teaches to disabled college students through Project LEEDS, Leadership Education to Empower Disabled Students. First, reflection: "We need to take time to think of where we've been and where we're going," he says.

Chelberg maintains that reflection must take place individually as well as within a group, that no one can exercise leadership without first having some sense of his or her identity. And for disabled people, he stresses, that means coming to an understanding and an appreciation of the disability that sets them apart. It reverses the traditional medical/rehabilitation model of disability by proclaiming that the individual, not the doctor or rehab specialist, is the "agent of remedy."

Yet once the individual reflection has begun, community becomes vital. "Disabled people have fought for the past twenty years or so to secure their rights, and we must continue to make sure they're available. But now we also have to think of our responsibilities, not only to the disabled community but to the nondisabled as well," he says.

His affiliation with the Disabled Student Cultural Center at the University of Minnesota helped him and other disabled students understand the power of creating alliances, as well as the importance of recognizing the dynamics behind sharing the power. These are among the issues he will address in a new project designed to acquaint students and Student Affairs personnel with ways to hold accessible events and to welcome disability.

"Leadership has sort of happened within the disabled community," he says, citing the case of a man who wanted to go to college when few disabled people had enrolled. This man's actions started the Independent Living movement at Berkeley. "Rather than being thrust into the middle of things all the time," Chelberg says, "we need to take our time, step back, and chart our course." He thinks reflection is a central piece of teaching leadership.

Chelberg helped arrange a ground-breaking event for disabled students: "Disabled and Proud: The 1993 national gathering of college student leaders with disabilities." Attended by people from across the country, the event, he says, "was unbelievable. I still hear people refer to it and say that it changed their lives."

MOTIVATION THEORIES

We all know or have seen people we consider to be great motivators. Successful leaders know how to motivate others, and they do this in large part by having an understanding of the needs of those they are trying to lead. Over the past 100 years, there has been an ever-growing body of research that has attempted to understand motivation and its core elements. What follows are brief descriptions of some of the most influential motivation theories and their application to leadership.

Hierarchy of Needs

You may have already learned about Maslow's **Hierarchy of Needs.** Psychologist Abraham Maslow claimed humans possess certain levels of needs. He postulated that one's primary needs—for food, shelter, sex, and safety—have to be met before higher-order needs for esteem and self-actualization can be satisfied. By the same token, one cannot be motivated to achieve high-order tasks if lower-order needs have not been met.

As Figure 2–2 shows, this motivation can be accomplished in a variety of ways. For example, suppose you are in a volunteer group, attempting to coordinate efforts for a fund-raiser. The other members of the group have rushed to the meeting without any chance for dinner. Maslow's theory suggests you won't be able to motivate them by appealing to their self-concepts if their stomachs are growling.

Maslow's ideas are discussed in greater detail in *Maslow on Management*. For a summary of this work, see Appendix II.

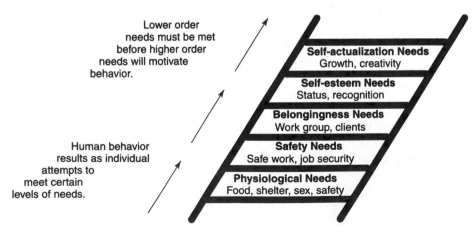

Figure 2–2 Maslow's Hierarchy of Needs

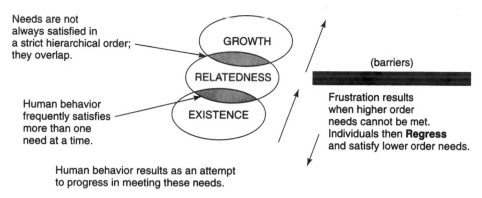

Needs are not always satisfied in a strict hierarchical order; they overlap.

GROWTH

RELATEDNESS

(barriers)

Human behavior frequently satisfies more than one need at a time.

EXISTENCE

Frustration results when higher order needs cannot be met. Individuals then **Regress** and satisfy lower order needs.

Human behavior results as an attempt to progress in meeting these needs.

Figure 2–3   ERG Theory

ERG Theory

The **ERG theory** refined parts of the Maslow model. Alderfer postulated that the main needs of humans are *existence, relatedness,* and *growth* (see Figure 2–3), which are comparable to Maslow's five areas. Yet Alderfer also suggested that we can do things to satisfy more than one kind of need at a time and our needs are not strictly hierarchical. For example, a person who has unmet relatedness needs (self-esteem needs in Maslow's model) may still look toward growth experiences (Maslow's self-actualization). In addition, the ERG theory notes that when an individual is frustrated in achieving a higher-level need, he or she may look to satisfying a lower-level one. This is termed a **frustration regression hypothesis.**

Although both Maslow's and Alderfer's theories are applicable to organizational settings, their work was primarily fueled by the desire to understand human needs across all settings. On the other hand, there are a number of theories that have placed primary emphasis on examining work-related needs. The most notable are the works of Frederick Herzberg and Douglas McGregor.

Herzberg's Dual Factor Theory

Herzberg began his research by asking a simple question: What do people want from their jobs? After surveying accountants and engineers, he concluded that certain factors tended to be associated with job dissatisfaction while a separate set of factors was linked with job satisfaction. He called this the **Dual Factor theory** (see Figure 2–4).

Herzberg termed the factors whose absence can lead to dissatisfaction **hygiene factors.** They include job security, quality of supervision, interpersonal relationships, working conditions, and adequacy of pay and fringe benefits. If these factors are present in an organization, employees are not necessarily satisfied; however, Herzberg contended that their absence would be associated with high levels of dissatisfaction reported by many employees.

Those factors that portend satisfaction he called **motivational factors.** Among these are opportunity for achievement and advancement, responsibility, job

Satisfaction		No satisfaction
	Motivation factors • Achievement • Recognition • The work itself • Responsibility • Advancement and growth	
Dissatisfaction		No dissatisfaction
	Motivation factors • Supervisors • Working conditions • Interpersonal relations • Pay and security • Company policies and administration	

Figure 2–4   The Two-factor Theory of Motivation

challenge, and recognition. Although these factors in and of themselves do not predict job satisfaction, Herzberg noted that it was unusual to find highly satisfied employees where these factors were not present.

LEADERSHIP SKILLS FOR THE TWENTY-FIRST CENTURY

COGNITIVE FACTORS AND PERSONALITY

Leaders help people care, say Dean and Mary Tjosvold (1995; for a summary of their book *Psychology for Leaders* see Appendix II), well-known authorities on leadership and team building. If followers are not motivated to accomplish a task, they suggest that leaders should be "psychologically savvy." They must have the kinds of interpersonal skills that let them get others involved and working together in what they call the "cooperative bottom line."

Effectively pulling in others to participate in a shared effort addresses individuals' needs to work toward self-actualization. But the Tjosvolds point out that it also is a good business strategy. "Life is aspiration. Learning, striving people are happy people and good workers. They have initiative and imagination, and the companies they work for are rarely caught napping."

McClelland's Trichotomy of Needs

According to McClelland, individuals differ in their need to control events and influence people. His **Trichotomy of Needs theory** identifies three main motives behind workplace behaviors—power, drive and achievement, and affiliation.

Drive for Power   Those with high drives for power are characterized by three traits: vigorous action and determination to use their power, thoughtfulness (some would call it scheming) about how to influence others' thinking and behavior, and concern about their standing with others (McClelland, 1975).

As we will see in the political science chapter (Chapter 6), both those who are leading and those who are following exert power at different times. Some theorists draw a further distinction between personalized power drives, in which people want power for their own reasons, and socialized power drives, in which people look to use their power for the good of others.

CREATE YOUR OWN THEORY: IMPLICATIONS OF UNDERSTANDING DRIVES FOR PRACTICING LEADERSHIP

As you engage in both leader and follower behavior, it's instructive to understand why you are making the effort to influence others. Those with personalized power drives are less likely to act as effective leaders, less emotionally mature, and more apt to try to manipulate others for their own goals. Those with socialized power drives, on the other hand, tend to be more open to questioning and advice and less defensive. They also tend to see the bigger picture rather than the short-term snapshot.

Drive and Achievement Motivation   Again, both followers and leaders can exhibit drive, or a strong pull toward getting things done. Some people demonstrate a high achievement motivation; that is, they love to be challenged and enjoy accomplishment for its own sake. People with strong achievement motivation have been described as consistently taking responsibility for success or failure, competitive, looking for feedback on their performance, taking moderate risks, and planning and setting goals for themselves.

By contrast, people—again, both leaders and followers—with weak achievement orientations are less motivated by solving problems, are not as satisfied by accomplishing the assigned tasks, and are looking for easier tasks.

Need for Affiliation   The third drive or need is for belonging, love, and connection with others. People with high affiliation needs work well with others and may be motivated by the interaction. According to McClelland, although people exhibit all three needs to varying degrees, only one usually motivates individuals at any given time.

McGregor's Theory X and Theory Y

Assumptions about what motivates collaborators can significantly affect the decisions that leaders make. Influenced by Maslow's work, Douglas McGregor proposed a continuum of beliefs held by managers about the motives of employees. At one end of the continuum, which he named **Theory X,** is the belief that people are motivated primarily by basic needs. Theory X leaders and managers hold the following assumptions:

- People inherently dislike work, and whenever possible will try to avoid it.
- Since people dislike work, they must be coerced, controlled, or threatened with punishment to achieve goals.
- People will avoid responsibilities and seek formal direction whenever possible.
- Most people place security above all other factors associated with work and will display little ambition.

A **Theory Y** leader, on the other hand, thinks that people are motivated by higher-order needs. Theory Y leaders base their behaviors on the following four assumptions:

- People can view work as an activity as natural as rest or play.
- People will exercise self-direction and self-control if they are committed to the objectives of the task.
- The average person can learn to accept and even seek responsibility.
- The ability to make innovative decisions is widely dispersed throughout the general population and is not necessarily the sole province of those in management positions.

Leaders should constantly evaluate their assumptions about the motives of others. Although no individual is likely to be a "true X" or a "true Y," the assumptions one makes can significantly affect the ability to practice leadership and inspire others.

Equity Theory

In this approach, people are thought to be influenced by their perceptions of the fairness of rewards for certain performances. Based on social comparison theory, **equity theory** suggests that people evaluate their own performance and their attitudes by comparing them to others. Developed by J. Stacy Adams at the University of North Carolina, equity theory posits that people consider two primary factors in evaluating equity:

1. The ratio of their outcomes to their inputs
2. The ratio of another's outcomes to inputs

Notice that these judgments are based on perceptions rather than objective data. A problem arises when a leader puts into place policies that are intended to be equal and fair, but that employees may see as preferential for some. This theory challenges leaders to consider the policies from the standpoint of the workers, both individually and collectively, in terms of fairness. Leaders will ask themselves whether some sectors are rewarded more than others, and in which situations resentments are likely to occur.

Equity theory further proposes that people will seek to equalize the ratios of outcomes (such as pay, recognition, job status) to inputs (such as effort, age, gender, experience, and level of productivity). Thus, if people feel they have been working very hard without receiving enough recognition for their efforts, at some point they will likely begin to produce less, moving the outcome/input ratio closer to 1. Conversely, when people feel they are being rewarded too much (a rare occurrence!), they will start to work harder so they can offset the inequity. Figure 2–5 outlines the basic tenets of this theory.

Expectancy Theory

Psychologist Victor Vroom first proposed the **expectancy theory** of motivation in 1964. Leaders benefit by having an accurate sense of the expectations employees bring to specific situations—they can use the information to help motivate performance.

As depicted in Figure 2–6, Vroom claimed that three principal components influence motivation:

1. Expectancy—an individual's perception of the likelihood that effort will improve performance

2. Instrumentality—an individual's perception of the likelihood that specific outcomes will be linked to their performance

3. Valence—an individual's perception of the worth of certain outcomes

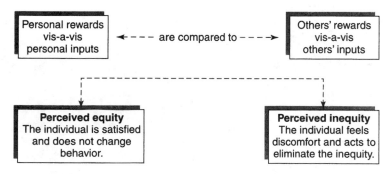

Figure 2–5   Equity Theory

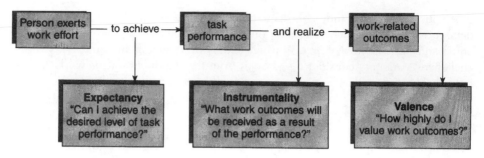

Figure 2–6 Expectancy Theory

Leaders can influence each of these components. For example, leaders can help collaborators improve their skills and abilities, thereby influencing expectancies. Leaders can also affect instrumentalities by offering support and advice. Finally, leaders can influence valences, or perceptions, by listening to others and helping them achieve the specified outcomes.

Reinforcement Theory

Based on the notion that behavior results from consequences, **reinforcement theory** looks at the role of positive and negative reinforcers, not at people's needs or reasons for choices. There are three major divisions of reinforcement theory—classical conditioning, operant conditioning, and social learning theory. **Classical conditioning** was developed by Pavlov around the turn of the twentieth century through experiments in which he trained dogs to salivate when a bell was rung, thus associating two normally unrelated stimuli—the bell and salivation (see Figure 2–7). The

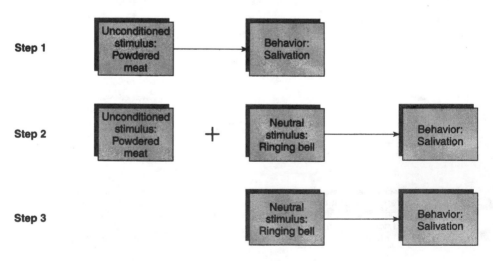

Figure 2–7 Pavlov's Conditioning Experiments

dogs learned over time that whenever the bell would ring food was to follow. The application to motivation is that humans will be motivated if they associate certain situations with desirable outcomes.

B. F. Skinner and other proponents of **operant conditioning** claimed that classical conditioning might be useful for dogs and primitive learning, but could not explain more complex learning. Skinner asserted that rewards are the major determinant of behavior; that is, behavior that is reinforced will tend to recur. Seen in this light, motivation can be thought of as finding the appropriate reward for the behavior that is desired. Obviously, this conditioning can go both ways. For instance, teachers have long known that praise or good grades or, in some cases, more concrete rewards such as stickers or candy or opportunities to engage in favorite activities can shape a student's behavior. However, canny students have learned that looking incredibly interested, asking questions, and general "brown-nosing" can help shape instructors' attitudes, and perhaps even their grading. The same operant conditioning dynamic exists between followers and leaders.

Modern behavioral learning theory has expanded on the classical and operant models to produce **social learning theory**. According to its proponents, such as Albert Bandura, learning is an active process and the learner has more control than classical or operant conditioning would suggest. A person's cognitive processes affect his or her response to the environment. In social learning theory, reinforcements or incentives are also seen to affect behavior. Most complex learning takes place via observing others and then imitating them. A common example is a young child taking cues from an older sibling and attempting novel behavior that previously has been neither reinforced nor punished.

The Effects of Human Differences on Motivation

As if understanding the aforementioned intricacies of motivation isn't difficult enough, the range of human differences adds significantly to the mix. With our increasingly diverse population, including differences in race, gender, religion, physical ability, country of origin, age, personality style, and sexual orientation, the overwhelming interplay of factors becomes obvious. Not that we can understand and predict all of the effects of these differences on motivation, but we can at least recognize their presence and seek advice about the implications.

Cultural preferences, for example, can turn what is intended as friendly eye contact into what is perceived as rude and offensive behavior. A reward that is clearly motivating for a young adult may be meaningless or denigrating to an older person. And expecting the same degree of physical effort from a person who may be weak from religious fasting but who prefers not to mention this is doomed to failure.

The Leader's Role in Motivation

In *Tough-Minded Leadership* (for a summary of this work, see Appendix II), management consultant Joe D. Batten says, "We must get rid of the old idea that a leader can give motivation. All motivation is self-motivation. We simply cannot and should not want to install motivation externally. The excellent leader goes all out to provide the climate, the stimuli, and the example, but all real motivation is self-generated. Only growing, actualized individuals can reach out beyond themselves in ways essential to true synergistic teams....We can know and lead others only when we are progressively learning how to know and lead ourselves."

The Dale Carnegie folks know all about this kind of motivation. In their book, *The Leader in You* (1993, pp. 51–52), Stuart R. Levine and Michael A. Crom discuss an employee going the "extra mile" to satisfy a customer:

> And people will only want to perform like that if they feel like an important part of the organization. That's why employees need to be respected and included in a corporate vision they can embrace. That's why people need a stake in their work lives. That's why their successes need to be rewarded, praised, and celebrated. That's why their failures need to be handled gingerly. Do these things. Then stand back and watch the results roll in.

They go on to list three underlying principles that must be addressed for motivation to be effective:

1. Employees must be included in all parts of the process, every step of the way. Teamwork is the key here, not hierarchy.

2. People must be treated as individuals. Always acknowledge their importance and show them respect. They're people first, employees second.

3. Superior work must be encouraged, recognized, and rewarded. Everyone responds to expectations. If you treat people as if they are capable and smart—and get out of the way—that's exactly how they'll perform. (p. 52)

In the highly competitive world of professional sports, the difference between winning and losing often rests not on which individual or team has more talent (although this never hurts!), but on which team has the greater will to win. Essential to creating and sustaining winning teams is the presence of a head coach with the ability to motivate his or her players. What follows is a profile of one of professional basketball's acknowledged master motivators, Los Angeles Lakers' head coach Phil Jackson.

PHIL JACKSON: MASTER MOTIVATOR

After a one-year hiatus, acclaimed coach Phil Jackson returned to the National Basketball Association in 1999 to become the new head coach of the Los Angeles Lakers. The author of *Sacred Hoops*, Jackson had combined Zen techniques with a ruthless competitive streak to guide the Chicago Bulls to six championships during the 1990s.

Of course, critics said, having Michael Jordan on your team can make anyone look like a brilliant strategist. Even though Jordan's brilliant play was indisputably a major factor in the Bulls' dominance during Jackson's tenure, Jackson's ability to convert the Bulls from a one-man show to a fully functioning team was arguably even more important. Players discarded by other teams—most notably Dennis Rodman, who was viewed by most as "uncoachable" prior to his entry to the Bulls and whose career essentially ended after Jackson departed—became important cogs in the Bulls' machine, each playing his role to near perfection. Never the conventional coach, Jackson incorporated Zen techniques into his practices and gave different players different books to read based on their personality and perceived need. Said former Bull Jud Buechler, "I think his strong suit is his personal relationship with the players. He really knows how to treat each guy and he handles each guy differently, which he has to on a team like this. He's very positive with each guy and really makes every guy on the team feel like they're part of something. He keeps everyone involved and the Zen and yoga that we do, it's fun because it's different."

Added NBA guard Ron Harper, who has played for Jackson in both Chicago and Los Angeles, "He tends to tell the guys, 'Just go out and do the job. Don't try to do some things you don't know how to do. Go out and stay in the team framework and do the job.'"

The Lakers team Jackson inherited was much like the Bulls team he had first encountered a decade earlier. Each team included one established superstar (Michael Jordan and Shaquille O'Neal) who had made millions off the court but had yet to win a title, a young burgeoning star (Scottie Pippen and Kobe Bryant) who at times resented being perceived as second fiddle, and a solid but unspectacular supporting cast.

The Lakers were a talented team on paper, but had folded under pressure the previous two seasons, losing four games to zero in the playoffs to teams with perhaps less talent but better team play. From the beginning, Jackson made his motivational strategy clear: "I'd say the key word here isn't sacrifice, but submit." Jackson said in a 1999 interview, "These players are going to have to change not only the way they play the game but also the way they approach it. They've tried to win with 'me'; now, we're going to try as 'we.'"

The results were immediate. Suddenly, players known mostly for scoring looked first to pass. Whereas once the Lakers' offense was characterized by throwing the ball to O'Neill while the other four players watched, now all five players appeared in constant motion, each with a defined role in an offense geared toward team play. And, perhaps most important, in times of stress, such as during the decisive seventh game of a playoff series with rival Portland, with the winner set to advance to the NBA Finals, his team remained calm and confident while Portland self-destructed. Portland's onetime 15-point lead evaporated into a 5-point Los Angeles win in the game's final minutes. Said Laker forward A. C. Green, "He's a man who feels a lot of peace and calm that transfers to the team. When guys out on the floor are starting to get crazy, he settles things down. He just doesn't seem to get rattled."

The composed Lakers went on to capture the 1999–2000 NBA crown, a testament to Jackson's ability to bring together a disparate group of millionaires into a unified group willing to sacrifice individual statistics for a common goal.

Section Summary

This section highlighted a number of leading theories that attempt to understand what motivates individuals to behave in certain ways. There are no universal truths. Each theory takes a unique perspective on motivation and each needs to be understood within the context of a society made up of individuals from widely divergent backgrounds and beliefs. Skillful leaders do not subscribe strictly to any one of these theories, but rather seek to understand and adapt these approaches to their own home and work relationships.

SUMMARY

In this chapter we explore some of the major contributions made by the field of psychology to our understanding of leadership. Specifically, we examine the impact of two subareas of psychology—personality research and motivational research—on our understanding of human behavior.

How do psychological principles apply to leadership? We'll let the Tjosvolds (1995) have the last word here:

> Leadership is a "we" thing that requires both leader and employee. So too does using psychology. You will be more efficient if you involve your employees, colleagues and friends in helping you develop your psychology skills and strengthen your leadership competence. Learning unites leaders and followers in a common journey of self discovery and team development....Leadership today is too complex and challenging to be left to one person; it's only successful when done together.

CREATE YOU OWN THEORY

In this chapter, you have been exposed to a number of theories both on the nature of personality itself and on how leaders can best motivate individuals and groups to achieve desired ends. Now it is your turn to consider to what extent you accept the premises put forth by these different theories. Are leaders born, or are they made? Under what conditions does the development of one's "true" personality best thrive? If you were to try to motivate your classmates to achieve a certain end, which approach would best suit you? What do you think people are looking for in leaders and what skills do you have that meet these needs? These are but a few of the questions we encourage you to consider in reflecting on this chapter.

Now let's reconsider the Leadership Moment at the beginning of the chapter. Based on your emerging theory of leadership, how would you analyze the changes that are taking place in Wally's work performance and how can these be addressed? Do you feel that he is simply a "lost cause," or are there interventions that could result in an improved performance? How would the issue of motivation play a factor in your analysis?

KEY TERMS

personality
nature/nurture debate
tabula rasa
attitude
stereotyping
selective perception
perceptual defense
attribution
Hierarchy of Needs
ERG theory
frustration regression hypothesis
dual factor theory

hygiene factors
motivational factors
trichotomy of needs theory
Theory X
Theory Y
equity theory
expectancy theory
reinforcement theory
classical conditioning
operant conditioning
social learning theory

QUESTIONS FOR DISCUSSION AND REVIEW

1. What is the "nature/nurture" debate? What evidence supports each side? Where do most psychologists fall on the nature/nurture continuum?

2. Describe a situation in which your initial perception of a situation turned out to be inaccurate. What are the implications of personal attitudes and perceptions on leadership?

3. What is selective perception? How does it differ from stereotyping and perceptual defense?

4. What distinguishes Alderfer's ERG theory from Maslow's Hierarchy of Needs?

5. What does Alderfer consider to be the primary human needs?

6. What are some of the distinctions between Theory X and Theory Y leaders? Do you know anyone who meets the criteria for either of these styles?

7. What is the primary difference between personalized and socialized power drives?

8. Is equity theory based on objective data or perceptions?

9. According to Vroom's expectancy theory, what three components influence motivation?

10. Compare and contrast Bandura's social learning theory with Skinner's operant conditioning theory and Pavlov's classical conditioning theory.

ONLINE SELF-ASSESSMENT TOOL

The Keirsey Temperament Sorter is perhaps the most well-known and widely used self-assessment tool that examines individual personality traits. To learn more about this instrument and to take two short personality quizzes (one focuses on temperament, the other on character), we encourage you to visit http:///www.keirsey.com.

CHAPTER 3

Management, Quality, and Team Building

LEADERSHIP MOMENT

You are the coach of your ten-year-old daughter's youth soccer team. After winning its first game, the team hit a rough patch, losing six games in a row. Several of your assistant coaches, as well as several other parents, are becoming increasingly bothered by this trend and are lobbying you to "instill more discipline" in practice and to start playing weaker team members less. Your players, at first indifferent to whether they won or lost, are now catching on to their parents' unrest at your last practice there were two different times when players screamed at each other for perceived mistakes, with one saying, "You're the reason we keep losing." You thought that coaching was going to be relaxing, but you're starting to realize that if this team does not start pulling together—and winning—soon, the season may be a real unpleasant one.

1. *What would you do?*

2. *Which would you place a greater emphasis on, winning or team building? How are they interrelated?*

3. *How would you address the multiple coaching philosophies of the parents of your team members?*

4. *How would you address the increased fighting among team members?*

As the opening Leadership Moment highlights, leadership often involves navigating through competing influences and impulses. As noted in Chapter 1, much of where we are in our understanding of leadership is a function of where we once were. This chapter provides some anchoring points as you progress on your leadership journey, providing information on three key areas that have been very influential in creating and continuing to shape leadership theory—management, quality, and team building.

MANAGEMENT

Peter Drucker (1974) wrote:

The emergence of management in this century may have been a pivotal event in history. It signaled a major transformation of society into a pluralistic society of institutions, of which managements are the effective organs. Management, after more than a

37

century of development as a practice and as a discipline, burst into public consciousness in the management boom that began after World War II and lasted through the 1960s. (p. 2)

[Every developed society] has become a society of institutions...every major task, whether economic performance or health care, education or the protection of the environment, the pursuit of new knowledge or defense is today being entrusted to big organizations designed for perpetuity and managed by their own management. On the performance of those institutions, the performance of modern society—if not the survival of each individual—increasingly depends.

Although the effects of management were first felt more than one hundred years ago during the Industrial Revolution as factories developed, it is only in the twentieth century that we began to systematically study its impact. **Management** has been defined as the coordination of human, material, technological, and financial resources needed for an organization to reach its goals (Hess and Siciliano, 1996, p. 7). Or, to return to Drucker (1974, p. 17), management is "a multipurpose organ that manages a business and manages managers and manages workers and work."

With such far-reaching definitions, just what is it that managers do? It is commonly agreed that five functions make up a manager's job: planning, controlling, organizing, staffing, and leading (see Figure 3–1). The addition of continuous improvement as a sixth function of management is a relatively new phenomenon.

Although these charts seem fairly straightforward, defining management becomes much more difficult because none of the functions is really discrete; they are all interconnected. Further, not every manager is involved in each of the functions. One way to distinguish between management functions is to designate different levels of managers. Top-level managers, for instance—the chief executive officers,

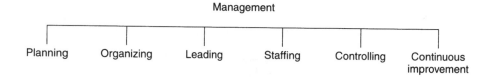

Shriberg's view of management vs leadership

Figure 3–1   Traditional Functions of Management (including Leadership)

presidents, and senior vice presidents—spend most of their time in the two functions of planning and organizing. They oversee the "big picture."

First-line, or front-line, managers, on the other hand, are typically involved in the "nitty gritty" of daily operations. These are the foremen, crew chiefs, and supervisors. Thus, first-line managers tend to spend much of their time in leading and controlling.

Leadership versus Management

Perusing the bottom half of Figure 3–1 prompts a very basic question for this text—indeed, for any participant of a class in leadership. Is leadership merely a subset of management? Just as we see with other disciplines—such as psychology, communications, political science, and military science—some management proponents might argue that, yes, leadership is one facet of management. The military, for example, asserts that leadership is a totally definable skill, a science that can be learned. Their training manuals outline the behaviors that typify leadership, so that to lead one must simply acquire those skills and behaviors (see Chapter 7 for a detailed discussion on military leadership).

We disagree. Along with other leadership theorists, we maintain that leadership is a piece of the pie, a part of management, but that there is a good bit of leadership that cannot be considered a subset of management. Leadership and management share some characteristics, but each is also separate and distinct. For a useful depiction of the distinctions between leadership and management, see Tables 3–1 and 3–2.

These tables do not define leadership and management, as neither is synonymous with nor a subject of the other. They describe leadership as both a process and a property (Jago, 1992). The process of practicing leadership is integral to this text, because it envisions leadership as a noncoercive influence that shapes an organization's culture and people and motivates participants toward a common goal. The property is the characteristic attributed to the people who are perceived as leaders (Yukl, 1995).

A person, then, may be skilled as a leader or manager or both—or neither. The skilled leader definitely needs to understand the principles of management. This brings us to the question: What is doing management all about?

While there is no one correct answer to this question, it is a beginning for our discussion. Table 3–3 lists Mintzberg's (1979) ten primary roles of a manager. Do you agree with this list? What would you add, change, or remove?

Much of the current debate on leadership has evolved from competing theories on management, as the next section describes.

The Evolution of Leadership from Scientific Management

Most management historians see leadership theory evolving from classical management work—most prominently the work of Taylor, Fayol, and Weber—in the late nineteenth and early twentieth centuries.

TABLE 3–1 **Distinctions Between Management and Leadership**

Activity	Management	Leadership
Creating an agenda	**Planning and budgeting.** Establishing detailed steps and timetables for achieving needed results: allocating the resources necessary to make those needed results happen.	**Establishing direction.** Developing a vision of the future, often the distant future, and strategies for producing the changes needed to achieve that vision.
Developing a human network for achieving the agenda	**Organizing and staffing.** Establishing some structure for accomplishing plan requirements, staffing that structure with individuals, delegating responsibility and authority for carrying out the plan, providing policies and procedures to help guide people, and creating methods or systems to monitor implementation.	**Aligning people.** Communicating the direction by words and deeds to all those whose cooperation may be needed to influence the creation of teams and coalitions that understand the vision and strategies and accept their validity.
Executing plans	**Controlling and problem solving.** Monitoring results vs. plan in some detail, identfiying deviations, and then planning and organizing to solve these problems.	**Motivating and inspiring.** Energizing people to overcome major political, bureaucratic, and resource barriers to change by satisfying very basic, but often unfulfilled, human needs.
Outcomes	Produce a degree of predictability and order and has the potential to consistently produce key results expected by various stakeholders (e.g., for customers, always being on time for stockholders, being on budget).	Produces change, often to a dramatic degree and has the potential to produce extremely useful change (e.g., new products that customers want, new approaches to labor relations that help make a firm more competitive).

Source: Reprinted with permission, by The Free Press, a Division of Simon & Schuster Inc. from *A Force for Change: How Leadership Differs from Management* by John P. Kotter. Copyright © 1996 by John P. Kotter, Inc.

In the 1890s, **Frederick Taylor,** the father of scientific management, felt that workers performed below their true abilities and that what they needed was proper direction and support. He drew on his engineering background to find the most efficient way to perform specific tasks. Applying his scientific management principles to the task of loading slab steel onto railroad cars, he meticulously analyzed each component of the job, then trained a hand-picked man to follow his directions precisely for each part of the task. Further, Taylor agreed to pay this man on a per-piece basis, a significant departure from standard practices at the time and one he predicted would encourage greater productivity. As a final step, Taylor arranged for the worker to focus only on the specific task of loading the steel, and Taylor, as the manager, oversaw related aspects, such as when and how the railroad car would be moved. The productivity gains were remarkable: productivity for this worker increased nearly fourfold. Taylor's experiment won over many who had been skeptical about such scientific approaches to work.

TABLE 3–2   **Distinctions Between Managers and Leaders**

Personality Dimension	Manager	Leader
Attitudes toward goals	Has an impersonal, passive, functional attitude; believes goals arise out of necessity and reality	Has a personal and active attitude; believes goals arise from desire and imagination
Conceptions of work	Views work as an enabling process that combines people, ideas, and things; seeks moderate risk through coordination and balance	Looks for fresh approaches to old problems; seeks high-risk positions, especially with high payoffs
Relationships with others	Avoids solitary work activty, preferring to work with others; avoids close, intense relationships; avoids conflict	Is comfortable in solitary work activity; encourages close, intense working relationships; is not conflict averse
Sense of self	Is once born; makes a straight-forward life adjustment; accepts life as it is	Is twice born; engages in a struggle for a sense of order in life; questions life

Specifically, Taylor called for:

1. A "science" for every job, including standardized work flow and work conditions
2. Carefully selected workers with the right ability to do each job
3. Careful training with proper incentives
4. Clear planning by managers

In 1916, **Henri Fayol** helped to further delineate the principles of management by setting forth five major management elements: planning, organizing, commanding, coordinating, and controlling. In the 1920s, sociologist **Max Weber** brought to the study of management the concept of bureaucracy, including a clear division of labor, a hierarchy of authority, formal rules and procedures, impersonality, and merit-based evaluations. Weber's notions of bureaucracy had none of the negative connotations that bureaucracies have today.

After World War I, when there was a tremendous increase in the demand for consumer goods, the **Hawthorne effect** was conceptualized. Simply put, as Ellen Mayo (1953) explained, if management increased its attention to workers, productivity also increased. From these findings the human relations movement evolved (discussed in Chapter 2), drawing on Maslow's hierarchy of human needs and McGregor's Theory X and Theory Y. Leadership theory continued to develop from these early works.

Beginning in the 1940s, the **quantitative management** perspectives (management science) emerged. This approach centers on applying mathematical models and processes to decision-making situations. **Operations management** focuses directly on applying management science to organizations. All leaders depend on

TABLE 3–3 Mintzberg's Roles

Role	Description
Figurehead	The manager, acting as a symbol or representative of the organization, performs diverse ceremonial duties. By attending Chamber of Commerce meetings, heading the local United Way drive, or representing the president of the firm at an awards banquet, a manager performs the figurehead role.
Leader	The manager, interacting with subordinates, motivates and develops them. The supervisor who conducts quarterly performance interviews or selects training opportunities for his or her subordinates performs the role of leader. This role emphasizes the social-emotional and people-oriented side of leadership and deemphasizes task activities, which are more often incorporated into the decisional roles.
Liaison	The manager establishes a network of contacts to gather information for the organization. Belonging to professional associations or meeting over lunch with peers in other organizations helps the manager perform the liaison role.
Monitor	The manager gathers information from the environment inside and outside the organization. He or she may attend meetings with subordinates, scan company publications, or participate in company-wide committees as a way of performing this role.
Disseminator	The manager transmits both factual and value information to subordinates. Managers may conduct staff meetings, send memorandums to their staff, or meet informally with them on a one-to-one basis to discuss current and future projects.
Spokesperson	The manager gives information to people outside the organization about its performance and policies. He or she oversees preparation of the annual report, prepares advertising copy, or speaks at community and professional meetings.
Entrepreneur	The manager designs and initiates change in the organization. The supervisor who redesigns the jobs of subordinates, introduces flexible working hours, or brings new technology to the job performs this role.
Disturbance handler	The manager deals with problems that arise when organizational operations break down. A person who finds a new supplier on short notice for an out-of-stock part, who replaces unexpectedly absent employees, or who deals with machine breakdowns performs this role.
Resource allocator	The manager controls the allocation of people, money, materials, and time by scheduling his or her own time, programming subordinates' work effort, and authorizing all significant decisions. Preparation of the budget is a major aspect of this role.
Negotiator	The manager participates in negotiation activities. A manager who hires a new employee may negotiate work assignments or compensation with that person.

Source: These roles are drawn from H. Mintzberg, *The Nature of Managerial Work* (Englewood Cliffs, N.J.: Prentice-Hall, 1979).

information and management science as the basis for much of the information used by decision makers. One of the century's leading theorists on management, W. Edwards Deming, began his career as a physics instructor and then moved on to statistics. From this base, he molded the highly influential principles of quality. (Deming and the quality movement are discussed later in this chapter.)

Management information science, commonly referred to within organizations as MIS, is a fairly recent subset of the management science perspective. In MIS, problems are examined and solved via quantifiable analysis.

Since the 1960s, we have seen other developments in management that have directly affected leadership. For instance, leadership scholars have examined management skills at different levels with an understanding of the impact of technical, conceptual, interpersonal, and diagnostic skills on top managers, middle managers, and first-line managers, as shown in Figure 3–2. The discussion has yielded useful information for both leaders and managers.

Similarly, the debate over whether management (and leadership) is a science or an art has also influenced the dialogue. Those who argue that leadership is a science believe that the issue can be approached in a logical, rational, objective manner. They stress the use of management science and "hard" data. Others, however, who feel that intuition, experience, and instinct are crucial, rely heavily on interpersonal and conceptual skills.

Contemporary Management Issues

Among the more contemporary management issues, the systems approach to organizations has had significant effects on leadership theory. This approach depicts a system as a set of interrelated parts that work together as a whole to achieve goals. In this view, organizations were originally considered **closed** systems; that is, they were not affected by outside events or situations. In reality, all organizations are **open systems.** They must deal with the environment to survive.

Clearly, then, individuals can't lead unless they have a thorough understanding of the organization as an open system, along with an appreciation of the makeup of the external and internal forces impinging on it. From the systems theorists came the word *synergy,* which describes the product of separate parts working together, making something more than merely the total of the separate parts by themselves.

The systems approach also suggests that managers consider the organization's internal forces, such as the subgroups and the effects of these subgroups on the

Management skills—different skills are needed at different levels			
Conceptual	Technical	Diagnostic	Interpersonal
Top management	XXXXXXXXX	XXX	XXXXXXXXX	XXX
Middle management	XXXXXX	XXXXXX	XXXXXX	XXXXXX
Front-line management	XXX	XXXXXXXXX	XXX	XXXXXXXXX

Figure 3–2   Management Skills—Different Skills Are Needed at Different Levels

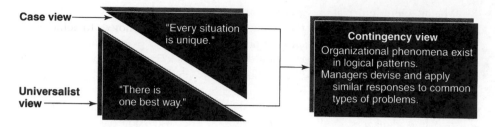

Figure 3–3   The Contingency View of Management

Source: Figures from *Management,* Third Edition, by Richard L. Daft; Copyright © 1994 by the Dryden Press. Reprinted with permission.

entire organization. (For example, see Chapter 4 for a discussion of the grapevine and its potential impact on organizational communication.)

Although classical management theory states that there is only one best way to resolve an issue, today there is widespread agreement with the **contingency theory,** which suggests that appropriate behavior in a given situation depends on a wide variety of variables and that each situation is different. What might work in one company with one set of issues, employees, and customers might not work in a different company with different issues, employees, and customers. See Figure 3–3.

Although it is impossible to address the impact of globalization on management and leadership theory in a few short paragraphs, it's indisputable that the impact of markets across the world on U.S. business has meant a significant change in perspectives. Organizations are being affected by the increasingly broad sweep of day-to-day life. How can it be considered anything but a sea change when we can electronically access the latest figures on the Hong Kong stock market and in the next minute communicate via the Internet with a consultant in Eastern Europe? Never again can business ignore global implications for organizations, as the U.S. auto makers learned to their peril in the 1980s.

Management has formed a key basis for leadership theory. Both classical and contemporary issues have provided vital data and insights for leaders and followers.

Two individuals who have successfully applied management concepts to practicing leadership in corporate settings are John E. Pepper, chairman of the board of Procter & Gamble, and Maureen Kempston Darkes, president of GM Canada. What follows are some of their thoughts on the characteristics of effective leadership.

LEADERSHIP

JOHN E. PEPPER

Leadership is an intriguing subject for me, and I'm happy to offer my observations about its development. First, a definition. Leadership to me is the particular process of guiding, directing, and motivating an organization to outstanding achievement in the organization's fundamental purposes.

Leading, then, involves articulating the appropriate vision, helping to develop what I call "stretching" objectives, making the right strategic choices to achieve the objectives; and implementing effective deployment plans to ensure that the resources and other necessary means are available to reach those objectives.

Leaders must also set the standards that guide the growth of the organization's culture and its results. Further, leaders must communicate with people so as to inspire them to exceed their previous achievements.

Clearly, the kind of leadership I'm describing pertains to all manner of activities, including a football team, an industry, a city, a nation, a household.

In my experience, I've found that certain qualities characterize the most effective leaders. I've identified four major benchmarks.

A Compelling Vision

Every effective leader I've known has possessed a personally felt vision and goals. Deep commitments that they are not only willing, but anxious to share with others.

There's almost a spiritual dimension to the conviction these leaders have about the purpose of the organization for which they are responsible. Think about the great football coaches Lou Holtz, George Allen. They both had unwavering commitments to their teams' excellence.

Simply put, if you don't believe in something passionately, you cannot be an effective leader. Yet it goes well beyond the passionate belief, to a concern for achieving the organization's basic purpose—its highest values—at the highest possible level. And then constantly improving that performance.

At P&G [Procter & Gamble], this means serving the consumer, winning in the market place, and achieving both financial and share leadership. It also means building a place of employment that attracts the best people around and helps them fulfill their ambitions. This aspect of leadership focuses on one's belief in innovation, growth, continuing improvement, and contribution to the company.

The most effective leaders at P&G, then, are those who believe deeply in the aforementioned values and who continually define what they mean, as well as how best to achieve them. Of course, these central values are shared by others at the company.

The question becomes, how does one develop this compelling vision? Let me address that on a personal level. I've worked at defining my personal goals as well as those of my department/subsidiary, and as the years have gone by, the company.

I have found a personal mission and priority statement very helpful in defining my goals long before they became so trendy. More than twenty-five years ago, I started what has become a personal tradition. I write down on a piece of paper what I want to do and what I want to contribute; where I need to improve; and what lessons I've learned. For these twenty-five years I've pulled out that piece of paper every six months or so.

It has been more than just a reminder to me. It has helped me build a deeper commitment to certain purposes and values and priorities, including superior products for the consumer, innovation, taking the offensive, and respect for the individual.

Personal commitment to a mission is vital, and it simply can't be manufactured. No matter what area you pursue, the capacity to be completely dedicated to a career or mission or strategy or tactic is all-important to its success. For the capacity to be totally dedicated is the foundation of a compelling vision, one that can be shared by others.

The kind of true leadership that involves taking risks and putting oneself forward as an example requires that the individual have deep convictions about a set of principles or a project that needs to be done.

The Ability to Inspire

Once the vision is in place, a leader must then have the capacity to inspire others in its pursuit—not blindly or unquestioningly, but with enough fervor to achieve the goals.

In my experiences, I've found leaders with different characteristics who persuade others to pursue the vision. Part of this infectious nature of leadership is due to the importance of the mission itself. Yet part also comes from a burning desire within the most effective leaders for action—to win—to contribute—to serve.

This brings us to the question of appetite. The appetite for pushing oneself to be the best we can be and to help others be the best they can be. This drive springs from different sources within us, and from a mixture of sources. Many people's drive is sparked by a deep commitment to serving others.

All of us, I believe, are pushed by the drive to win, to be our best selves. To keep improving.

For me, the three greatest drivers in my work and life have been to serve, to be the best I can be, and to win.

Winning is something we all understand. In our highly competitive business, people won't succeed if they aren't winning against the competition. Competition provides a great benchmark, and, frankly, it spurs the adrenaline. Winning is fun.

Service is another great motivator—service to consumers, shareholders, our communities, and employees. Better service than before, better service than our competitors, better service in the absolute. That points to the quality of our products, and in having major preferences in consumer acceptance versus competition. It comes down to the value of our products.

Going into a country in Eastern Europe where we've never sold before, providing products of a quality consumers have never seen before—that's service. That's rewarding.

And it's service to employees, employees who stake their lives with the company, to offer them the training and the environment where they can grow to their fullest. In Eastern Europe, China, and Russia, young men and women can contribute in ways they've never before imagined.

It's service, too, to the communities where we work. We're involved in education and in other fields where the leadership of P&G can help. In addition, we serve the environment directly through our products and our processes.

That drive to be all you can be keeps you learning and growing. Each of the strongest leaders I've known would describe these drivers—the ones that enable them to inspire others in their vision—somewhat differently. Yet in all cases the drives are honestly felt and experienced, and ones we must nourish.

Initiative, Focus on Results, Courage, and Tenacity

The most effective leaders I've known take the initiative to make the biggest personal difference, the most significant personal contribution they can. Whatever action they're focused on, they're fully engaged in trying to make things better than they are at present. Real leaders don't wait for permission. And their willingness to jump into the situation makes work fun for them, and for those around them. Their initiative also produces results that are recognized and rewarded.

These men and women have a laser-like focus on results. Their inner drive propels them to make things happen and get things done, producing a better tomorrow than today. They display an enormous amount of energy and capacity.

True leaders have the kind of personal courage that fuels their pursuit of their convictions, even when this means persisting against significant opposition. They're unafraid to say and do what may be unpopular. To do what they're convinced is right. These leaders are transparent

They are forceful advocates for what they believe in, even—indeed, especially when that goes against the grain.

Most of the biggest decisions I've been involved in have been controversial. The decisions have come about because someone had the courage to persist with a point of view.

Many of P&G's largest brands today were subjects of controversy when they began. Take Bounce Dryer-Added Fabric Softener. There were many who wondered whether putting a sheet in a dryer would appeal to consumers. In fact, the patent was turned down by other companies and almost by P&G until someone with a strong conviction that this could be made into a high-performing, high-value product persuaded the company to proceed. And now Bounce is one of our most successful brands, highly accepted by consumers and providing excellent returns to Procter & Gamble.

In the same way, these leaders have the courage to take command, to be decisive, to ask for action. After they've reviewed all the options and the discussions and debates have run their course, these leaders reach the point where they must step out and exercise their own responsibility.

One example we encountered in the 1980s was the need to bring a regional focus to our operations in Europe. Through much of our history, we had operated almost as separate fiefdoms—each country on its own. That was fine in some respects, but it became clear that it was necessary to focus our research and development efforts against a narrower group of projects if we were to achieve true performance and value breakthroughs for the consumer. We also had to rationalize our production sourcing in Europe so that we could achieve greater reliability and lower costs for consumers. That required a major change in mindset in the way we operated. It was very controversial. Ultimately, as the head of European operations, I needed to make the decision that this was the right way to go in the future.

In order to carry out this responsibility for decision making, it is essential to deal with problems head-on and not avoid them. Overcome difficult obstacles rather than put them off. With that conviction, I've always aimed to tackle the toughest problems first.

Persistence

Finally, my great leaders don't give up. They push on and on. It reminds me of my favorite story about Winston Churchill. After he retired from public office, he was asked to address the students and faculty at his grammar school. As you can imagine, the headmaster was very excited and told the students to prepare to hear one of the greatest talks they'd ever hear in their lifetimes.

The day arrived and Winston Churchill walked out on the stage with a small piece of paper, on which was written a few notes. He peered down at the audience, over his glasses, and said:

"Never, never, never, never give up."

And with that, he turned around and went back to his seat. Initially, the audience was surprised and let down. They'd expected so much more. But in time, they came to view it as the most important talk they could have heard. It summarized a lifetime of experience in just six words.

I've never forgotten this. I never will.

MAUREEN KEMPSTON DARKES: VALUING DIVERSITY AT GM CANADA

Maureen Kempston Darkes assumed the presidency of GM Canada on July 1, 1994. As the first woman to head Canada's largest industrial company, she has attracted intense media scrutiny. Her young administration boasts several ground-breaking changes in GM Canada's corporate culture.

The former vice president of corporate affairs and general counsel for GM Canada notes that she always enjoyed setting direction and trying to create something of value. From her early days with GM, she has been very interested in ensuring that people could have a voice in the company.

"I was a founding member of the Women's Advisory Council," she says, explaining that the group works to ensure that employees can genuinely participate in the business. "It's a very strong group that provides me with feedback and insight about a number of issues." Kempston Darkes credits the Council with helping her develop new policy, such as the flexible working hours and alternative work schedules recently adopted by the company.

"What's interesting about the flexible working arrangement," she says, "is that we originally looked at it for women. It turns out, however, that it's really been used more by people moving toward retirement age. It helps them transition. Every time we become more flexible we serve more people, and we develop a better product."

Valuing Differences

A leader, says Kempston Darkes, must provide clear vision, motivation, and guidance. "But leadership is also about counseling and mentoring. The end result is creating an environment where people can fully participate."

"People, after all, are our most important resource. Unless we can focus on their unique abilities, we're not fully utilizing our resources," she asserts.

Dealing with diversity is a key component of leadership to her. "To me, the challenge is creating a culture where people can contribute to the company regardless of sex, cultural difference, age, any other kind of difference. When we can create this climate, we can better understand our workforce, the marketplace—the whole environment."

She stresses the connection between diversity in the workforce and the increasingly diverse marketplace. "If I have a very diverse sales force, I can better relate to that market. Or take a look at the college graduates. I want to attract and retain talent. That means recruiting them, but also once they're here, making sure they're respected and considered. So this is not just about managing diversity. It's about valuing diversity. And there's a quantum leap between the two."

She has directed her senior management staff to examine every aspect of GM Canada's corporate culture in an attempt to value diversity. "We're very much in the beginning stages here. Our goal is to have a fully empowered workforce."

Listening

"For me," she says, "real listening begins with understanding the customer base. So any leader should be prepared to be out in the field. I spend a considerable part of my time in the field."

Listening makes good business sense. "Sloan said it best: 'The quickest way to profit is to serve the customer in ways the customer wants to be served.' We do that and then ask ourselves, 'How can we exceed that?'"

"If we're pushing up market share, it's because we listen to the customer better and translate what he/she wants into products or services."

One example is twenty-four-hour roadside assistance offered on any new car or truck purchased from GM Canada. "Why do we know that's important to the customers? Because they told us," she says.

Leaders must also listen to the workforce, Kempston Darkes says, and they must be willing to appreciate constructive feedback. "Our business is so competitive, you can't have a huge ego. You have to continually get better, and you can't do that sitting still."

To promote accessibility, she shuns the traditional grand executive office in favor of a smaller, less imposing one with a glass conference room next door. "It's symbolic that I and my senior managers are quite open."

GM Canada has also instituted a less formal dress code, which the employees monitor themselves. Depending on outside contact, the employees don't have to wear ties. Further, there is no executive dining room, no preferred parking. "It's symbolic, of course," she says, "but we're trying to promote the idea of openness and teamwork."

Insisting that she wants to hear what employees have to say, she adopts what she calls "a no fuss routine." On her frequent stops at dealerships and plants across Canada, she talks to people, asking them questions and giving them the chance to offer their own ideas and suggestions.

"I come back and work on those ideas. Empowered people have so much to contribute. Most people want to be able to contribute. The most frustrating thing in the world is to have an idea but no one willing to listen to it."

Finally, Kempston Darkes asserts that leaders must have a sense of balance. "Home and family are very important. Workaholics get a lot accomplished, true, but they can be too hard on others. You're more able to understand your employees when you search for the balance yourself." She and her husband have recently built a log home an hour north of Toronto, where they try—not always successfully, she admits—to escape for quiet time together.

THE QUALITY MOVEMENT

In recent years several proponents of a more comprehensive approach to ensuring quality in products and services have emerged. The teachings of these quality gurus often contrast starkly with the prevailing beliefs of managers. In the 1950s, as Japanese business tried to rebuild after World War II, these quality teachers were well received, but they were shunned in the United States until the 1980s, when Japanese companies exerted tremendous pressure on American business. Apparently, necessity is also the mother of radically new approaches to leadership, as industrial leaders in both countries only adopted the new approaches when they were desperate.

W. Edwards Deming

The best-known quality pioneer worldwide was Dr. W. Edwards Deming of the United States. Deming (1900–1993) was raised on a homestead in Wyoming with a strong ethic not to waste anything. He was quite a scholar, studying engineering and math before completing a Ph.D. in physics. During summers between school sessions, the young Deming worked in sweatshop-style factories, where he developed a deep sympathy for the working person. Although Deming started by teaching statistical quality control, he gradually developed a system of fourteen points. Fittingly, he tinkered with the wording and explanation of some of these points up to his death at age 93. Deming believed that while minor improvements might be possible by choosing to perform some of the points, skipping any of them would greatly diminish the total success. **Deming's 14 points** form a manifesto of what is wrong with traditional Western-style management (Deming would not call traditional practices leadership; he would call them management). Because many leaders initially found Deming's points counter to their normal way of thinking, they rejected them. Others willingly accepted some points, but disagreed with others. The fourteen points are shown here in Deming's own words, although many other writers have adapted them. Numerous books, articles, study groups, and seminars have been devoted to understanding Deming's ideas. For a man who had minor influence in his own country until age 80, Deming will long have a profound influence on the United States and the world.

Deming's Fourteen Points[*]

1. Create constancy of purpose toward improvement of product and service, with the aim to become competitive and stay in business, and to provide jobs.

2. Adopt the new philosophy. We are in a new economic age. Western management must awaken to the challenge, must learn their responsibilities, and take on leadership for change.

3. Cease dependence on inspection to achieve quality. Eliminate the need for inspection on a mass basis by building quality into the product in the first place.

4. End the practice of awarding business on the basis of the price tag. Instead, minimize total cost. Move toward a single supplier for any one item, on a long-term basis of trust.

5. Improve constantly and forever the system of production and service, to improve quality and productivity, and thus constantly decrease cost.

6. Institute training on the job.

7. Institute leadership. The aim of supervision should be to help people and machines and gadgets to do a better job. Supervision of management is in need of overhaul, as well as supervision of production workers.

8. Drive out fear so that everyone may work effectively for the company.

9. Break down barriers between departments. People in research, design, sales, and production must work as a team, to foresee problems of production and use that may be encountered with the product or service.

10. Eliminate slogans, exhortations, and targets for the work force asking for zero defects and new levels of productivity. Such exhortations only create adversarial relationships, as the bulk of the causes of low quality and productivity belong to the system and thus lie beyond the power of the work force.

11. Eliminate work standards (quotas) on the factory floor. Substitute leadership. Eliminate management by objective. Eliminate management by numbers, numerical goals. Substitute leadership.

12. Remove barriers that rob the hourly worker of his right to pride of workmanship. The responsibility of supervisors must be changed from sheer numbers

[*]W. Edwards Deming, *Out of the Crisis* (Cambridge, Mass.: MIT Center for Advanced Engineering Study, 1986), pp. 23–24.

to quality. Remove barriers that rob people in management and engineering of their right to pride of workmanship. This means *inter alia*, abolishment of the annual or merit rating and of management by objective.

13. Institute a vigorous program of education and improvement.

14. Put everybody in the company to work to accomplish the transformation. The transformation is everybody's job.

Joseph Juran

Dr. Joseph Juran was born in Romania, came to the United States as a boy just before World War I, and spent his youth performing odd jobs to earn money for his family. Trained as an engineer, he worked for Western Electric Company in a variety of engineering and quality-related assignments. Juran and Deming were influenced by some of the same people and ideas early in their careers. Juran received a law degree working at night, then worked for the U.S. government during World War II and taught engineering for several years. In 1951, Juran published his acclaimed Quality Control Handbook, which many people still consider to be the quality "bible." On numerous occasions Juran traveled to Japan, where he taught middle and upper managers the importance of direct managerial involvement in improving quality. Management, he told them, was as important to quality as the statistical approaches they had already started to use. In fact, the combination of statistical and management approaches has proven exceedingly effective in Japan and elsewhere.

In contrast to Deming's demands for an overthrow of Western-style management systems, Juran focused on improving current management systems, thereby showing concern for practical quality improvement issues.

Juran's quality improvement model, sometimes referred to as a breakthrough sequence, consists of the following tasks:

1. Convince important decision makers that the improvement is needed.

2. Set logical improvement goals based on a reasonable plan.

3. Organize a project team to reach the goals with specific guidance on what to do.

4. Provide the team adequate training.

5. Identify the causes of the problem.

6. Develop a set of possible approaches to solve the problem, select one approach, and implement it on a small scale.

7. Evaluate the results.

8. Improve the approach, if needed, and implement it.

9. Overcome the resistance that some people are bound to have concerning the new methods.

10. Standardize the approach to maintain the improvement through training, control charts, and so on.

Juran has proven to be very accurate in predicting the direction of quality. As far back as the middle 1960s, he warned the Western world that Japan would overtake them in quality and productivity because of their quality improvement efforts. Now Juran calls the twentieth century the Century of Productivity. By the end of the century there was greater worldwide supply than demand of most products and services. The result, he says, is that customers can increasingly demand excellent quality, and companies that do not produce it will go out of business. Juran believes this trend will be so strong that he has already named the twenty-first century the Century of Quality!

Now that we have scratched the surface of the ideas of two leading quality experts, what lessons for leaders can we draw from them? We envision the lessons grouped under four primary paradigms.

Paradigms

1. **Quality must be a systematic approach.**
   Minor improvements may result from using some of the quality concepts and tools, but major improvement requires that they be used as an integrated whole. The Malcolm Baldrige National Quality Award in the United States has become the most common framework for describing the various parts of Total Quality Management. The Baldrige framework states that leadership is what fuels a quality effort. Without active, direct leadership, improvement will not happen.

2. **Customers are the reason we do everything we do.**
   Every time we answer the phone, fill out a piece of paper, cut metal, or answer a question it is because someone needs the output of that action. That someone is a customer, either external or internal to our organization. We need to identify that customer and his or her needs and treat satisfying those needs as our reason for existing.

3. **Leaders must understand long-term thinking.**
   Because our goal must be the long-term viability of our organization, we must frequently make decisions that help in the long run, but may cost us money or inconvenience now.

4. **Quality improvement requires a series of different thinking patterns.**
   Instead of always thinking in linear logic, we must frequently think first in a divergent manner such as brainstorming possibilities, then in a convergent manner such as prioritizing or selecting.

Teams develop in a predictable progression that leaders must understand and plan for. Leaders generally need to develop more influencing skills for dealing with teams rather than just directing them. For example, teams often make decisions using consensus for which all team members must truly agree. Teams also need to be empowered to make some decisions that previously may have been made at levels higher in the organization. If leaders suggest teams will get to make decisions, but then do not actually let them because the decision does not conform to what the leader wants, all efforts are likely to backfire. Finally, measuring team process and results and establishing appropriate reward and recognition systems place demands on leaders (see Figure 3-4).

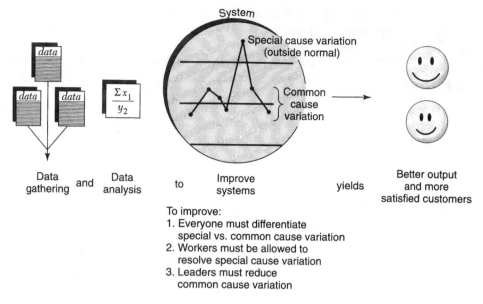

| Data gathering | and | Data analysis | to | Improve systems | yields | Better output and more satisfied customers |

To improve:
1. Everyone must differentiate special vs. common cause variation
2. Workers must be allowed to resolve special cause variation
3. Leaders must reduce common cause variation

Figure 3–4   Using Facts

Organizations, Teams, and Leadership

Leadership and management theorists have long struggled with the issues of meeting the needs, concerns, and expectations of the organization and each of its stakeholders as they balance individual needs. The organization is seen as an entity just as each individual is. The organization has a life cycle, its ups and downs, and its "personality"— just as each person involved does. The field of Organizational Development systematically studies these issues.

In recent years, increasing emphasis has been placed on teams, teamwork, and "teaming." Teams may be single or multipurpose. They may be led autocratically, democratically, or be self-directed. They may be single focus or multifunctional. They may exist for brief periods of time or be expected to continue indefinitely. The leadership challenge is different depending on the team's mission, life cycle, size, purpose, and so on.

In understanding leadership roles for a team, it can be studied as a static or dynamic entity. As a static entity, group processes are often reviewed to ensure that the various group roles are being played and that the group's and each member's needs are being attended to.

Dynamic teams are often looked at in terms of their stages of development.

The Stages of Group Development   All organisms go through various stages of development on their journey to maturity. The team organism is no different. There is an emerging belief that teams go through five stages of development on their journey to maturity. These stages are forming, storming, norming, performing, and adjourning.

Forming   **Forming,** the initial stage of team development, is marked by a period of acclimation. It is during this time that individual team members begin to form impressions about their colleagues' personalities, work habits, social habits, and thinking styles. This is also a time filled with great uncertainty in the minds of individual group members who are then often accepting of the authoritative role of a leader.

Storming   The second stage of group development is known as **storming.** During the storming phase, individual group members begin to feel more comfortable in the presence of other group members. It is under these circumstances that individual personalities begin to come to the surface. Team members will begin to voice their expectations and opinions, along with their vision, for the group as a whole, as well as for themselves as participating members of the group.

The storming stage is a time typified by conflict, disagreement, and a seeming lack of organization and agreement. The storming stage can be a perilous time for the group and therefore for the leader as well. Without properly dealing with the tide of ideas and conflict, which accompany the storming stage, group dynamics may be inadvertently damaged or destroyed. Under these circumstances, it is the role of the leader to promote the open sharing of ideas and opinions, while at the same time maintaining a level of conflict that is healthy and productive.

Norming   The **norming** stage of team development arises out of the conflict that is present in the storming phase. During the norming phase, conflict is resolved and team members begin to accept and understand one another. The roles that the team members must take on in order to achieve success are identified. A sense of team identity emerges, and the goals and objectives of the team come to the forefront. It is the role of the leader during the norming stage to promote group unity.

Performing   During the **performing** stage there is a strong emphasis on the accomplishment of the team's goals or tasks. The roles of each individual team member and the procedures the team will follow have been established, so the performing stage is marked by conflict resolution and open communication, which are embraced for the purpose of task accomplishment. During the performing stage, team members show a high commitment to the team and the team's goals. Leaders should focus on directing actions toward task accomplishment.

Adjourning   Not all teams go through the final stage of team development, known as **adjourning.** During the adjourning phase the team prepares for termination. Permanent teams may never experience this stage. For those teams that do, however, there is an emphasis on finishing up the final details surrounding the team's goals. Team performance becomes less of a priority. Team unity is often very high. Individuals going through the adjourning phase usually experience a high degree of contradictory emotions. On one hand, there is a great deal of pride in the accomplishment of the team task. On the other hand, the individual may feel despair and regret at the loss of closeness and purpose that the team represented. The goal of the leader in the adjourning stage is to help team members to transition into new roles by providing a sense of closure as well as praise and thanks for the successful completion of the task.

Advantages to Working in Teams

Teams often provide many benefits, including some that they were not expecting. One of the major benefits and reasons for adopting the team approach is the enhanced performance that this structure provides.

Teams often produce a higher quality and quantity of output than the combined output of each individual member working alone. There are a number of reasons for this. First, a team provides for a diverse set of knowledge and skills that a single individual could never have alone. Also, the team approach allows members to deal immediately with problems as they arise, rather than dealing with the delays that departmentalization can cause, as well as the fact that several people will be working on the same project. This allows mistakes to be caught and corrected more readily.

Teams also provide for a higher degree of innovation. Teams are comprised of multiple individuals who each bring an exclusive set of skills and knowledge, and bring a unique perspective. This allows a team to deal with situations in a way that a lone individual might not consider.

Another benefit that teams provide, and one that often comes as a pleasant surprise in organizations, is an increase in employee satisfaction and motivation. As a member of a team, employees are often able to see the results of their contributions. This tends to have a motivating effect on the employee. And, as a result, many organizations see a decline in turnover and absenteeism, even if that was not the original objective of the team design.

Barriers to Effective Teamwork

There are also some potential hazards that all leaders should be aware of when dealing with teams.

One such hazard is called **groupthink,** which is the impairment in decision making and sound judgment that can occur in highly cohesive groups. It can be identified when group members dismiss information that undermines their position, shun dissidents, and unify around a decision that may be unfounded.

Another potential problem with teams is the phenomenon known as **social loafing.** Social loafing is the tendency for individuals to lower their level of effort when it is believed that the results of their efforts won't be directly attributed to them, but will instead be shared by the team as a whole. In essence, people tend to hide in groups when they think they won't be noticed.

The field of leadership is moving from an emphasis on individuals to the concept of dealing with all kinds of teams, from self-directed multifunctional work teams to more traditional single-focus teams with a designated leader. These challenges and opportunities are being defined in the contemporary explorations of team leadership. The following two profiles highlight successful leaders who understand the importance and power of effective teams.

DEAN SMITH: TEACHER OF TEAMWORK

Since arriving at the University of North Carolina, Chapel Hill, in 1961, former head basketball coach Dean Smith has fashioned one of the leading college athletics programs in the country. Not only are the Tarheels arguably the most successful college basketball team of all time, but the program has also avoided scandal and managed to have an excellent record for graduating its basketball players both during and immediately following Smith's tenure.

Smith's teams were known for their cunning defenses, their discipline, and above all, their unselfishness. Coach Smith stressed teamwork as the highest priority. No matter how talented the players are individually—and he has coached Michael Jordan, James Worthy, Jerry Stackhouse, Vince Carter, and dozens of others who have gone on to successful NBA careers—Smith wanted no part of a "star system" at UNC. Instead, he placed a higher value on assists than points. As a result, few of his players have averaged 20 points per game, and that's more than okay with him.

He reportedly has never promised playing time, even to stellar prospects. When the newcomers arrive on campus, he assigns them an underling role to upperclassmen. For instance, they may be asked carry the film projector and chase loose balls in practice.

In addition to the stress on unselfish play and teamwork, Smith has instituted many other innovations, including huddling at the free throw line before foul shots and allowing tired players to take themselves out of the game.

Despite an incredible overall win/loss record (851–247) and coaching the 1976 U.S. Olympic team to a gold medal performance, Smith for years was dogged by the media for never winning an NCAA title, even though his teams made repeated trips to the Final Four and the championship game.

When asked about it, he said "If we win, I won't be a better coach."

When the 1981–82 team finally obtained the coveted NCAA title with a last-second win over Georgetown, Smith's players were happy to have won for him. Guard Jimmy Black, who had endured his mother's death and his own near-fatal car accident, said, "In my times of tragedy, he [Smith] has always been there to lean on. This is our way of repaying him for being a shoulder."

Frequently deflecting praise to his players, Smith that night asserted that his protege, Georgetown's John Thompson, had outcoached him. "And I don't think I'm a better coach now because we've won a national championship....If we lost, I'd have another shot; I'd feel for those kids who wouldn't have another chance. Just because they won, I won't like them any more than last year's team," he said.

Despite the effect on future seasons, Smith has repeatedly counseled those juniors projected to be among the top five picks in the NBA to enter the draft. This has meant losing the services of such notables as Jordan, James Worthy, and many others, most of whom have returned to earn their degrees.

Long after they've left the team, the players frequently return to visit Smith and keep in close contact with him and with each other. Michael Jordan, for instance, gave Smith his 1991 NBA championship ring. They report that more than simply being a coach, he has been a friend and a teacher, concerned with their lives beyond basketball.

A shoe contract he signed with Nike near the end of his coaching career was far different from the contracts many coaches sign: it covered the entire athletic department of the university, providing shoes and apparel for twenty-four university teams; funded the basketball team's international exhibition tour; and paid the university as well. Rather than pocketing the money himself, as most coaches do, Smith donated the entire signing bonus ($500,000) to charity. He also earmarked $45,000 of his annual $300,000 endorsement salary from Nike to a fund that helps former players finish their degrees and divided the rest among his assistants and office staff.

BARRY AND ELIOT TATELMAN: FUN, FAMILIES, FURNITURE

Most companies would give anything to have Warren Buffet call them "one of the most phenomenal and unique companies that I have ever seen. The reputation . . . from their employees, their customers, and the community is unparalleled. This company is a gem!" Chairman and CEO of Berkshire Hathaway Inc., Buffet offered this high praise for Jordan's Furniture, a decidedly unconventional furniture operation centered in the Boston area. Buffet's comments came with the announcement that Jordan's Furniture would merge with a Berkshire Hathaway subsidiary.

Brothers Eliot and Barry Tatelman celebrated the merger in a typically innovative way: they gave every member of their 1,200-person organization a bonus of 50 cents for every hour worked for Jordan's. Since most of the employees have been with the company for 10 or 20 years and more, it meant a tidy little sum. The longest-term employee pocketed $40,000.

Such generosity is nothing new to the Brothers Tatelman. In 1970, they inherited the store begun by their grandfather Samuel Tatelman (and subsequently run by their father, Eddie Tatelman) in 1928 in Waltham, Massachusetts, and have exercised a variety of employee-pleasing options ever since. Recently, a spontaneous staff holiday meant flying the company's 1,200 employees to Bermuda for a day-long beach party and barbeque.

The investment has been worth it, not only in being able to hire excellent salespeople during an unusually tight labor market, but also in keeping customers happy to return to Jordan's.

"You're only as good as your weakest link," says Barry. "Our stores are exciting, our values are good, the entertainment factor is there, the service is incredible." But what stands out above all else is Jordan's staff. "Our people smile and are genuinely happy to be where they are," he says.

And who could blame them? Jordan's four sites are nothing like stuffy furniture stores—they're theme parks that emphasize family fun and good corporate citizenship. The company is affiliated with a host of local charities, including local Big Brothers and

Big Sisters and the Massachusetts Adoption Resource Exchange. For the latter, Jordan's hosted an "adoption party" that drew more than 2,000 people and resulted in at least six children finding adoptive families. Staff members get involved in the charity events, deriving a sense of satisfaction that mere paychecks can't supply.

The stores themselves are marvels: a Bourbon Street simulation complete with Dixieland band and Mardi Gras regalia, a $2.5 million laser-enhanced thrill ride called the "Motion Odyssey Movie," in-house full-service family restaurants, and hourly animatronic entertainment versions of the Beatles, Elvis, and the Supremes.

The Tatelmans use "Las Vegas-style" marketing designed to bring people into their stores in the same way casinos use entertainment to lure people to gamble. "We were going to bring people to a furniture store for something other than furniture and make them walk through the whole store," explains Eliot.

Especially for families, the stores have become weekend destinations, and they also sell furniture—enough so that 1999 sales figures neared $250 million. Jordan's has incredible market identity despite spending only 1 to 2% of their gross revenues on advertising.

One industry analyst attributes their success to credibility. "The number one reason for their success is that people believe in the company," says Britt Beemer with America's Research Group in Charleston, South Carolina. "The more you get people to believe in the company, the less you have to keep lowering and lowering and lowering your prices to get people to buy from you."

SUMMARY

This chapter touches on three areas of study that have shaped the growing field of leadership. Management, like leadership, can be characterized by a variety of definitions. The ambiguity, in fact, has spawned some controversy over whether leadership is a subset of management or vice versa. The authors review this issue and assert that, although the two fields share many features, each has its own separate elements. The beginnings of scientific management are traced and contemporary systems approaches are described.

Following John Pepper's remarks about leadership and a profile on Maureen Kempston Darkes, the chapter continues with a discussion of the quality movement and two of its early quality leaders, W. Edwards Deming and Joseph Juran. A final section on the implications of the quality movement for leadership addresses the stages of group development and teamwork.

CREATE YOUR OWN THEORY

Are you a manager or a leader? Or perhaps a combination of the two? In what situations do you find it easier to lead? What is your perspective on the attributes of quality circles? Do leaders always need to be team players? In what contexts is teamwork paramount? Is working well in teams consistent with your view of the attributes of the ideal leader for the twenty-first century?

Now let's revisit our opening Leadership Moment. If you were coaching a girls' soccer team, which would be more important to you—winning or developing teamwork skills in your players? Does one lead to the other? Would you be likely to share the viewpoints of some of the parents that certain players should get less playing time because they are not as skilled as the others, or do you have the perspective that at age 10 all of the girls should play for approximately equal lengths of time (including your own daughter)? Would your answer be different if the girls were 5 years old? How about if they were all 16? What if you were coaching a team of boys instead of girls? What distinctions might you make? What does that say about your leadership style?

KEY TERMS

management
Frederick Taylor
Henri Fayol
Max Weber
Hawthorne effect
quantitative management
operations management
closed systems
open systems
contingency theory

Deming's 14 points
Juran's quality improvement model
forming (stage of group development)
storming (stage of group development)
norming (stage of group development)
performing (stage of group development)
adjourning (stage of group development)
groupthink
social loafing

QUESTIONS FOR DISCUSSION AND REVIEW

1. What does Fayol identify as the five key functions of management?

2. What are some key roles of managers as identified by Mintzberg? In which situations might each role be most effective?

3. What is the primary distinction between early management theories (i.e., Taylor, Fayol, Weber) and contemporary theories?

4. Do you see management as being more an art or a science? Why?

5. According to Deming, what were the key historical factors behind Japan's embracing of modern quality principles before U.S. managers did?

6. What are some common themes linking Deming's fourteen points? Which points seem particularly important to you, and why?

7. What are some of the paradigms that Total Quality Management demands of leaders?

8. To what extent do you feel that TQM principles will be a factor in leadership development and practices in the twenty-first century?

9. What are the stages of a team's development?

10. What are groupthink and social loafing and what threats do they hold for effective team functioning?

ONLINE SELF-ASSESSMENT TOOL

Are you cut out for teamwork? To find out, take the short quiz offered by Barbara Reinhold at http://content.monster.com/tools/quizzes/teamplayer/.

EXERCISES

Exercise 3.1   Leading vs. Managing

You are the Regional Director of the American Heart Association. As such you are responsible for the 18 local offices in your territory. Listed on the next page are a number of typical activities. Please identify them as management or leadership by placing a check mark in the appropriate columns. Some activities could fall in either category. In that case, identify which it should be based on the way you would actually perform the activity.

Exercise 3.2   Leading vs. Managing: Follow-up

1. Which activities/functions in the previous exercise could be classified as either management or leadership, in your opinion?

2. In two or three sentences, explain why each of those activities/functions could be an example of both management and/or leadership.

3. Briefly explain why you classified those particular activities/functions the way that you did.

4. Were there any activities/functions for which you disagreed with the answer key's classification?

5. If so, why?

ACTIVITY/FUNCTION	MANAGEMENT	LEADERSHIP
1. Supervising the development of the budget at each of the local offices.		
2. Hiring, firing, and evaluating the 18 local directors.		
3. Conducting an annual retreat with the local directors to set specific objectives for the coming year.		
4. Preparing and submitting quarterly reports to the national executive director about the work of each chapter.		
5. Mediating conflicts at the local level and between the 18 directors.		
6. Visiting each chapter monthly in order to motivate and inspire each staff.		
7. Speaking at endless Rotary, Kiwanis, Lions' Clubs and other civic groups in the region in order to articulate the mission and need for the American Heart Association.		
8. Solving problems that local directors are unable to.		
9. Monitoring the budgets of the local chapters closely since there are few contingency dollars if budgets aren't met.		
10. Spending quality time on substantive, long-range plans for the association.		
11. Attempting to influence policy at the national level because of the changes observed locally.		
12. Forming ad hoc teams from various local offices to deal with unexpected/unusual or regional issues and opportunities.		
13. Reviewing and adjusting the fund raising time-line for each office.		
14. Participating in the selection of key leaders in each local fund campaign.		
15. Keeping local directors and staff members energized and excited as the long months of fund raising continue.		
16. Keeping the local directors and staff focused on final details after the fund campaign ends.		
17. Continually searching for new and innovative ideas about solving the age-old problems in not-for-profit organizations.		

ACTIVITY/FUNCTION	MANAGEMENT	LEADERSHIP
18. Developing and implementing the high-risk strategies if they have the potential for big payoffs.		
19. Scheduling personal "thinking time" each week to try and remain focused on the big picture and removed from the food of daily minutia.		
20. Reading and promptly responding to the numerous reports, correspondence, and requisite forms from local offices, national headquarters, and constituent groups in your five-state region.		

KEY

1.	M	6.	L	11.	L	16.	M
2.	M	7.	L	12.	L	17.	L
3.	M	8.	M	13.	M	18.	L
4.	M	9.	M	14.	M	19.	L
5.	M	10.	L	15.	L	20.	M

CHAPTER 4

Communication

LEADERSHIP MOMENT

George Ruth of Ruth's Consulting firm has a crisis brewing. For years, his consulting firm has made its reputation on its ability for "rapid-response." Now, as the company has grown and expanded to different cities across the country, communication break-downs occur almost daily. As the owner, George has emphasized team-based decisions and has worked very hard to empower the firm's employees so they don't come to him with every little decision. Yet, rather than enjoy their freedom, some employees still seek his approval for every move, slowing down the organization's response rate. Meanwhile, other employees are starting to take liberties and make decisions that affect the entire business without consulting anyone. In addition, George is having trouble finding ways of rapidly reaching all of his employees, who by now are spread out in offices in Boston, Chicago, Minneapolis, and Washington, DC. All employees have e-mail accounts, but many check them only sporadically. The companywide voicemail system is only a little better—often individuals will leave voicemails rather than walk down the hall and converse with that person.

All these factors are combining to diminish the firm's reputation for rapid-response. If these communication breakdowns continue, Ruth worries, the whole business might collapse.

1. *What would you do?*
2. *What types of communication breakdowns are taking place? How would you label them?*
3. *Could some of these communication breakdowns have been avoided? How?*

Communication is in many ways at the heart of leadership. One can create an ingenious plan for reinvigorating a company, but if one is not able to communicate this plan, it is not worth the paper it is written on. Successful leaders understand the nuances of communication and are able to alter their communication styles to meet the demands of specific situations. This chapter will introduce you to some major communication theories and demonstrate the existence of many levels within communication. We urge you to consider which forms of communication are most comfortable to you and why and to think about the situations in which certain types of communication channels (e.g., e-mail versus phone calls) are most effective.

Let's begin with some communication fundamentals.

BASIC COMMUNICATION THEORY: TRANSACTIONAL MODEL OF ENCODING, CHANNELS, AND DECODING

Human communication is best viewed as a **transactional** process. That is, communication involves an exchange in which both sender and receiver determine the meaning of the communication. Here is how transactional communication works. When a communication is made, it passes through several points between the sender and receiver (see Figure 4–1). When information is communicated, the first step toward interpreting that information is called **encoding.** The encoding process translates the communication into a set of meaningful symbols (language) that express the communicator's purpose. The resulting message is then transmitted through an available **channel.** Among the many channels of communication within organizations are face-to-face communication, memos, computer messages, and nonverbal cues such as facial expressions. The channels we use include such devices as telephones, fax machines, computers, and, in face-to-face communication, our senses, especially hearing, sight, and touch. Culture affects our choice of channels. For example, for messages with emotional content, some cultures ascribe more import to tone of voice than to facial expression. Others, such as some African cultures, may place a higher value on touching while conveying a message.

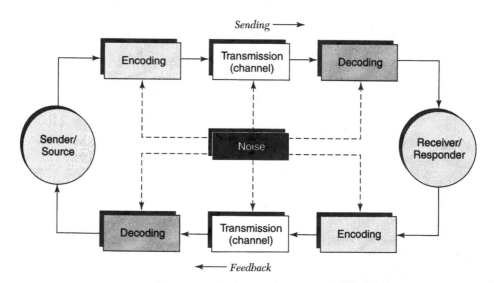

Figure 4–1   A Model of the Interpersonal Communication Process
Source: P. L. Hunsaker and C. W. Cook, *Managing Organizational Behavior,* Reading, Mass.: Addison-Wesley, 1986, p. 197. Copyright 1986 by Phillip L. Hunsaker. Reprinted by authors' permission.

A story about a Turkish friend illustrates the disastrous effects possible when cultural differences interfere with communication. Gungor was an extremely outgoing, friendly person Art had met in the 1960s. He came to visit in New York City and was particularly excited about seeing the United Nations. Art showed him how to use the bus and told him that he'd see him that evening. When Art returned home that evening, his usually high-spirited pal was in the dumps. He said that he had been bitterly disappointed. It was then that Art realized that he should have given him some communication pointers.

First, he should have warned Gungor to avoid sitting next to someone else on the bus if empty seats were available and not to make eye contact with other people much less try to engage them in conversation. Gungor thought that people disliked him, but they were actually protecting their space and their sense of safety—two elements vital to anyone who has ever ridden public transportation in New York City!

The final step in the transactional process is decoding. **Decoding** is a process of interpretation performed by the receiver of the message. Based on that interpretation, the receiver may structure a response, which then goes through the same process of encoding, transmitting (through one or more channels), and decoding. In our previous example, Gungor had tried to be friendly, but his message was lost in decoding.

Filters and Sets

We communicate to bring about a variety of outcomes such as understanding, pleasure, and influence. But, as we all know, what we are attempting to say and what is actually heard by the receiver of a communication can be quite different! The original intent of a communication can be affected by a host of factors including filters and sets. **Filters** are the physical and psychological factors that affect the message. For example, from a physiological standpoint, a person literally may not be able to hear a message if he or she has a hearing impairment. Other major filters include exposure to the language being spoken, cultural differences in language usage, and the use of slang. Thus, the original intention of a message may get lost in translation, leaving both sender and receiver confused and/or angry. Typically, though, filters aid communication. Since we are not robots, we all use filters as a way of placing information in context or forming additional meanings to communications.

Sets, which are more elaborate forms of filters, describe a predisposition to respond in a certain way. For instance, people from the Middle East typically stand much closer to each other (6 to 12 inches) than people from the United States (18 to 36 inches). The distance cultural set had major implications during recent negotiations about the Middle East. One Egyptian diplomat complained to the press that an American diplomat must not have been truly concerned about the negotiations: when the American talked to him; he stood far away, a clear sign to the Egyptian that he was withdrawing. The American, of course, was surprised by this accusation, asserting that he stood where he was comfortable. Neither the American nor the Egyptian diplomat had an adequate understanding of the other's cultural set and a miscommunication ensued.

Interference

Interference or **noise** refers to anything that distorts the message or distracts the receiver from accurately hearing the message. Beyond the usual kinds of noise we experience such as loud music or the sound of jackhammers on the street, interference can include nonsound factors such as the room's stuffiness or lack of light or other people's distracting behavior or strange dress. The more channels we use, the greater the chance for interference. For instance, speaking on the phone deprives us of seeing the other's facial cues. Communicating via e-mail involves its own set of established protocols but eliminates tone of voice as well as facial cues and gestures.

Types of Communication

Throughout history, the methods through which communication is delivered have become increasingly sophisticated. For example, a politician may devise a formal 40-minute speech to deliver in Congress, a five-page press release for the media, a one-page letter to her supporters, and a 30-second sound bite to include in speeches in her home district—all on the same topic. Each form of communication has a different thrust and is intended for different audiences.

But one does not need to be a politician to devise different ways to communicate messages. We all use different forms of communication to meet our needs. What follows is a brief description of some of the major ways in which communication can be classified.

Verbal versus Nonverbal Communication   In some ways this is the most basic communication distinction. **Verbal communication** describes communication put forth via speech. However, this is not the only way in which messages can be conveyed. It is said, in fact, that a message is conveyed more by **nonverbal** means (e.g., facial gestures, body language) than by actual words. When someone smiles while simultaneously saying he is angry, most of us would assume that this person is not really angry. Nonverbal cues can also be ambiguous and open to disparate interpretations: a smiling angry person, for instance, could be squinting, trying to soften the anger by smiling, or expressing contempt. It's also quite possible that the entire meaning of an extended verbal communication can be changed by one subtle wink or smile, indicating that the speaker was only kidding.

Intentional versus Unintentional Communication   Like the distinction between verbal and nonverbal communication, the difference between intentional and unintentional communication is quite intuitive. That is, **intentional communication** refers to communication that was consciously and purposefully delivered. When you receive a call from your partner and he or she asks you if you wouldn't mind picking up some milk on your way home from work, that is likely an intentional communication aimed at achieving a certain outcome—fresh milk. However, it is possible that this same communication could have **unintentional** components. Your partner might not have thought about this communication beyond thinking, "I would like to have some milk," but you, as the receiver, might add some further meaning. If you felt that your partner sounded somewhat annoyed on the phone, you might take this message to mean that he or she is annoyed by always doing the grocery shopping and may be testing you to see if *you* will do the shopping. You may even come home with an armload of groceries, astonishing your partner who wanted only milk.

Every communication has an intended message, but depending on the context and to whom the communication is offered, it also may offer unintended messages as well. Skilled leaders are aware of this phenomenon and are always on the lookout to see if their communications are being received in the spirit in which they were intended.

Formal versus Informal Communication   A **formal communication** is built within the framework of an organization and follows a stated procedure. For example, circulating memos or posting information on the company Web site is for many organizations a formal mechanism for distributing information. On a smaller scale, staff meetings may be used for formal discussions on topics.

Informal communication channels are not formally sanctioned or created by the organization; rather, they emerge within its everyday life. Similarly, informal groups in the workplace may take root across and within levels and departments and serve the interests of the members. Among the more common manifestations of informal communication is the **grapevine.** Rumors and beliefs—often given more credence than communication from higher management—are passed along the grapevine. This channel serves the social needs of group members but may be disliked by those managers or leaders whose communications are inadequate. These leaders may see the grapevine as creating much noise and distorting their messages. Table 4–1 describes some primary characteristics of the grapevine.

Upward versus Downward versus Lateral Communication   In the traditional workplace setting, a status differential often exists among those who are conversing. Thus, the same words may take on a different meaning if they are spoken by the CEO as opposed to an entry-level employee. Communication can take three different directions in a hierarchical structure. **Upward communication** consists of feedback given by employees to others higher in the corporate chain of command. This feedback can be given in a number of ways, such as via direct communication, surveys, memos, e-mail, and so on. Upward communication is to be encouraged. Managers who place rigid guidelines on upward communication and discourage feedback from lower-level employees stymie creativity and lose access to valuable ideas and suggestions.

Downward communication is feedback given by managers to their subordinates. Examples include performance evaluations, memos, policy statements, and so on. This information must be presented clearly and its relevance to the audience highlighted to ensure that they do not ignore it.

Lateral communication is organized communication with peers. When done effectively, it serves to heighten the efficiency, clarity, and quality of information and further strengthen existing communication networks.

Figure 4–2 displays some of the core objectives for using upward, downward, and lateral communication.

TABLE 4–1 Observations about the Grapevine

1. The grapevine is a significant part of an organizational communication system with regard to (a) quantity of information communicated and (b) quality of information, such as its importance and its effects on people and performance.

2. The quality of management decisions depends on quality of information inputs that management has, and one useful input is information from the grapevine.

3. Successful communication with employees depends on (a) understanding their problems, (b) understanding their attitudes, and (c) determining gaps in employee information (the grapevine is a valuable source of these kinds of inputs).

4. The quality of management decisions is significantly affected by management's success in listening to and interpreting the grapevine.

5. The quality of management communication programs is significantly affected by management's capacity to understand and to relate to the grapevine.

6. The grapevine cannot be suppressed or directly controlled, although it may be influenced by the way management relates to it.

7. The grapevine has both negative and positive influences in an organization.

8. The grapevine can provide useful inputs even when information it carries is known to be incorrect.

9. In normal organizational situations, excluding situations such as strikes and disasters, the grapevine on the average carries more correct information than inaccurate information.

10. The grapevine carries an incomplete story.

11. Compared with most formal communications, the grapevine tends to speed faster through an organization, so it can affect people very quickly.

12. Grapevine communications are *caused*.

13. Men and women are approximately equally active on the grapevine.

14. Nonverbal communication is significant in interpreting verbal grapevine communication.

15. Informal leaders often serve as message centers for receiving, interpreting, and distributing grapevine information to others.

16. Typical grapevine activity usually is not a sign of organizational sickness or health; that is, grapevine activity is a normal response to group work.

Source: From P. V. Lewis, *Organizational Communication: The Essence of Effective Management*, 3rd ed. (New York: Wiley, 1987), pp. 47–48. Reprinted by permission of the publisher.

LEADERSHIP SKILLS FOR THE TWENTY-FIRST CENTURY

COMMUNICATION AND THE INTERNET: AN INTERVIEW WITH LOUIS KRUGER

The explosion of technology in recent years has led to an increasing availability of methods by which communication can take place. Whereas once we were limited to telephone, mail, fax, or—*gasp*—face-to-face conversations to com-

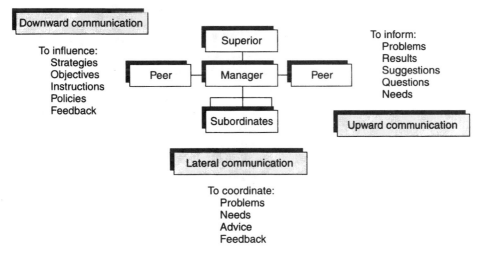

Figure 4–2   Directions of Communication and Their Objectives

municate, the continuing widespread use of online methods, particularly e-mail, to communicate and enhance professional and personal development has led to a whole new set of communication challenges—and opportunities. Woe to the aspiring leader who does not understand the communication dynamics of e-mail!

A leading expert on Internet communication within a professional development context is Dr. Louis Kruger of Northeastern University. Dr. Kruger is the Director of the Global School Psychology Network (GSPN), an Internet professional development group for school psychologists. For the past several years, Dr. Kruger and a team of researchers have worked both to create an online environment through which school psychologists can meet and learn from one another in a safe environment and to study the ways in which participants have utilized the online options available to them through the GSPN. The following is an excerpt from an interview conducted with Dr. Kruger in August 2000.

Q: What obstacles to communication does the Internet and, in particular, e-mail, create?

A. One of the most important barriers is the lack of subtle cues characteristic of face-to-face communication. Cues, such as facial gestures or voice inflection, may be subtle but often play a pivotal role in expressing emotion and clarifying the content of our verbalizations. The GSPN uses several strategies to decrease the emotional distance and impersonality of e-mail. For example, we attempt to create a friendly and warm environment by sending all newcomers a welcome message. The message describes the values of the community and suggests how the person might introduce himself or herself to the other members of the community. Our online facilitators also do an excellent job modeling good communication skills and monitoring the environment for potential misunderstandings.

Q: *Why do people join the GSPN and what motivates them to become frequent users and contributors?*

A. Similar to any other type of community, including neighborhood communities, people invest time in the GSPN if they feel their needs are being met. People are very particular about how they use their time, and school psychologists are not interested in idle chatter. Our research suggests that most school psychologists join and revisit the GSPN if they believe the community is furthering their professional development.

Q: *Have there been times when conflict has arisen among members? If so, how were these conflicts resolved?*

A. Conflicts have been infrequent. The research team was all too aware of some of the destructive scenarios that have occurred on many other Internet discussion groups. Therefore, we strove from the very beginning to create a psychologically safe environment, where novice school psychologists as well as novice Internet users would feel comfortable. The online facilitators have been very vigilant, and have done an excellent job of intervening early and tactfully. In general, we use online, private consultations to arrive at the best solution. If anything, we have erred on the side of creating too safe of an environment.

Q: *What advice would you offer to future leaders about using and understanding Internet communications?*

A. Many of our best leaders are reluctant to assume leadership positions in Internet groups. In addition, many of the young professionals feel more comfortable using the medium than do their more senior colleagues. Thus, there is the danger of wisdom and generation gaps occurring on the Internet. This is unfortunate because many of the skills that are required in face-to-face groups also are needed on the Internet. One of the early difficulties I experienced was applying my knowledge of teams and groups to the Internet environment. For example, developing positive social norms is just as important (and possibly more important) in Internet groups as it is in face-to-face groups. The Internet will only grow in significance for group communication. It's a moral imperative that our leaders master this new communication medium.

To learn more about the Global School Psychology Network, you can contact Dr. Kruger at counsel@neu.edu or visit the GSPN's Web site at http://www.dac.neu.edu/cp/consult/.

STRATEGIES FOR FACILITATING COMMUNICATION: THE ROLE OF LISTENING

While much attention is given to the role of the sender in communication, only recently have we begun to focus on the critical importance of listening in effective communication. We all know that listening and hearing are quite different: hearing involves physiologically receiving the sound waves and neurologically processing the stimuli. Listening, on the other hand, involves understanding, assigning meaning to what we hear, and remembering (short-term or long-term). Listening is a complex process that we in the Western world are only just beginning to understand. The Japanese language has seven words that describe levels of listening. Try to think of any synonyms to listening in English!

Levine and Crom (1993, p. 985) assert that listening is the "single most important of all the communication skills. More important than stirring oratory. More important than a powerful voice. More important than the ability to speak multiple languages. More important even than a flair for the written word."

Listening is an active process. It takes not only sustained concentration on what the other person is saying but also attention to such nonverbal cues as gestures or other forms of body language. Nonverbal cues convey the message that you are listening and concentrating on what the other person is saying. Active listening can produce huge benefits. People everywhere love to be listened to, to find a receptive audience for their thoughts and concerns. Active listening does much to nourish a relationship and convey the sense that you respect that person. Table 4–2 provides guidelines for active and effective listening.

TABLE 4–2 Guidelines for Effective Listening

1. Stop talking. It is impossible to listen and talk at the same time.
2. Listen for main ideas.
3. Be sensitive to emotional deaf spots that make your mind wander.
4. Fight off distractions.
5. Take notes.
6. Be patient. Let others tell their stories first.
7. Empathize with other people's points of view.
8. Withhold judgment.
9. React to the message, not the person.
10. Appreciate the emotion behind the speaker's words.
11. Use feedback to check your understanding.
12. Relax and put the sender at ease.
13. Be attentive.
14. Create a positive listening environment.
15. Ask questions.

Source: Phillip L. Hunsaker and Anthony J. Alessandra. *The Art of Managing People.* New York: Simon and Schuster, 1986. Copyright 1986 by Phillip L. Hunsaker and Anthony J. Alessandra. Reprinted by authors' permission.

Dean Rusk, former secretary of state under President Lyndon Johnson, understood the power of listening. His experiences in negotiating with political leaders across the globe convinced him that listening is "convincing people with your ears."

Factors Leading to Breakdowns in Communication

Any number of factors can cause noise and thus contribute to the breakdown of communication. Sometimes these distortions are deliberate and other times they are simply a component of human nature. Donnelly, Gibson, and Ivanecevich (1995) have identified the following factors as leading to communication breakdowns:

- Differing frames of reference
- Selective perception
- Semantic problems
- Filtering
- Constraints on time
- Communication overload

Differing frames of reference refers to the fact that senders and receivers bring to any communication diverse experiences and expectations, offering the potential for message distortion. What the sender intended to convey may not be interpreted in the desired manner because the receiver is approaching the message from a different perspective.

Selective perception occurs when the receiver attends to a certain portion of a message and ignores the rest. People generally attend to statements that reconfirm their beliefs and often ignore or distort disconfirming statements. When people make these types of value judgments, they are selectively attending only to those portions of communication that are important to them. If people have poor source credibility, receivers often distort or ignore the message because the senders are not seen as reliable sources of information. Do we always believe what the boss tells us?

Sometimes poor communications can be attributed to **semantic problems,** which are misunderstood word meanings. This is a particularly salient problem when the sender and receiver hail from different cultures. Words with double meanings or culturally specific meanings run the risk of being misinterpreted by the receiver. Along the same lines, words can take on special meaning within a group and then be misunderstood by those outside the group because the sender has not clearly communicated their special meaning.

Earlier in this chapter, *filtering* was described as a process in which the receiver breaks down information from larger to smaller bits. In the context of factors leading to breakdown in communications, filtering takes on a different meaning. Instead of being a process used by the receiver of a communication, filtering in this context means the sender manipulates the information with the goal of restructuring it to be more pleasing to the receiver. Negative filtering can occur for a number of reasons, most commonly to cover up for a mistake or to try to impress another.

Time pressures can also contribute to distortion, because important words or steps in the communication may be omitted to obtain a desired outcome more quickly.

Finally, **communication overload** occurs when a person simply has too much information to decode in a reasonable time frame. The recent explosion of the electronic media often means we arrive at the office to find dozens of messages waiting on the computer! A deluge of information limits our ability to absorb and respond effectively.

Improving Communications

Just as there are a number of potential impediments to communication, so too are there a number of ways to improve communication. The first step is to create a **supportive communicative climate.** According to Gibb (1961), this involves:

1. Using descriptive, as opposed to evaluative, speech

2. Taking a collaborative approach to problem-solving

3. Communicating with spontaneity, rather than from hidden strategies or agenda

4. Demonstrating empathy—going beyond hearing what someone says and attempting to view the situation from the other's frame of reference

5. Promoting equality across and within levels of an organization

6. Trying to hear all sides of a debate rather than simply sticking to one's own agenda

Another important aid to communication beyond effective listening (discussed earlier in this section) is using feedback to increase understanding. Organizations with an extremely hierarchical structure or limited opportunities for interaction across levels frequently encounter communication problems because no feedback is given. People in these cases falsely assume that their messages are being heard in the manner intended, when it is likely that just the opposite may be occurring. In other cases, people may not feel free to offer accurate information so they filter their message to obtain a more positive response.

Leaders must understand the importance of both giving and receiving feedback. Table 4–3 offers guidelines for this process. Leaders also need to model giving effective feedback—that is, feedback that helps others improve their performance. See Table 4–4 for a comparison of effective and ineffective feedback.

Expressing Feelings and Solving Conflicts People express their feelings in a variety of nonverbal ways, such as laughing, yawning, complaining, and gritting their teeth. A goal of effective communication is to set a climate in which it is permissible, even expected, for people to express their feelings directly and openly. When people stop suppressing their feelings, others can understand more of what is going on and speculation shrinks. To do this, we must feel safe. We must trust that others will value what we say and try to understand our feelings and reactions from our perspective.

TABLE 4–3   **Guides for Giving and Receiving Feedback**

Criteria for Giving Feedback

1. Make sure your comments are intended to help the recipient.
2. Speak directly and with feeling, based on trust.
3. Describe what the person is doing and the effect the person is having.
4. Don't be threatening or judgmental.
5. Be specific, not general (use clear and recent examples).
6. Give feedback when the recipient is in a condition of readiness to accept it.
7. Check to ensure the validity of your statements.
8. Include only things the receiver can do something about.
9. Don't overwhelm; make sure your comments aren't more than the person can handle.

Criteria for Receiving Feedback

1. Don't be defensive.
2. Seek specific examples.
3. Be sure you understand (summarize).
4. Share your feelings about the comments.
5. Ask for definitions.
6. Check out underlying assumptions.
7. Be sensitive to sender's nonverbal messages.
8. Ask questions to clarify.

Source: Phillip L. Hunsaker and Anthony J. Alessandra. *The Art of Managing People.* New York: Simon and Schuster, 1986: pp. 202–213. Copyright 1986 by Phillip L. Hunsaker and Anthony J. Alessandra. Reprinted by authors' permission.

Charismatic Leadership

Many call themselves leaders, but only a select few can truly be called charismatic leaders. In modern parlance, **charismatic leadership** involves a relationship between a leader and the persons being led in which the leader is believed to possess inspirational charismatic qualities. Currently a thriving area of research within leadership studies, the term *charismatic leader* brings to mind vivid images for many. For some, it may evoke images of influential religious or spiritual leaders, such as

TABLE 4–4   **Characteristics of Effective and Ineffective Feedback**

Effective Feedback is…	Ineffective Feedback is…
• Meant to help	• Meant to disparage
• Clear, specific	• Vague, ambiguous
• Immediate (if possible)	• Slow in coming, not tied to event
• Sensible and appropriate	• Inaccurate, inappropriate

Martin Luther or Mother Theresa (see Leadership Profiles in Chapters 1 and 10). Others may think of great political leaders, such as Thomas Jefferson or Nelson Mandela (see Leadership Profile in Chapter 1). Still others may picture less well-known men and women, such as a mother who through the sheer force of her own personality influences changes by a school board or a child who seems to make friends easily and is a "natural leader." Charismatic leadership is at once a familiar and an elusive topic, one that does not easily fit into any particular definition, category, or discipline. We have chosen to discuss charismatic leadership in our chapter on communication because one common link among charismatic leaders is that skilled use of communication is central to their leadership. Their perceived charisma is based on their ability to communicate.

The word *charisma* is derived from the Greek, meaning *divinely inspired gift.* Once used only in reference to religious figures, the term was expanded by sociologist Max Weber to include secular leaders. Weber argued that societies feature three types of authority structures. In a **traditional authority system,** authority is granted based on traditions and unwritten laws separate from the individual personalities of the power-wielders. A classic example is the passing of the crown to the eldest male upon the death of a king. A **legal-rational authority system** is characterized by the presence of a bureaucratic structure that governs the use and transition of power, as exemplified in the transfer of power to the vice president upon the death of the president of the United States.

A **charismatic authority system** is fueled by society's belief in the leader's powers and abilities. Often seen as nearly superhuman, charismatic leaders are given power based on personal authority rather than by laws or traditions. Examples run the gamut from heroes to villains, from the Dali Lama to Adolf Hitler.

MODELS OF CHARISMATIC LEADERSHIP

Within the leadership literature, a number of theoretical models attempt to define and describe charismatic leadership. Halpert (1990), in analyzing the nine characteristics of a charismatic leader put forth by House in 1976, determined that charismatic leadership is based on three dimensions: referent power, expert power, and job involvement. **Referent power** is based on the use of interpersonal skills to influence others. Referent power is not derived from formal authority, but rather is obtained through the formation of a relationship in which others come to trust and respect the individual with referent power. **Expert power** is similarly not necessarily based on a formal title or position, but rather is due to a person's specialized knowledge or skills. For example, we would not expect to find receptionists at the top of any company power chart, yet they are often the ones who know best how to get things done in the organization. That explains why smart individuals may bypass managers and turn to receptionists when they need help in specialized areas. The last component, **job involvement,** reflects the ability charismatic leaders possess to understand the organizational and social culture and inspire others to be invested in their work.

According to Jay A. Conger, charismatic leaders are effective communicators who use specific communication styles to communicate their visions. The two dominant styles are **management by inspiration** and **management by anecdote.**

Management by inspiration occurs when leaders distinguish themselves in such a way that others feel inspired to follow them. Common rhetorical techniques that serve this purpose are using metaphors and analogies and adjusting one's message for different audiences. Management by anecdote, in which leaders use real or fictitious stories to communicate a point, is similarly a rhetorical technique that many charismatic leaders use to their advantage. Abraham Lincoln was well-known for his skillful use of anecdotes—some real, many invariably fiction—to rebut arguments made by his rivals.

What happens when a charismatic leader is able to influence a large number of individuals and how does change come about? According to Conger (1988; see Appendix II for a summary of Conger and Kanungo's 1998 work entitled *Charismatic Leadership in Organizations*), charismatic leaders possess an ability to introduce quantum change in an organization. Conger suggests that these leaders progress through four stages, beginning with sensing opportunity and formulating a vision. Their strong sense for the needs of consumers and their equally powerful ability to dissect the flaws in the current organizational strategy help them develop a vision that is both exciting and realistic.

The second stage is articulating the vision. Charismatic leaders use their advanced communication skills to portray the vision's core aspects.

The third stage is building trust in the vision. As important as promoting the vision is, it is equally important that charismatic leaders sell themselves so that others see them as skilled and trustworthy. This trust-building is not accomplished by coercion, but rather via methods such as personal risk-taking, unconventional expertise, and self-sacrifice. Supporters of charismatic leaders not only subscribe to the vision, but they also respect the leaders and trust their ability to accomplish the vision.

The final stage is achieving the vision. Empowerment is instrumental in this stage, since it imbues followers with a sense of self-worth and belief in their competence to overcome obstacles. If followers believe in the vision and in their ability to overcome potential obstacles, they stand a far greater chance of achieving success.

From a different perspective, Hackman and Johnson (1996) believe that leaders must demonstrate communication skills in three primary areas—monitoring the environment and building relationships (linking), thinking and reasoning (envisioning), and influencing others (regulating). They conclude that charismatic leaders excel in all three areas, possessing superior skills in building personal alliances, creating an exciting vision, and inspiring others to help them to achieve this vision.

Is Charismatic Leadership Always Beneficial?

At the extreme, a charismatic leader can inspire others to overthrow a corrupt leader or to turn around a failing business. Charismatic leaders are our heroes—they possess the skills, intellect, and courage to view the world differently and to inspire others to follow them in seeking change.

However, throughout history charismatic leaders have also played pivotal roles in mass killings, as in mass cult-related suicides and in the Holocaust. Failures of charismatic leadership are typically less dramatic, though, and result from sources such as an underdeveloped or otherwise impractical vision or implementation of the vision and/or unchecked egoism leading to resentment among followers. When power is based largely on the leader's personal communication and persuasion skills, the danger exists that followers of charismatic leaders can become blinded to the equally valid ideas or opinions of others or will reject the charismatic leader after unfavorable events occur. Succession after the death or retirement of a charismatic leader is often problematic, particularly if the leader has not trained a replacement (which is often the case) and was not also a transformational leader (this term will be discussed in more depth in Chapter 9)—meaning that his or her efforts did not result in a system in which followers emerged more capable of leading themselves.

Charismatic leadership can come from a variety of sources. What follows are Leadership Profiles of several charismatic leaders—some who are now internationally respected and admired and others who are equally loathed and condemned.

DAVID KORESH: CHARISMATIC CULT LEADER

The leader of the religious sect known as the Branch Davidians, Koresh was originally named Vernon Wayne Howell. He chose the new name to reflect King David. Koresh is the Hebrew name of a Persian leader. After a schism in the sect, Koresh moved his followers to a primitive camp in east Texas, where he gathered his "family" every day for lessons and sermons.

Koresh's rule was absolute: he not only owned everything in the camp but he also had the right to have numerous wives and mistresses. An articulate speaker with a reportedly phenomenal knowledge of the Bible, Koresh traveled across the country recruiting followers to join the "family" in Texas.

He preached that Armageddon was imminent and he and his followers dug tunnels, built watchtowers, and heavily armed the camp. They began referring to the camp as "Ranch Apocalypse."

Alcohol, Tobacco, and Firearms agents eventually found out that the camp contained more than 8,000 pounds of ammunition that included M16 rifles and grenade launchers.

After a 51-day standoff between the ATF forces and the Branch Davidians, the federal agents tried to smoke Koresh's group out with tear gas. Although the events are disputed, the FBI maintains that Koresh ordered his followers to ignite the lamp fuel. Whatever the cause, a horrible fire swept through the compound, killing 78 people, among whom were 17 children. Many were the children of Koresh.

BARBARA JORDAN: HER WORDS WORE BOOTS*

My first thought on hearing of Barbara Jordan's death was, "She was too young." She was only 59 when she died. Yet she long ago became one of our society's elders, a wise woman for our national village, a deeply rooted moral touchstone for an increasingly rootless nation.

She had always been wise beyond her years. She was only 29 when she became the first black woman elected to the Texas Senate, elevating the collective IQ of that chamber by several hundred points simply by showing up.

She was only 37 when, on the House Judiciary Committee, her eloquence lifted the squalid mess of Watergate out of the shadows of petty partisan politics and into the sunlight cast by our Constitution. As the measured tones of this stolid young black woman pealed across this nation, the oh-so-powerful white men of Watergate began to shrink into a foul-mouthed smallness totally unworthy of the offices they held. As she said then, Barbara Jordan was not willing to be an idle spectator of our nation's government. She knew to her bones that she was the government, she and the rest of us "We the People." She was that truly rare thing: a thinking patriot.

Why did she touch us so? I think it was because she always connected her prose to this passion, and thereby exalted both. Her words always wore boots, treading powerfully into our hearts and minds.

Blacks and women especially were enlarged and empowered by her words and example, but her wisdom and humor transcended race and gender. No one ever mistook Barbara Jordan for some mere token. She was wholly and completely herself. Moreover, she did not suffer fools gladly. I often saw her silence buffoons with a look—a skill that came in handy in the Texas Senate.

When her illness struck her in the late 1970s, we were bereft, mourning what might have been, perhaps even the first female and first African-American president.

But to mourn then was to underestimate Barbara Jordan. She had just come home, she hadn't given up. As she assumed the mantle of elder stateswoman and scholar, her influence continued to be felt in Texas and in Washington. Powerful men and women flew into Austin to sit at her feet, and she gave them all the same thing: unsparing honesty.

Her vast intellect was matched by her courage and integrity and, often, tempered by her wit. Even as her illness attacked her body, that magnificent voice went on. When he was about four years old, my nephew Nicholas heard her on the radio and asked me, "Is that God?"

I replied, "No, but it should be."

I think the idea of God as a black woman would have tickled Barbara Jordan. Now I find myself imagining all the great conversations going on up there on heaven's front porch—Barbara and God, voices rolling like thunder, laughter sparkling like rain.

We're gonna miss her for a long, long time.

°Written by Katie Sherrod, 1996.

RONALD REAGAN: THE "GREAT COMMUNICATOR"

[I] won a nickname, "The Great Communicator." But I never thought it was my style or the words I used that made a difference: It was the content. I wasn't a great communicator, but I communicated great things...

—Ronald Reagan in his farewell address, 1989

In this era when public distrust—if not outright antagonism—toward U.S. leaders runs rampant, it is easy to forget that it was not that long ago when a U.S. president inspired confidence in many people through his phrases, stories, and unshakable optimism about the future. Reagan believed that God had given the United States a special place in history.

As discussed in this chapter, vision is an integral component of charismatic leadership. As former Reagan speechwriter Peggy Noonan wrote in *Time* magazine's "100 Most Influential Individuals of the Twentieth Century" series: "Ronald Reagan knew, going in, the sentence he wanted, and he got it. He guided the American victory in the Cold War."

And boy, could he communicate that vision. Reagan's vision of America as a nation of destiny was tied to a speaking style that emphasized simplicity. He was fond of saying that "there are simple answers—there are just not easy ones." Although many might not agree with him, when Reagan spoke, we understood what he meant. He fully believed that the United States was in the right and that it would emerge victorious in the Cold War. He inspired millions—including other key heads of state—to believe in him. Said former Canadian Prime Minister Brian Mulroney in a 1998 interview in *Vanity Fair*: "You know, when you've got a quarterback who can run, who can throw, and who can take a hit and he's out there in the rain every Sunday—well, that idea got through to the allies. And when it did, everything jelled."

Born of humble origins in Tampico, Illinois, Reagan burst upon the national political scene late in the 1964 presidential campaign when he gave what is still referred to in some Republican circles as "The Speech." He defended free enterprise and railed against communism so successfully that David Broder has called this speech "the most successful national political debut since William Jennings Bryan electrified the 1896 Democratic convention with his 'Cross of Gold' speech."

Reagan possessed such a charisma that often even his political detractors were drawn to him. The charisma carried him to high rates of popular support despite scandals such as Iran-Contra during his second term. Wrote Greg Senf, "When those little red lights on the cameras lit up, he glowed like a man welcoming his best friend, and somehow he made you feel like you were his best friend."

Now *that* is a charismatic leader!

For more about Reagan and leadership, we recommend James M. Strock's *Reagan on Leadership: Executive Lessons from the Great Communicator,* Rocklin, Calif.: Prima Publishing, 1998.

HOWARD STERN AND OPRAH WINFREY: MEDIA MOGULS

Oprah and Howard—an unusual pair recognizable by their first names. One is the self-proclaimed "King of All Media" and the other's book recommendations become instant best-sellers. Both reach millions daily and have inspired a series of imitators who have not neared their level of success. One show provides its listeners with a seemingly endless stream of naked women, unusual persons, and celebrity gossip. (Stern has called himself "the man who has put the 'sin' back in syndication.") The other has explicitly rejected "tabloid television" and may be America's most well-known and effective advocate for a host of causes.

Born less than three weeks apart in 1954, both Winfrey, an African-American female from rural Mississippi, and Stern, a Jewish male from Queens, burst upon the national scene in 1986 with syndicated talk shows bearing their names. Both began rather conventionally but quickly made detours that led to superstardom. As a sophomore at Tennessee State University, Winfrey broke barriers when she became the first female and the first African-American news anchor in the Nashville market. After graduation, she continued as a news anchor in Baltimore but found that the role of the detached news reporter was not for her. By age 22, she was hosting a TV talk show entitled "People Are Talking" and a career was launched.

Similarly, Stern graduated Magna Cum Laude from Boston University, having majored in broadcasting and film. Never the traditional disc-jockey, Stern stated in a 1984 *People* magazine article that in his first professional job postgraduation "It dawned on me that I would never make it as a straight deejay. So I started to mess around."

At the time of Oprah's emergence on the national stage, Phil Donahue was the undisputed king of daytime television talk shows. Among the best at utilizing the now ever-present format of the host moving across the audience with a microphone, Donahue's shows were based largely on providing viewers with information. Invited guests were recognized experts and discussions were rarely personalized. Oprah's style was different. Utilizing what Deborah Tannen terms "rapport talk"—the back-and-forth conversation that Tannen believes to be the basis of female friendship—Oprah also brought in experts, but also shared her own secrets. Said Winfrey in a 1986 interview, "The difference between Donahue and me is me. He's more intellectual in his approach. I appeal to the heart and relate personally to my audiences." Through the years, Oprah's viewers have received updates on her love life and struggles with weight and she has divulged information ranging from the mundane to the deeply personal, such as disclosing that she was raped as a child. By sharing herself with her audience, Oprah has allowed many people to form a connection with her that transcends television.

Similarly, people have come to learn much about Howard Stern through his radio and television shows and via his autobiographical book and movie *Private Parts*. Said Stern in a 1997 interview: "I always resented the label of 'shock jock' that the press came up with for me because I never intentionally set out to shock anybody. What I intentionally set out to do was to talk just as I talk off the air, to talk the way guys talk sitting around a bar." With its endless stream of scantily clad or naked females, Stern's show appears to be the ultimate "guy" show, but his charisma and relentless honesty and openness have produced an extraordinarily loyal audience that often transcends gender.

Thus, although their personal interests and their shows' content remain as divergent as ever, Winfrey and Stern have both built huge media empires based on charisma and openness. An unlikely pair, Winfrey and Stern have nevertheless been able to maintain their audiences' rapt attention since 1986 and counting.

SUMMARY

Leadership in many ways begins with communication. Leaders who cannot communicate their ideas will rapidly find a diminishing audience for their efforts. Communication is something that we all know something about, yet is not easily defined. This chapter provides an introduction to basic communication theory and its application to leadership. At its core, communication involves a transactional process between sender and receiver, each of whom acts on information based on perceptions of what is being communicated. Communication can be verbal or nonverbal; intentional or unintentional; formal or informal; and upward, downward, or lateral, depending on who the senders and receivers are and in what context the communication is expressed.

Leaders know how to listen. In recent years, more attention has been given to interpersonal barriers to communication and the role that active listening can play in facilitating communication. Communication will never be a wholly objective process, but skilled leaders are sensitive to the underlying dynamics and are adept at effectively utilizing the media through which communication can be offered.

CREATE YOUR OWN THEORY

Throughout this chapter, we have explored the many different ways in which communication can be put forth. As you reflect on these different approaches, which do you find to be your strengths? Are you, for example, an e-mail person or do you prefer to talk face-to-face? In what context would either of these options be preferable?

Also important to consider is the role that distortion can play in receiving a message. How well do you handle basic communication theory? What personal filters and sets do you bring into interpersonal interactions? What types of feedback are you primed to hear and accept and what are your blind spots?

Are you a charismatic leader? If so, why, and if not, why not? Who are some of the charismatic leaders you have known and what made them so? What are some of the perils of a leadership style based largely on the charisma of the leader?

Finally, what are the implications of all these considerations for your own theory of leadership? In our opening Leadership Moment, we presented the fictitious case of George Ruth, who finds that as his firm expands in terms of staff size, communication media available, and geographic locations of employees, effective communication is becoming more and more difficult. In this era, when many of us already feel overloaded with access to communication (quick: how many e-mail accounts, phone numbers, pagers, and mailing addresses do you have?), how should leaders work to reduce barriers to communication and ensure that others are able to receive information in the most effective way?

KEY TERMS

transactional model of communication
encoding
communication channel
decoding
filters
sets
interference/noise
verbal communication
nonverbal communication
intentional communication
unintentional communication
formal communication
informal communication
grapevine
upward communication
downward communication

lateral communication
differing frames of reference
selective perception
semantic problems
communication overload
supportive communicative climate
charismatic leadership
traditional authority system
legal-rational authority system
charismatic authority system
referent power
expert power
job involvement
management by inspiration
management by anecdote

QUESTIONS FOR DISCUSSION AND REVIEW

1. Describe how communication is a transactional process. What are the steps within this process?

2. What are some examples of communication sets?

3. Describe three situations in which interference has impeded communication.

4. Describe three situations in which nonverbal signals can alter the meaning of a verbal communication.

5. What is the primary distinction between upward, downward, and lateral communication?

6. How is active listening different from hearing?

7. What are some of the major factors that can lead to a breakdown in communication?

8. What are some of the characteristics of a supportive communicative climate?

9. What is charismatic leadership? Is it always desirable? Why or why not?

10. Describe Conger's four stages of charismatic leadership.

ONLINE SELF-ASSESSMENT TOOL

To learn more about the effectiveness of your communication skills, try the self-assessment tool at http://www.psychtests.com/communic.html.

CHAPTER 5

Cultural Anthropology

LEADERSHIP MOMENT

You work for a mid-size company that has recently merged with a larger, international organization. As part of the merger, you will now be sharing office space with employees from this larger company and, over a period of six months, the two groups will be collapsed into one large team. Although this has been a friendly merger, current management is concerned about complications that might arise. You have been asked to put together an action plan for ensuring a smooth transition in your department, which you will continue to head after the merger is complete.

1. *What would you do? Where would you begin?*
2. *What thoughts do you have about the likely events of the next six months?*
3. *How might your personal values play a role in this process?*

*I*n the movie *The Matrix*, a small crew of individuals discovered that their society was a virtual reality created by computers. Their everyday world, though it seemed real, was actually a computerized matrix that hid the shocking truth that computers controlled the world. There was hope, however, that humans could regain control as long as they could find *The One*—the only human who could embody the matrix. Able to understand and communicate with computers, *The One* was the person beyond all others who could *lead* humans to triumph over the computers.

Have you ever seen a leader like *The One*?—someone who seems to have an innate sense of what is successful and not? Have you been around leaders who are able to read people so accurately that their every word and behavior seems perfect for accomplishing their goal?

How about the opposite? Have you ever had substitute professors who just didn't seem to jibe with the culture of your class? Everything they said or did seemed opposite to your normal professor? Or have you worked in a company where a new CEO is hired? You think it must be some mistake because the new CEO seems inept at communicating well with associates and wants to change everything.

Although sometimes we may feel like substitute professors and new CEOs automatically fit these molds, it's not true. All substitute teachers and CEOs are not incompetent. Similarly, nobody has innate leadership skills. Rather, society and culture play a significant role in developing leadership styles and skills. Cultural anthropology is a social science that can shed light on this.

This chapter examines the contributions of cultural anthropology to our current understanding of leadership. Specifically, the following pages provide insight on three questions:

1. What is cultural anthropology?
2. What are some broad-ranging definitions of culture?
3. How do culture and leadership influence each other?

At the end of the chapter you will be able to revisit the above scenarios to evaluate them with a newfound understanding of the relationship between culture and leadership.

CULTURAL ANTHROPOLOGY

Cultural Anthropology studies human cultures and their development, which is tough since **culture** is not easily defined and there is no consensus on what it means. The definition has been an ongoing conversation for centuries.

To explore the link between culture and leadership, an important first point is that *our definitions of culture affect the meanings we ascribe to leadership*. This chapter illustrates this.

To learn what leadership today requires, early in this chapter we examine two current definitions of culture and the types of leadership they promote. Additionally, we introduce in depth some cultural skills that top leaders today exhibit.

However, these definitions of culture would not be as clear or impactful if we did not realize how significantly different they are from past definitions. Therefore, in ending this chapter we provide a historical definition of culture to compare the type of leadership it promoted to what we admire today.

In essence, we begin to see that one skill of a leader at any point in history is the skill for introducing leadership that positively influences our culture. Also, it is about creating a culture, which promotes a successful sense of leadership.

So how are the two linked? Let's begin to explore this complex dynamic.

CULTURE

The first definition of culture that we explore is provided by *Webster's Dictionary*. This definition of culture gives the impression that culture is all encompassing—it is "the totality of socially transmitted behavior patterns, arts, institutions, and all other products of human work and thought." The sheer expanse of this definition can be impressive, daunting, and confusing.

Docs that mean that a chair is culture? A desk? The way we talk? Is anything *not* culture? And, if everything is culture, who cares?

If you have asked these questions and had these thoughts, you are not the only one. In fact, many anthropologists in history steered headlong into these questions, attempting to create exhaustive universal lists of the content of culture.

We could propose, however, that there is value in this all-encompassing definition. If our definitions of culture do promote certain types of leadership, what does this broad, open-ended definition promote?

This self-reflection is important for you throughout the chapter. As we dissect another modern definition of culture, stop every once and a while to consider, "What does this have to do with leadership?"

Perhaps one aspect of the above definition that we can value is how clearly it leaves all options open for what culture is. It seems to recommend that as we read, we should behave as the definition does. We should keep an open mind to the possibilities of what leadership means.

NATURE/NURTURE DEBATE AND CULTURE

The definition of culture that we use as a working definition for this chapter comes from anthropology. It is, "Culture is *elements of learned behaviors* and meaning systems common to a human society." Let's explore **learned behaviors.**

The **nature/nurture debate** explained in the psychology chapter (Chapter 2) introduces this also. The debate poses an age-old question: Is culture genetic or acquired through real-life experience? The most common belief is that human behavior is a combination of biological (nature) and environmental (nurture) influences. Many would go one step further to say that culture is primarily *nurture.*

Every day we learn social lessons and behaviors. In fact, we can't get away from them. How we choose to sleep, bathe, and eat all reflect these social lessons and ultimately are our culture.

For instance, in Japan people sleep on futons, whereas in the United States most people sleep on mattresses. As well, Japanese bathing methods are different from the showers people take in the United States, and so is the food. So if you are Japanese, you learn one set of standard behaviors, whereas if you are American it is likely you have a different set. These behaviors describe and contribute to our culture.

We learn our culture by mimicking the behaviors of those who teach us when we are children. And this is one link to leadership. What does being a leader mean to you? Where do you get the answers that pop into your head as we consider that question? Can you hear your father describing his sense of leadership? Your teacher? Television?

In large part, our nurture (which is culture) forms our definition and behaviors for leadership. For instance, when we choose to be a leader, we typically express this by molding our behaviors to act according to how we were taught.

Let's explore two different lessons on leadership and examine how they ultimately translated into differing behaviors. During World War II, Japanese fighter pilots called *Kamikaze* were taught that honorable leaders give their life so that others may survive. In enacting this type of leadership, *Kamikaze* pilots were specific. Do you know what they did?

These pilots would dive their booby-trapped planes into enemy territory. However, rather than exiting the planes, the pilots would stay in them and crash. They would give their lives so that their country could win the war. In Japanese culture, these pilots were considered brave and became legends.

On the other hand, in the United States fighter pilots were taught that honor involved dedication to staying alive so they could continue to help their platoon. As a result, U.S. fighter pilots always evacuated if their plane went into a dive. Committing suicide would have been considered weak and dishonorable.

As we can see, "different strokes for different folks" applies to leadership. And culture is what helps determine our different leadership strokes.

That is not to say that *nature* does not play a role. Our behaviors in part are determined by our physical capabilities. For instance, how we walk is determined by the fact that we have two legs. How we talk is determined by the fact that we have a mouth with vocal chords. So, though there is great variety in behaviors across the world, in at least one way our cultures are limited and commonly shaped.

This has been our first lesson. When you think and act like those around you, you are learning culture. In fact, when you join the club of similar behaviors and thoughts, you are also propagating the culture.

Described this way, it sounds easy to receive and live our cultural lessons. But is it? Later in this chapter, we address this topic by describing lessons we learn. Sometimes cultural lessons are positive and at other times they can be painful and negative.

Additionally, we look at how these lessons relate to becoming a leader. If we are taught appropriate cultural behavior, isn't it easy to become a leader? What if our lessons do not match other leadership ideas?

MEANING SYSTEMS

The definition of culture we use for this chapter also says that culture is "*meaning systems* common to a human society." Let's look at *meaning* and *systems* individually.

Meaning identifies a certain relationship between two things. For instance, the word *cat* connotes a certain meaning. When I say *cat*, you may visualize a furry, four-legged animal that meows. The reason you visualize this is because your society has agreed upon this meaning relationship. The word *cat* has become the sign for the animal.

If we never experienced a foreign language, it may never occur to us that the sound *cat* may mean something entirely different in another country. In fact, it may not even be a word. Or if we had learned a foreign language, we might know a different word for describing what we see as a *cat*. However, we may be surprised to find that different cultural meanings are ascribed to the same animal.

For instance, in the United States cats are typically pets and definitely take a lower social standing than humans. In Egypt, however, cats were used to represent gods and were often given better accommodations than humans.

So what is the implication for leadership? It is simple. *Culture is the meanings (signs and symbols) that we apply to tangible objects and behaviors.* It is how we describe what we see, do, and think. And because what we see, do, and think has been ingrained in us throughout our life, we often think of culture as just our reality.

At this juncture the implications of culture for leadership crystallize at a deeper level. Leadership is like the cat above. It is socially constructed and looks different depending on the meaning our society ascribes to it. Just as *cat* can mean one thing in one culture and something entirely different in another, so too can leadership be defined differently. Remember, each of us has a unique reality. As such, we also have a unique perspective of what leadership is.

So you may ask, why do people in the United States tend to have a somewhat common definition of leadership? This is where a closer look at the word *system* comes in.

Our societies are made up of standard venues of education and relationships that we call systems—our educational, media, and family systems are a few. When a specific meaning is fortified through books, media, and education, it becomes broader than just an individual's thought. Instead it becomes a common definition.

In the United States, our systems have created a somewhat common definition of leadership so that if you asked two different U.S. citizens to describe leadership, it is likely there would be some commonalities. Let's take a look at how common thought leads to common leadership.

CHARACTER

According to Ralph Waldo Trine (1908), our leadership character is a result of our thoughts, actions or behaviors, and habits.

Thoughts include our assumptions, beliefs, and values, of which we have many. Some of these relate to our definition of leadership. For instance, one thought we might have is that being a good leader involves motivating others. What is a thought you have about leadership? What do you assume good leaders do? What do you value about leaders?

This is important to know because our thoughts form the foundation for our actions. In other words, our thoughts drive our behaviors. For instance, for me leadership is about behaving in ways that will motivate others. How do you behave in order to implement your thoughts on leadership? And when you do implement your thoughts, are they successful or do they seem to fail time and time again?

Our thoughts and behaviors are not successful in all situations just because we have them. Can you think of an example where you acted out your recipe for leadership, and it seemed out of place? I remember when I moved to Japan during college, I cleaned my host family's kitchen while they were out. Taught that good household leaders clean up after themselves, I was confused and shocked when my actions were met with my host-mother's embarrassment and humiliation. She thought that her kitchen had been too dirty for me.

What happened? If I had been home and done the same thing I would have been praised. However, my Japanese host mother and I had different thoughts about cleanliness, the role of guests, and personal space. Why? We were raised with different stories. We learned different lessons from our teachers about what is good and bad, successful and not.

What stories did you learn about leadership while growing up? What behaviors were promoted in your stories? What behaviors were punished in your stories?

If we are Christians, we might have learned the link between leadership and motivation from a story about Jesus. For many people He is considered so capable because He was able to motivate a group of disciples to follow Him even in the face of danger. Our lessons probably were not limited to the Bible either. They came from lots of sources.

The Little Engine That Could, my favorite childhood book, taught me that succeeding against all odds requires self-motivation. The main character was a train that motivated itself to carry a heavy load over a mountain by repeating the phrase, "I think I can, I think I can, I know I can...."

With time and repetition, the lessons in these stories become imprinted in our minds. Our culture shapes us, and we begin both to represent it and to propagate the lessons we learned.

One way we propagate these lessons is by filtering. For instance, if we read a book that has the opposite lesson from what we were taught, we may doubt its value.

Have you done this? Have you purposely not shared a story because you felt it was inappropriate for representing your idea of positive leadership? Let's put it another way: Would you read *The Little Engine That Could* and feel good if the train said "I think I can't, I think I can't, I know I can't"?

CULTURE AS AUDIOTAPES—AN ACTIVITY

When we are growing up, we learn important lessons from our parents, teachers, and friends. These lessons are typically repeated so that they become ingrained. In fact, sometimes we can hear the lessons playing in our heads like voice tapes.

My most typical tape sounds like my mother's voice and says things like, "Stand up straight. No elbows on the table. Don't talk with your mouth full."

What are examples of cultural lessons that play like audiotapes in your head? How do they affect your behavior? How do they affect your leadership?

Just as we develop firm thoughts about leadership, we also develop firm **behaviors.** We learn through trial and error what the leaders around us think success looks like, and we behave like they do repeatedly. Over time and through repeated behavior, we develop **habits.** What is one example of a leadership habit you have developed?

I know one habit I have developed is to smile and make eye contact when I greet people. After all, while I was growing up my mom did this, my favorite television and book characters did this, and it always worked. To this day, I am still amazed that a straight gaze and an authentic smile can do so much to motivate colleagues.

But, once again, this did not work in Japan. There, downcast eyes are considered respectful accompanied by deep bows. So once again we see that our behaviors, which can become habits, may work in some situations and not in others. What does this say about leadership? What would a good leader be able to do?

Repeated habits form our **character.** If we were to ask ourselves to describe our character, what would many of us say? We would likely say that we are "leaders." And what would this mean? Only now might we begin to realize that leadership is not a vague concept. Rather leadership, at least at some level, is very specifically the behaviors and habits we use to exhibit our thoughts.

Additionally, we may consider that leadership is about flexibly mimicking and ultimately learning and leveraging behaviors that are different from our own. Many of our behaviors might be successful within the context where we were raised. But would they be successful elsewhere?

It seems that leadership, to a degree, is also about learning and using appropriate behaviors for accomplishing goals within a certain context. But does that mean we should mimic all behaviors to be successful? What if we seriously disagree with a behavior or thought?

STAYING ABOVE-BOARD

Two work departments can think similarly that leadership involves motivation. Yet they can exhibit different motivational behaviors. For instance, one department might boisterously cheer its employees while another views quiet recognition as appropriate for motivating. It's not difficult to imagine that the two departments probably look different even though they both value motivation.

One contention might be that as long as the end goal has been accomplished, leadership is productive. What do you think? What if the behaviors you enforce to accomplish a goal are not positive? Are you a leader then?

Chapter 2 introduces McGregor's **Theory X and Theory Y,** which prompts this line of thought. McGregor believed there are two types of employees:

Theory X Employees

- Inherently dislike work, and whenever possible will try to avoid it
- Must be coerced, controlled, or threatened with punishment to achieve goals

Theory Y Employees

- View work as an activity as natural as rest or play
- Exercise self-direction and self-control if they are committed to the objectives of the task

As we see, McGregor proposes behaviors to motivate both types of employees. But do you agree with him? What would you do to motivate the Theory X employees? Would you choose coercion as McGregor recommends? What does your choice have to do with *leadership character?*

LEADERSHIP SKILLS FOR THE TWENTY-FIRST CENTURY

As we have learned, our *thoughts* drive our *behaviors*, which become *habits* that reflect our *character*. Let's examine what this looks like personally by using the chart to fill in personal examples.

Thoughts	Behaviors	Habits	Character
I think…	*As a result, I…*	*I have the habit of…*	*Therefore, I…*
Leadership requires thoughtful decision making	Gather information that helps me make fair decisions	Researching a situation from many angles	Am an evaluator

INTEGRATION OF KNOWLEDGE

In the Theory X and Theory Y example, we may think there is a simple answer, or we may not. The truth is that leadership is not always simple. In large part this is because our thoughts are not exclusive of each other. Rather, we *integrate* lessons we learn in our lifetime, so that we are constantly building a new repertoire of thoughts and behaviors for navigating life. For leadership, this is an important concept because integration of thoughts can have both positive and negative outcomes.

The overall consensus of theorists is that our ability to integrate thoughts and actions is positive. In fact, it is critical for our development from child to adult. Albert Einstein's genius is attributed in part to his skill for integrating information. Research on his brain illustrates that he had more neural connections by far than most of us ever have.

As we grow and integrate more cultural information into our brains, we are able to answer questions that are more complex. We are able to see the nuances of relationships where differing thoughts, behaviors, and characters interface. We are also able to make mistakes in how we use our lessons. Here's an example to consider.

Industrial sociologist Edwin Nichols describes this scenario about gender stereotypes in lectures throughout the business world:

A lead employee resigns when she decides to stay home with her baby after maternity leave. Her office must hire another associate. Among the candidates are Susan, a young married woman with superb qualifications and Charles, a young man with much less experience who was only partly impressive in his interview.

The staff knows they need someone who can work independently from the start and who will stay for at least three years. They have convened to make their final decision:

MARK: We need to hire the most competent candidate because we have so much business and none of us has time to train someone.

SAM: We also need someone who will stay with the company for at least three years because we are in such an important growth phase.

MARY: I think we need a strong employee we can count on for consistency and even-keel performance. I think Charles is the man for the job.

SAM: I have to agree on this one. Even though he is less experienced, I think he will be able to pick up speed quickly and won't hold us back.

MARK: Why don't you think Susan could do the same thing? She is more qualified!

As we consider Mark's question, let's examine the influence of **cultural integration.** What caused Mary and Sam to dismiss Susan as a viable candidate?

In this scenario three people described the characteristics they desire in an employee and agreed on several. Competency was one and others included the ability to learn and contribute quickly and a likely commitment to stay at the company for three years.

It seemed that Mary and Sam assumed that Susan would be unable to learn quickly or stay three years to contribute to the company's growth even though her qualifications are far superior to Charles's. The question is, how did they come to this conclusion?

An answer may lie in the cultural lessons they were taught. Here is a likely *cultural deduction process:*

1. The previous employee was a woman.
2. The woman became pregnant.
3. The woman made an emotional decision to stay home with her baby.
4. The emotion interrupted the woman's stay at the company.
5. The company can benefit from significant tenure of good employees.
6. The business needs someone who can learn and contribute quickly.
7. The new candidates include a woman and a man.
8. The woman is young and married.
9. The woman might want to have a baby.
10. Babies cause emotion.
11. Emotion interrupts business.
12. Women are emotional.
13. Women have to take time to recover from their emotions.
14. Men are not emotional, and are taught to recover quickly from negative situations.
15. The man is the best person for the job because he will not be emotional and will learn quickly.

This is just one example of the way our minds can work to deduce a series of false assumptions by integrating our thoughts. Do you think this is natural? What does this mean for leadership?

OUR FILE CABINETS

As we learn and use lessons our teachers share with us, we put these lessons into our brains, which are like *file cabinets.* And as we face new situations and recognize that there can be value in applying past lessons, we automatically dig into our file cabinets. Why is this process important for leaders to be aware of?

We can make assumptions that are not accurate. On average we make 11 assumptions every 7 seconds about what we see and experience, and most of them are wrong. However, sometimes we prove them right and so we are encouraged to depend on our file cabinets again.

Where leadership comes in to our file cabinet process is a personal choice. Some people may rely completely on their immediate impressions and thoughts to make decisions. After all, it is easy. Would you? Do you?

We can imagine that all of us have. Similarly we can consider whether it is best. We may choose to believe instead that the best type of leadership involves implementing informed and thoughtful integration. In other words, instead of acting on our immediate impressions, we step outside of them to consider alternatives. What could Mark, Sam, and Mary do to implement informed integration? What benefits are there for leaders in using this skill?

NEGOTIATION

Sometimes as leaders we have to be our own devil's advocate to ensure that we fully examine our decision making. This is what Mark did in the above scenario. He didn't settle for Mary and Sam's initial decision, but rather posed the provocative question, "Why not Susan?"

Other times, we may find ourselves in situations with no shortage of alternative opinions! Have you ever been in a room trying to build a unified vision among vastly different perspectives? This is where the skill for cultural **negotiation** comes in.

Cultural negotiation is the alternative to mere mimicking. It is about personal assessment and taking a personal stand. For instance, when we talked earlier about Theory X and Theory Y, we posed a question. How would you motivate people who dislike work? Would you accept McGregor's recommended method of coercion? Or would you work to find an alternative so that you could behave in a positive, more authentic way while still having an impact?

Not all differences in opinions are as negative as Theories X and Y, but negotiation questions we might ask ourselves are still the same. *Negotiating involves making a decision about your standards as a leader.* If you have a leadership philosophy and someone tempts you to behave in a way that is opposite, what do you do? To what degree are you willing to bend? Do you have to bend or are there ways you can leverage other commonalities to come to an agreement?

Let's look at an example to bring these questions to life. A common example of cultural negotiation is the conversations between doctors and their patients. A physician is trained in medicine and possesses cultural information about patient care, illness, and disease that comes from experience in medical school, residency, and practice. In contrast, patients may know little about medicine but a great deal about how they view illness and accept treatment.

To come to a mutual decision about care, doctors must listen to patients and patients must listen to doctors. Simultaneously, each must assess what they feel is critical for the interaction. For instance, the doctor may recognize that an antibiotic is absolutely necessary for making the patient well. And so perhaps the doctor recommends penicillin.

The patient determines that she is open to any antibiotic except penicillin, to which she is allergic. What should go through the physician's mind to come to a common ground?

In this process of cultural negotiation, it is easy to see that both individuals were leaders. In other words, both individuals were taught lessons on leadership that drive particular behaviors. Also, both individuals have set boundaries based on what they are familiar with, comfortable about, and trusting of. And in the end, both worked together to build an aligned solution.

We may also recognize another dynamic of this interaction—one that relates to credibility.

CREDIBILITY

Credibility, like leadership, is accomplished differently according to cultural lessons. Yet, in essence it means one common thing. Credibility is a level of trust granted to a person by other people.

In the United States, professionals who have certain educational credentials are typically granted a certain level of positional credibility. For instance, in the scenario above, one dynamic facilitating the cultural negotiation is the credibility typically granted to doctors.

Aside from graduating with special credentials, what else can you do to build credibility? What role does credibility play in being a good leader?

One thought is that given the complexity of culture, a leader can benefit from being competent at negotiating across different cultural models. Why? Leaders who are culturally flexible can build rapport with people who have different thoughts, behaviors, and habits. Then, by leveraging commonalties, these individuals can begin to build the familiarity, comfort, and trust inherent in credibility.

When people feel trusting of others, research reveals they are more likely to consider alternative perspectives. For instance, a patient who trusts her doctor might reconsider her boundaries for care at his advice.

For further discussion on credibility and its import to leadership, please go to Appendix II and read the summary of *Credibility*, a popular book authored by leadership experts James M. Kouzes and Barry Z. Posner. See also the special essay by Kouzes and Posner later in this chapter.

JIMMY CARTER: AMBASSADOR TO THE WORLD

This native of Plains, Georgia, is known more for his activities after leaving the White House than for the term he served as president. The Iranian hostage crisis, the worst oil embargo in U.S. history, and an economic recession marred his administration.

After losing the 1980 election to Ronald Reagan by one of the most lopsided margins in U.S. history, the 56-year-old Carter retreated to Georgia where he sold the family peanut business to repay its huge debts. He and his wife Rosalynn spent the next few years raising funds for the nonprofit, nonpartisan Carter Center dedicated to conflict resolution, human rights, and improved health care around the world.

The title of their 1987 book, *Everything to Gain: Making the Most of the Rest of Your Life,* illustrates their determination to find meaning in their post–White House years. Together, the Carters have created an impressive legacy in international good works, traveling to 115 countries to monitor elections, working to alleviate poverty, and promoting childhood immunizations.

A devout Baptist, Carter uses his carpentry skills to help build homes for people in Habitat for Humanity. As distinguished professor at Emory University, he lectures on politics, health care, and human rights. In addition to his extensive travel and his domestic work, Carter has written 14 books since leaving office. His schedule is so rigorous in "retirement" that he wears out Secret Service agents, according to historian Douglas Brinkley in *The Unfinished Presidency.* Brinkley compares Carter's postpresidential life with that of John Quincy Adams, whose 16 years in Congress were devoted largely to struggling against slavery.

Defining retirement as "liberation from mandatory duties," Carter took up skiing at age 62. He has climbed Mounts Kilimanjaro and Fuji and he and Rosalynn jog around the airport during layovers on their many plane trips. He enjoys teaching his grandchildren to fly fish.

The day following his defeat in 1980, Carter told reporters he would never use his status as a former president to make money, and he has honored that commitment, donating his lecture fees to the Carter Center. The Carters live frugally in their modest ranch house built in 1961. They enjoy taking yearly Christmas vacations (using their frequent flier miles) with their four children and grandchildren.

CESAR CHAVEZ: THE AMERICAN GANDHI

Cesar Chavez attended 65 elementary schools and never graduated from high school, yet he became an internationally known organizer of agricultural workers. Born near Yuma, Arizona, in 1927, Chavez saw poverty and grinding working conditions first hand. Having lost their 100-acre ranch and its adobe house during the Depression, the Chavez family traveled the country as migrant laborers. From age 10 on he worked in the fields.

In 1962 he founded the National Farm Workers Association, an organization that later became the United Farm Workers (UFW) of America. The union drew from the mainly Mexican American and Filipino farm workers in California and the Southwest. He served as UFW president until his death in 1993.

In 1965 he organized the first successful American farm workers' strike against the California table grape growers. For this boycott he attracted the interest of civil rights groups and radical student activists. The country was galvanized when Chavez, a minister, and ten strikers were arrested, stripped, and chained together by local sheriffs. The strike ended in 1967 when California's largest winery agreed to proper contracts with the UFW and others followed suit.

Yet the disputes with the industry were far from over. Farm workers demanded such seemingly basic rights as clean water, toilets in the fields, decent hours, sleeping quarters without rats, and regular health inspections.

An advocate of nonviolent social change, he gained a reputation as the "American Gandhi." Chavez embarked on hunger strikes in 1968 (25 days), 1972 (24 days), and 1988 (36 days) to call attention to the need for nonviolence. At the time of his death (thought to have been hastened in part by the effects of the hunger strikes), he was leading another action to protest the use of pesticides harmful to workers.

CLEASTER MIMS: RAISING EXPECTATIONS

Cleaster Mims knew that something major was wrong with the public schools. As a high school English teacher, she felt that the urban system where she taught put students "on a conveyor belt from the schoolhouse to the jailhouse."

Her experience with high schoolers and with "boat people" and other immigrants to whom she taught English as a second language showed her that too many students were pigeonholed in terms of their socioeconomic status. Too many students who could achieve were left to languish because not enough was expected of them.

"Kids don't fail," she insists, "teachers fail. And colleges that turn out teachers who cannot teach fail."

The cost of low expectations to the individual is enormous, she said, but the cost to society is even more immense. "We assume someone coming from a certain environment can't achieve, and we end up pushing people to the back of the line who could find a cure for cancer or AIDS."

While listening to a talk by educator Marva Collins, Mims saw the parallels between her experience and the philosophy of Ms. Collins's West Side Preparatory School in Chicago: the pursuit of academic excellence. She determined to start a school in Cincinnati, Ohio, that would demand nothing short of that.

Working with volunteers in the community, she found space in a church basement and made do with cast-offs for supplies and furniture. "We didn't even have books the first year," she says, noting that she eventually bought the school's classical literature at a local Goodwill store.

Now, in the eighth year of the school's operation, what began as a basement program with 41 students has expanded to more than 300, and Mims is converting a recently purchased facility into a boarding component.

Asked about her leadership, Mims deflects credit: "I feel that I'm chosen. When God chooses you, you cannot not do it and find any happiness in life," she says. As the president, CEO, principal, and founder of the school, she says, "The buck stops with me. But I'm not above sweeping the floors."

Although her university teaching career as a professor in oral communications at Xavier University limits her to being at the school only two days per week, she says she has empowered the teachers to carry on without her. "I had a vision about the school and I've been able to pass it on."

She said, "One has not been successful until they have enough to give away."

She attributes much of her success to the hard work and persistence she learned from her upbringing in the South, where she benefited by attending black schools with high-caliber faculty. In those days, she explains, black professionals were severely limited in the types of jobs they could get, so all-black schools profited from their talents. She herself never felt the sting of lowered expectations, and she hopes to help other children avoid it as well.

"We need a metamorphosis of the mind."

RECAP

So far in this chapter we have learned that culture is the systems we create and propagate through our thoughts, behaviors, and habits. Additionally, we have learned that cultures can look vastly different, and therefore, so can the concept of leadership.

In today's world, which increasingly involves international communication and interactions at all levels of diversity, we have learned that leadership in large part is about developing skills for learning and interfacing successfully with new thoughts and actions. It is about developing an inclusive character with personal standards.

From here, we focus on three more culture-related leadership issues. First, we examine one reason why being an inclusive leader has its challenges. Second, we introduce a tool that you can use to self-assess your leadership style. Third, we prove once again that leadership is socially defined. And we illustrate that one common leadership skill today is being able to communicate cross-culturally.

CHALLENGES TO CHANGE

A primary reason that being an inclusive leader is challenging relates to our inherent dislike for uncertainty and change. Up to this point, we have discussed how we learn thoughts and behaviors in a somewhat sterile way. Teachers teach; you learn.

The reality is that we become emotionally and otherwise attached to our cultural lessons. And sometimes we may feel like we want to preserve and sustain them more than we want to learn other thoughts and behaviors.

We may feel there are certain incentives for maintaining our culture as it is. For instance, power is often granted to individuals with certain thoughts and behaviors, and we risk losing power if we adopt alternative perspectives and behaviors.

We have seen this on a small scale already. For instance, you may hold fast to your opinions in a meeting because they grant you power in the office. What is also worth seeing is self-preservation on a large scale. When we see the lengths to which people have gone in order to preserve their culture, it poses some important questions about leadership.

Is it our job to preserve our culture? Is it to change our culture? To what lengths will we go to maintain our culture? Are they worth it? A look at one significant culture change in history can help us ponder these questions in more detail.

ROMAN EMPIRE

One notable culture change in history relates to Rome. The Roman Empire began to collapse in 245 A.D. when Christianity became a viable alternative to worshipping pagan gods.

Considering *cultural negotiation*, we know that in most cases differing perspectives can be resolved. Repeatedly, however, from 245 A.D. to 330 A.D., discord between Christianity and pagan tradition reached levels of irreconcilable differences. Christianity too often threatened the politics of traditional Rome, and war was a constant fixture.

War is fascinating because it illustrates strategies individuals use to maintain their cultural views. This dynamic has to do with the **cultural normative process.** Because individuals are raised into a norm and become comfortable with it, they will work to maintain it. **Normative action** refers to bringing social pressures to bear on behavior that is considered abnormal and threatening to the status quo.

To proclaim the Roman Empire's domination over Christianity, numerous emperors implemented normative action. In many cases they enslaved or murdered Christians. Additionally, many emperors required Christians to publicly denounce their faith. Emperors conducted such practices for a precise purpose: to demoralize advocates of Christianity in lieu of promoting traditional Rome.

Reading this we may be horrified at the strategies emperors reverted to. In fact, we may feel like Christianity, in all its virtue, deserved to win. However, Christianity was not saintly either during this culture change.

When Christianity supplanted the Roman pagan tradition, Christians similarly leveraged normative action to exert their power. They stripped Roman architectural monuments of the valuable marble with which they were constructed, and then symbolically used the marble to build monuments to Christianity (Smitha, 1999).

Why can we sometimes go to such lengths to maintain our views? One reason relates to change. The scope and trauma of transition can be painful, uncertain, and slow. Individuals can suffer what feels like minor identity crises. And, in some cases, a change may represent a horrible alternative to some people.

What does this mean for leadership? If you know that good leaders need to be able to help individuals navigate and succeed in our ever-changing world, what skills do you want to build? How can you self-assess to ensure you are not implementing harmful normative actions?

FOUR CULTURAL WORLD VIEWS

This section introduces a tool that can help you interface with people who have different thoughts, behaviors, habits, and characters. Industrial sociologist Edwin Nichols researched ways to help individuals make sense of the variety of cultures in the world. Let's examine his research so that we can use it as a tool in becoming the best leaders we can be.

Nichols proposes that four world views can clarify the diversity in the world. Also, he has developed a tool for self-assessing our thoughts along 11 aspects of culture, depicted in Figure 5–1.

Nichols's premise in designing this tool was that thoughts are the layer of meaning that most significantly distinguish cultures from each other. He realized that two cultures may act differently, but at their core have similar thoughts. Understanding the differing thoughts is the first step in understanding cross-cultural difference.

My Cultural Patterns

1. Relationships, family, and friends   Nuclear |————| Extended

2. Time and time consciousness   Fixed |————| Fluid

3. Food and eating habits   Necessity |————| Experience

4. Beliefs and attitudes   Egalitarian |————| Hierarchical

5. Dress and appearance   Informal |————| Formal

6. Communication and language   Explicit/Direct |————| Implicit/Indirect

7. Sense of self and space   Distant |————| Close

8. Mental processes and learning styles   Linear |————| Lateral

9. Work habits and practices   Task |————| Relationships

10. Values and norms   Individual |————| Group

11. Emotions   Controlled |————| Expressive

Figure 5–1   Eleven Aspects of Culture Patterns
Source: Adapted from Gardenswartz and Rowe, *Managing Diversity: A Complete Desk Reference and Planning Guide.* Homewood, Ill.: Business One Irwin, 1993. © 2000 Global Lead Management Consulting.

EDWIN NICHOLS'S WORLD VIEWS—A HIKING ANALOGY

The primary difference among cultures is their thought about what success is. The premise of this analogy is that individuals in each world view would prioritize their hiking tool(s) according what they think would make them most successful on a two-day, overnight hiking trip. In other words, their behavior in selecting a tool would reflect their thought about success. Let's see the differences.

World View	Desired Tool	Thought
Member–Object	Good equipment (pack, clothes, food, etc.)	Obtaining identified objects will contribute most to my success.
Member–Member	A friend to take on a trip	Developing camaraderie with other people will contribute most to my success.
Member–Group	A group of people to join me	Being a part of collective, harmonious groups will contribute most to my success.
Member Great Spirit	A connection with nature to help me	A connection with nature will contribute most to my success.

Nichols's four world views are charted in the sidebar with a personal interpretation added. To simplify a complex theory, a hiking analogy is used to illustrate the differing cultural thoughts among the four world views Nichols has identified. As you look at your self-assessment along the 11 aspects of culture, where do you fall? Which world view do you feel you resemble most? What does this mean for your leadership behaviors? How might you successfully interface with someone from a different world view?

DEFINITION OF CULTURE AND ITS INFLUENCE ON LEADERSHIP

We have examined in depth the current definition of culture. A final topic to address is how the definition of culture itself affects our view of leadership. The easiest way to illustrate this is by comparison.

At the beginning of the chapter modern, inclusive definitions of culture are provided. Comparing these with a definition from the 1800s will let us see how different definitions ultimately advocate different notions of leadership.

The word *culture* derives from the Latin word *colere,* meaning to till, cultivate, or inhabit. In the 1800s, preeminent poet Matthew Arnold proposed that **cultivation** was the key to culture. Cultivation to him meant the improvement or refinement of people and implied the acquisition of traits associated with *his* culture.

TABLE 5–1   **Diverse Definitions of Culture**

Topical	Culture consists of everything on a list of topics, or categories, such as social organization, religion, or economy.
Historical	Culture is social heritage or tradition that is passed on to future generations.
Behavioral	Culture is shared, learned human behavior, a way of life.
Normative	Culture is ideals, values, or rules for living.
Functional	Culture is the way humans solve problems of adapting to the environment or living together.
Mental	Culture is a complex of ideas or learned habits that inhibit impulses and distinguish people from animals.
Structural	Culture consists of patterned and interrelated ideas, symbols, or behaviors.
Symbolic	Culture is based on arbitrarily assigned meanings that are shared by a society.

In other words, rather than an inclusive perspective, Arnold defined culture as "contact with the *best* which has been thought and said in the world." And, as an arrogant man, he believed his social standing and artistic talent deemed him the appropriate person to define what was "the *best*."

Using Arnold's definition, leadership looks much different from what is advocated today. According to Arnold's definition, the meaning of, "Our schools hope to *cultivate* an appreciation for art and music," might be self-centered:

1. Arnold would presume that *his* style of appreciation for art and music is superior to others.

2. He would develop the teaching curriculum to reflect *his* notion of art and music.

3. He would dub anybody who did not achieve *his* success as "uncultured."

This example illustrates that our definition of culture profoundly influences our definition of leadership. We have reviewed several definitions of culture. Look at Table 5–1 to see others and ask yourself what each definition says about the type of leadership it supports.

As you may see in reading the definitions, part of being a leader involves defining culture now and into the future. How would you define culture?

THE TEN MOST IMPORTANT LESSONS WE'VE LEARNED ABOUT LEARNING TO LEAD

JAMES M. KOUZES AND BARRY Z. POSNER

1. Challenge Provides the Opportunity for Greatness—in Leading and in Learning to Lead

Draw a line down the middle of a piece of paper. Now think of the leaders you admire. Write the names of leaders you admire in the left-hand column. In the right hand column, record the events or situations with which you identify these individuals. We predict that you will have associated the leaders from business with corporate turnarounds, entrepreneurial ventures, new product/service development and other business transformations. For those leaders in the military, government, the community, the arts or the church, clubs and student organizations, we predict a similar association with transforming events and times.

When we think of leaders, we recall periods of turbulence, conflict, innovation and change.

But we need not investigate well-known leaders to discover that all leadership is associated with pioneering efforts. In our research, we asked thousands of people, both individual contributors and those in management positions, to write "personal best leadership" cases. It struck us that these cases were about significant change. When the participants in our studies—be they college students or senior citizens, from communities or corporations, from the boiler room to the boardroom—recalled doing their "personal best" as leaders, they automatically associated their best with changing, innovating and overcoming difficulties. These personal best leadership cases illustrate that challenging opportunities provide "ordinary" people the chance to demonstrate extraordinary leadership actions. "The biggest lesson I learned from my personal best [involving his college baseball team]," Karl Thompson explained, "is that you will never know if something will work if you don't try it."

A similar realization came when we asked people how they learned to lead. They responded overwhelmingly: "trial and error." Experience, it appears, is indeed the best teacher—but not just any experience. To describe how their "personal best leadership" and learning experience felt, people used the words "exciting," "exhilarating," "rewarding" and "fun." Dull, routine, boring experiences—in the classroom or in the boardroom—did not provide anyone anywhere with the opportunity to excel or to learn. Only challenge presents the opportunity for greatness. Leaders are pioneers—people who take risks in innovation and experiment to find new and better ways of doing things. Learners are also venturers.

2. Leadership Is in the Eye of the Beholder

Constituents choose leaders. Leaders cannot be appointed or anointed "superiors." Constituents determine whether someone is fit to lead. Power and position may offer the right to exercise authority, but we should never, ever, mistake position and authority for leadership. Only when our constituents believe that we are capable of meeting their expectations will we be able to mobilize their actions.

When we view leadership from this perspective, the relationship is turned upside down. From this vantage, leaders serve their constituents; they do not boss them around. The best leaders are the servants of others' wants and desires, hopes and dreams. And to be able to respond to the needs of others, leaders must first get to know their constituents. By knowing them, listening to them and taking their advice, leaders can stand before others and say with assurance, "Here is what I heard you say that you want for yourselves. Here is how your own needs and interests will be served by enlisting in a common cause."

This notion of leaders as servants flies in the face of the leaders-as-heroes myth perpetuated in comic books, novels, and movies. Yet it is the single most important factor in that dynamic relationship between leader and constituent. Unless we are sensitive to subtle cues, we cannot respond to the aspirations of others. And if we cannot respond to their aspirations, they will not follow.

3. Credibility Is the Foundation of Leadership

We also researched the expectations people have of those whom they would be willing to follow. We asked more than 25,000 people from a range of organizations around the globe to tell us what they admired and looked for in their leaders. According to this data, people want leaders who are honest, forward-looking, inspiring and competent.

While these results aren't surprising, they are extraordinarily significant to all leaders, because three of the four characteristics comprise what communications experts refer to as "source credibility." When determining whether or not we believe someone who is communicating with us—whether that person is a teacher, newscaster, salesperson, manager, parent or colleague—we look for trustworthiness (honesty), expertise (competence), and dynamism (inspiration). Credibility is a leader's single most important asset, and it should be protected and nurtured at all costs. Personal credibility is the foundation on which leaders stand. We call this the *First Law of Leadership*—if you don't believe in the messenger, you won't believe the message. This is precisely what Michael Cole learned as a 16-year-old T-ball coach: "Once the kids [ages 4–8] saw that I wanted what was best for them as well as sharing in their excitement, they became a lot more trusting of me."

4. The Ability to Inspire a Shared Vision Differentiates Leaders from Other Credible Sources

While credibility is the foundation, leaders must envision an uplifting and ennobling future. The one admired leadership quality not a criterion of source credibility is "forward-looking." We expect leaders to take us to places we have never been before—to have clearly in mind an attractive destination that will make the journey worthwhile. "Leadership isn't telling people what to do," says Anthony Bianchi, who organized a ski trip to the Italian Alps for American college students studying in Florence: "It's painting a picture of an exciting possibility of how we can achieve a common goal."

To distinguish ourselves as leaders, we must be concerned with the future of our groups, organizations, and communities. If there is no vision, there is no business. The domain of leaders is the future. The leader's unique legacy is the creation of valued programs and institutions that survive over time.

Equally important, however, is the leader's capacity to enlist others to transform the vision into reality. We found that the ability to inspire others to share the dream—to communicate the vision so that others come to embrace it as their own—was what uplifted constituents and drew them forward. Leaders in any endeavor must demonstrate personal enthusiasm for the dream. Only passion will ignite the flames of our constituents' desires.

5. Without Trust, You Cannot Lead

While we asked people to recount *their* "personal best leadership" experiences, they typically came to realize that it wasn't really *"my* best; it was *our* best. Because it wasn't *me;* it was *us."* Leaders can't do it alone! In fact, no one ever achieved an extraordinary milestone all by himself or herself—it is a team effort (and notice there is no "i" in the word team).

At the heart of these collaborative efforts is trust. Leaders genuinely desire to make heroes and heroines of others. Without trust, people become self-protective and controlling. Similarly, when there is low trust, people are likely to distort, ignore and disguise facts, ideas, conclusions and feelings. People become suspicious and unreceptive. A trusting relationship between leader and constituents is essential to getting extraordinary things done.

Leaders create a caring climate—a climate of trust. For people to disclose their needs and feelings, to make themselves vulnerable, to expose their weaknesses, to risk failing, they must truly believe they are safe. For example, in learning to parachute jump, people will probably not be eager to jump if they do not trust the instructor or the equipment. Trust must be established before people will risk learning something new.

Another primary task of leadership is to create a climate in which others feel powerful, efficacious and strong. In such a climate, people know they are free to take risks, trusting that when they make mistakes the leader will not ask "Who's to blame?" but, "What did we learn?"

Involvement and participation are essential to create this climate. Giving free choice and listening to others are other important elements of a trusting environment. Leaders focus on fostering collaboration, strengthening others and building trust—on giving their power away—as the most effective strategies for enhancing the power of everyone.

6. Shared Values Make a Critical Difference in the Quality of Life at Home and at Work

Credibility—that single most important leadership asset we mentioned earlier—has at its root the word "credo," meaning a set of beliefs. Every leader must begin by asking, "What do I stand for? What do I believe in? What values do I hold to be true and right?" Through our research, we found that people who reported greater compatibility between personal values and the values of their organizations also reported significantly greater feelings of success in their lives, had greater understandings of the values of their managers and coworkers, were more willing to work longer and harder hours, and felt less stress at home and on the job. Shared values are essential for personal and business health.

Shared values provide a sense of alignment, so that, just like a rowing team, everyone is pulling in the same direction. Feeling aligned is empowering, creating a sense of freedom and personal integrity. When people feel that their personal values are in synch with those of their organization, our research indicates they are personally more successful and healthier. They feel liberated and in control of their lives. Shared values enable everyone to experience ownership in the organization.

7. Leaders Are Role Models for Their Constituents

When we asked people to define credibility behaviorally, the most common response was "Do what you say you will do." People believe in actions more than in words, in practices more than in pronouncements. It's simply not sufficient to communicate values and beliefs. We must live them, and leaders are expected to set the example for others.

Mindy Behse, for example, reported that when she was captain of her high school swim team, her teammates watched what she did: "I couldn't ask anybody to do anything I wasn't willing to do. I had to take practices very seriously." Blaine Thomas learned quickly that being captain of his baseball team meant that people not only watched what he did on the field, but off the field as well. And, he pointed out, "I couldn't be one kind of a leader, with certain standards on the field, and then be some other kind of person or leader off the field with different, especially lower, standards." As the team leader of a group of student painters during the summer, Mike Burciago observed that his willingness to do his share of the "grubby work" made it easier to get others to voluntarily do their share as well.

Credibility is earned minute-by-minute, hour-by-hour through actions consistent with stated values. Values are often considered the soft side of management, but based on our research, we would say that nothing is more difficult than to be unwaveringly true to one's guiding beliefs.

8. Lasting Change Progresses One Hop at a Time

When we asked Don Bennett, the first amputee to reach the 14,410-foot summit of Mt. Rainier, how he was able to climb to that height, he replied, looking down at his one leg and foot, "One hop at a time." When preparing for the climb, he would imagine himself on top of the mountain 1,000 times a day. But when he started to climb, he'd look down at his foot and say, "'Anybody can hop from here to there.' So I did."

Big results from small beginnings. "Our goal seemed enormous; so we broke it down into parts and gave one part to each member," is how Richard Cabral accounts for the success of his high school organization in hosting a dinner for more than 300 people, including parents and the city's mayor. Progress is always incremental. The key to lasting improvement is small wins. Choosing to do the easy things first—those that can be accomplished quickly and inexpensively by a team with a local champion—is the only sure way to achieve extraordinary things in organizations. Referring to his own struggles against the seemingly insolvable problem of South Africa's apartheid, Bishop Tutu noted: "You eat an elephant...one bite at a time!"

9. Leadership Development Is Self-Development

Leaders take us to places we have never been before. But there are no freeways to the future, no paved highways to unknown, unexplored destinations. There is only wilderness. If we are to step into the unknown, we must begin by exploring the inner territory.

Leadership is an art—a performing art. And in the art of leadership, the instrument is the self. A musician may have a violin, an engineer a workstation and an accountant a computer. But a leader has only himself or herself as the medium of expression. Leadership development, then, is essentially a process of self-development.

The self-confidence required to lead comes from learning about ourselves—our skills, prejudices, talents and shortcomings. Self-confidence develops as we build on strengths and overcome weaknesses. As Larry Olin, captain of his college tennis team, learned: "You must be confident in yourself before you can expect others to be confident in you."

People frequently ask, "Are leaders born or made?" We firmly believe that leadership can be learned. Certainly, some people are more predisposed to lead than others. But this is true of anything. Leadership is definitely not a divine-like grace given to a few charismatic men and women. It is a set of learnable practices. We believe it is possible for ordinary people to learn to get extraordinary things done. There is a leader in everyone, and the greatest inhibitor to leadership development is the belief that leadership cannot be learned.

Developing ourselves as leaders requires removing the barriers, whether self-imposed or imposed by the organization, and understanding that development is a continuous improvement process, not an event, a class, a book, or series of programs.

10. Leadership Is Not an Affair of the Head, It Is an Affair of the Heart

Leadership is emotional. Period. To lead others requires passionate commitment to a set of fundamental beliefs and principles, visions and dreams. The climb to the summit is arduous and often frightening. Leaders encourage others to continue the quest by inspiring them with courage and hope.

In our study of leadership, we often asked our interviewees how they would go about developing leaders, whether in school, business, government or volunteer organizations. Major General John Stanford, then Commander of the U.S. Army's Military Traffic Management Command, gave a memorable reply: "When people ask me that question, I tell them I have the secret to success in life. The secret to success is to stay in love." Not the advice we expected from a Major General or from any of the people we interviewed, but the more we thought about it, the more we realized that leadership is an affair of the heart. Constituents will not follow unless they are persuaded that their leader passionately believes in his or her view of the future and believes in each of them.

More than ever before, there is a need for people to answer the call for leadership—to seize the opportunities for greatness. Only by looking inside our hearts will we know when we are ready to take that first step along the journey to the future.

James Kouzes and **Barry Posner** are co-authors of two award-winning and best-selling books on leadership: *The Leadership Challenge: How to Keep Getting Extraordinary Things Done in Organizations* (San Francisco: Jossey-Bass, 1995) and *Credibility: How Leaders Gain and Lose It, Why People Demand It* (San Francisco; Jossey-Bass, 1993). Kouzes is CEO of The Tom Peters Group/Learning Systems (Palo Alto, Calif.) and Posner is Professor of Organizational Behavior and Managing Partner, Executive Development Center, Santa Clara University (Santa Clara, Calif.).

SUMMARY

Cultural anthropology studies cultures, of which there are many. Cultures differ in thoughts, behaviors, habits, and characters. In this time of increased internationalization, leadership may be defined in part as the ability to communicate effectively across cultures. Yet this is not an automatic skill. Instead it involves developing a personal leadership philosophy.

Individually we can benefit by recognizing the lessons on leadership that we learned growing up. Additionally, we can benefit by learning to leverage what we know about culture—that it is an ongoing process of creation, normative implementation, and negotiation.

As leaders we must develop personal standards and skills that facilitate successful interactions. And, just as *The One* in *The Matrix* never gave up on learning the skills that would allow him to lead, we must continue our personal journey of leadership throughout our lives.

CREATE YOUR OWN THEORY

Throughout this text, we have stressed the idea that leadership is in the eye of the beholder; that is, we all form our own views on what leadership is and how it is practiced most effectively. This chapter in particular has highlighted the idea that meaning is socially and individually constructed, based in large part on our formative experiences and continually refined through our interpretation of the events we experience each day.

Some questions to consider include: What are some of the different definitions of culture that are offered in this chapter and that speak to you most? What are some of your thoughts about culture and leaders? What can we take from history as we continue to formulate our own theories on leadership?

Let's move these ideas into a business context. In the opening Leadership Moment, you were placed in the position of supervising a merger of people and cultures between two departments that previously had worked in isolation. In this situation, what would your strengths and weaknesses be as a leader attempting to facilitate this change? What would your priorities be and around which potential issues would you seek support?

KEY TERMS

cultural anthropology

culture

learned behaviors

nature/nurture debate

thoughts

behaviors

habits

character

Theory X and Theory Y
negotiation
credibility

cultural normative process
normative action
cultivation

QUESTIONS FOR DISCUSSION AND REVIEW

1. What does it mean to say that culture is learned?
2. What is the concept of "meaning systems" and why is this important to understanding culture?
3. What are some common thoughts of the members of the group that you most strongly identify with?
4. What is leadership character?
5. What can happen when two organizations have radically different assumptions about culture?
6. Provide an example of a situation where a cultural deduction has been made.
7. What was Matthew Arnold's perspective on culture and whom did he believe to be the best arbiter on how to cultivate culture?

ONLINE SELF-ASSESSMENT TOOL

To read more about cultural anthropology and the power of narratives, we recommend that you visit www.armintl.com/stories/david-bio.html.

CHAPTER 6

Political Science and Presidential Leadership

LEADERSHIP MOMENT

You're Dean of the Graduate School and the administration's representative on a committee designed to address the concerns of graduate students. A small but growing group of graduate students has been pressing the university to provide larger stipends, to pay some or all of their health insurance costs, and to demonstrate more respect for the role of graduate students in the university. One of the graduate student representatives on the committee has sparked the ire of the committee's one faculty representative—an individual chosen without graduate student input. She reported in a meeting summary sent out to a graduate student organization e-mail list that the faculty member "seemed unsympathetic to graduate student concerns." At the next meeting, without any advance warning, the professor lashed out in a disrespectful and confrontational manner at the graduate student. Although you do think the graduate student could have exhibited better judgment by choosing her words more carefully, she certainly didn't deserve to be treated like this.

1. *What would you do?*
2. *What power issues are at play in this scenario?*
3. *How might your perspective change if you were the president of the university? What if you were a member of the graduate student government?*

*I*t is impossible to understand fully the notion of leadership without an understanding of certain fundamental principles of political science. Many would argue that leadership is about the exercise of power and political science is, at its core, a study of what constitutes power, who has it, and how it is exercised. As many have explained, politics, much like leadership, is about who gets what, when, and how. Understanding our own answers to these questions sheds lights on how we evaluate leadership regardless of whether we are referring to the competency of a president, the effectiveness of a dean, or the skills of a company's chief executive officer (as well as all the intermediate levels of leadership necessary in both a democracy and most good companies).

Just as good managers must consider the needs of their employees along with the needs of the company, a truly great president must be attentive to the needs of the people—as the position is elective—and to the larger needs of the nation and the public good. When discussing presidential leadership (which we will do in further detail), the question arises whether great leaders are born, are formed, or both. Are the presidents consistently ranked as great by academics and the public—Washington, Jefferson, Lincoln, and FDR—great because of their innate personality traits or because of the extraordinary times in which they served? Just as a so-called ordinary person like Miep Gies (profiled in Chapter 1) points to the times in which she lived as the trigger for her extraordinary actions, the great presidents seem to have been born with the necessary ingredients to respond to the clarion calls of history effectively.

POWER

Political theorists and scientists debate issues about power and its exercise. Theorists have articulated competing and complementary theories of the state, which have evolved in conjunction with the development of the modern state in the post-Machiavellian period. Power, in this sense, has to do with how to order society, whether we are referring to the power of Hobbes's *Leviathan* (discussed in Appendix I) or the power exercised by elective representatives. Power, as it relates to leadership, is more about regulating the relations of individuals to each other. **Power,** for our purposes, can be defined as the potential influence over the attitudes and behaviors of one or more target individuals.

Influence is the degree of actual change in the target person's attitudes or behaviors. **Influence tactics** are, therefore, behaviors one person uses to affect another's attitudes or behaviors. Examples of influence tactics include appeals to reason, emotion, and inspiration, as well as consultation, ingratiation, exchange of favors, the formation of coalitions to influence a particular target individual or group, pressure tactics, and more coercive tactics based on one's position of authority.

The power of individuals shapes the types of tactics they can use to influence others. Those with more power have a larger array of tactics from which to choose. In many ways a democracy is an exercise in influence tactics as those in power seek to influence others in positions of power and the broader public seeks to influence those with power to better represent their interests. In our country, those with more money and education are often more effective at influencing those in power, just as managers and upper-level employees are more effective at influencing a company's operations.

According to a workplace survey of 165 managers cited by Robbins (1993), the following seven strategies are the most common tactics used to obtain influence:

1. *Reason* (most often cited): using facts and data to make a logical or rational presentation of ideas
2. *Friendliness:* using flattery, creating goodwill, acting humble, and being friendly prior to making a request

3. *Sanctions:* using organizationally derived rewards and punishments such as preventing or promising a salary increase, threatening to give an unsatisfactory performance evaluation, or withholding a promotion

4. *Bargaining:* using negotiation through the exchange of benefits or favors

5. *Higher authority:* gaining the support of higher levels in the organization to back up requests

6. *Assertiveness:* using a direct and forceful approach such as demanding compliance with requests, repeating reminders, ordering individuals to do what is asked, and pointing out that rules require compliance

7. *Coalition building:* getting the support of other people in the organization to back up the request

The survey also found that managers chose influence tactics depending on four factors: their relative power, their objectives, their expectation that the other person would comply, and the culture of the organization. Effective leaders must understand the types of influence tactics being used in their organizations as they seek to develop a shared vision. In addition, those lower on the organizational totem pole should be aware of their managers' tactics so that they understand what is expected of them.

Figure 6–1 portrays a way of viewing the distinctions between power and influence.

Sources of Power

Before we talk about where power comes from, we should define power as it relates to our discussion of the intersection of leadership and political science. According to DuBrin (1995), organizational politics is defined as the informal approaches to gaining power through means other than luck or merit. French and Raven (1975) found that managers derive power, as such, from five sources. This model is worth discussing in greater detail because of its wide acceptance. We know that leaders have power, but almost all individuals have power in some form or other, which means that leaders and followers both exercise power from different sources simultaneously.

| | | **Basis of manipulation** | |
		Power	Influence
Type of manipulation	Positive	Inducement	Persuasion
	Negative	Coercion	Obligation

Figure 6–1   Different Forms of Political Manipulation

Source: Reprinted from *Business Horizons*, March–April 1987. Copyright 1987 by the foundation for the School of Business at Indiana University. Used with permission.

1. **Expert power**—based on knowledge or competence. The expertise could range from understanding how to make a strong presentation or how to get an invoice processed in an organization to demonstrating how to harness nuclear energy. Clearly, followers also can be experts, as when a mechanically adept student rescues the professor's class by fixing the video recorder.

2. **Referent power**—based on relationship and personal drawing power. Leaders who attract others by their style or charisma demonstrate referent power. For instance, a student dressed in a novel or unusual way may inspire others to dress similarly.

3. **Legitimate power**—bestowed by formal organization. Also known as *position power,* this type comes with the sign on the door and the title on the letterhead. However, the real power may lie elsewhere in the organization. Sometimes the most powerful person in an organization is the administrative assistant who controls the schedule and access of the titular head.

4. **Reward power**—the ability to offer and withhold types of incentives such as status, promotions, salary increases, or interesting assignments. Followers can reward leaders' behavior through their praise, enthusiasm, or obvious support.

5. **Coercive power**—the ability to force someone to comply through threat of physical, psychological, or emotional consequences. Parents generally possess this power, as do children, which is why they often get favorable results from throwing a tantrum in a crowded store.

In addition to understanding the different sources of power, it is equally important to assess the effectiveness of different types of power. According to Nelson and Quick (1996), reward and coercive power both might produce the desired results, as long as the manager/leader is present. Coercive power, however, has the potential unintentional consequence of placing the manager in the role of a "Big Brother" who must constantly monitor the actions of employees. Reward power also requires managers to watch over the shoulders of employees to determine who deserves a reward. Both types of power, therefore, foster growing dependence on managers. Those who expect to receive rewards or to be coerced into action take their cues from their managers.

Legitimate power—as embodied in the T-shirt slogan, "Because I'm the mommy, that's why!"—has its place but ultimately is less effective in helping organizations achieve their goals and in fostering employee satisfaction. Referent power and expert power are the most effective, especially from an organizational perspective. However, charismatic leaders must be careful not to lose sight of common goals. Expert power is most closely associated with task performance and employee satisfaction, which is not surprising since it can empower followers as much as leaders.

Position or Personal Power

Yukl (1994) and others describe power in different terms, asserting the existence of two types of power—position and personal power. **Position** (or *legitimate*) **power** is derived from one's place in the organization (see Figure 6–2). The amount of an

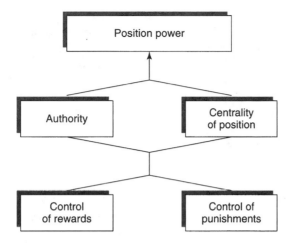

Figure 6–2   Position Power

individual's position power varies depending on organizational policies and union contracts. Position power gives individuals various kinds of power, including:

- Authority (the right to influence others in specific ways)
- Control over information
- Control over who does the work and where they do it
- Control over rewards and punishments

Personal power, on the other hand, is derived from an individual's personal attributes (see Figure 6–3). Leaders who have expertise, are likeable, and are attractive often possess this power, which they can use in interactions with subordinates as

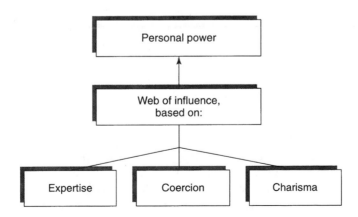

Figure 6–3   Personal Power

well as superiors. Personal power comes from a variety of sources, including referent and expert power. Control over information and its distribution can give an individual personal power. Association power, which occurs when an individual has influence over somebody else with power, also can provide an individual with personal power. Personal power cannot be gleaned by knowing somebody's title.

Which type of power—personal or position—do you think is more effective? According to Yukl, those who lead through personal power have more influence over us. Do you agree? Of course, many leaders, such as Margaret Thatcher of Great Britain and Lee Kuan Yew of Singapore (see the following Leadership Profiles), have successfully utilized both.

MARGARET THATCHER: BRITAIN'S "IRON LADY"

Margaret Thatcher was not only Britain's first woman prime minister, she was the first female prime minister of any European country. She surprised most political commentators when she led her Tory party to victory in the country's general election in 1979.

Growing up as the younger daughter of a lay Methodist minister, Ms. Thatcher learned early on to stand behind her own decisions regardless of other people's opinions. Unbounded determination helped her win a scholarship to Oxford, where she held leadership positions in the Conservative Association.

She continued working for the conservative position, and became the youngest woman candidate in the country when she stood for local election. Despite losing twice in a row, she managed to increase the conservative vote by nearly 50 percent and proved herself a capable, hard-working politician.

She married, had twins, went to law school, and practiced as a barrister specializing in taxation law, but she kept her eye on the goal of being elected to Parliament. After several disappointments, she reached her goal in 1959.

Ms. Thatcher rose to prominence in the conservative Tory party, and in 1961 was appointed secretary to the ministry of pensions and national insurance. From 1964–70, she emerged as an opposition spokesperson to the Labour party, then in power. As the minister of education (after the Conservatives won the 1970 general election), she was dubbed the "most unpopular woman in Britain" for her controversial views on education, including discontinuing free milk for students over seven and increasing school milk charges.

After Conservative Edward Heath lost in the 1974 general election, Ms. Thatcher announced that she would seek the party's leadership. Although no one took her seriously at first, she emerged the victor after two ballots.

Then, in 1979, she won a narrow victory in a no-confidence vote over James Callaghan, who became the first prime minister to be voted out of office since 1924.

Having campaigned on the promise to "turn the tide against socialism," she introduced legislation to reduce government spending in health care, housing, social security, and education while increasing support for the military and reducing taxation, particularly for the wealthiest people.

She was roundly criticized in Parliament and in the media for what her opposition called "the savage attack on the welfare state." Undaunted, she declared that the country was "sick and needed a dose of strong medicine."

Despite a major victory in quelling the civil war in Rhodesia and helping to hold free elections that resulted in black nationalist leader Robert Mugabe winning, she faced increasingly difficult times at home: massive unemployment, rising numbers of businesses closing, and widespread public uproar over her economic policies. Nevertheless, Ms. Thatcher won three consecutive general elections and held office continuously longer than any British prime minister since Gladstone.

She has been lauded and sneered at for her persistence and her willingness to challenge conventional wisdom. Indeed, even her rise to the top was a great challenge. She was the epitome of an outsider, coming not from the aristocracy of the party, but rather from a provincial town and middle-class parents. Most significantly, she was an outsider in terms of gender.

Writing in the *Atlantic Monthly* (Dec. 1991), Geoffrey Wheatcraft explains:

> She was cut off by the "homosocial" traditions of her party, which thirty years ago were very strong and are scarcely weak even now. It was a chaps' party—chaps who had known each other at school, at university, in the army, chaps who met to talk and drink in the House of Commons smoking room or the clubs of St. James Street. This was a camaraderie from which the lowborn were mostly excluded, and a woman was by definition entirely excluded. And so Margaret Thatcher had to plow her own furrow, make her own friends, and attack the citadel of power from outside.

LEE KUAN YEW: NATION BUILDER

The world's longest-serving prime minister, Lee Kuan Yew ruled Singapore from its inception as an independent country in 1959 until stepping down in 1990. Born in Singapore in 1923, he attended Raffles College there before going to England to study law at Cambridge.

After returning to Singapore in 1950, he threw himself into politics and rose to the top spot in the government in 1959. His accomplishments in Singapore are legendary: turning the economy from manufacturing to high-tech, transforming the infrastructure of the country to a modern-day exemplar, nearly eliminating crime and unemployment, and creating one of Asia's foremost health care and educational systems. Today, per-capita income in Singapore is higher than in England. Singapore boasts the world's busiest port and the third-largest oil refinery in addition to its role as a global center of manufacturing and service industries—all this in a tiny country almost totally lacking in natural resources.

His forthright, confrontational personality seems decidedly un-Asian. *Time International* describes Lee as "living by the conflict theory of management: you either dominate or are dominated." He experienced being dominated, first by British colonial rule and later by the often-brutal Japanese occupation in World War II.

When he came to power, he didn't hesitate to become the dominator. His style of governing was often described as "soft authoritarian," although his opponents might not agree with the "soft" designation. Lee promoted a culture that stressed discipline, avoiding drugs, and encouraging tolerance among the races.

In 1994, an American teenager convicted of a crime in Singapore was sentenced to caning. Despite torrents of opposition, including a personal plea from President Clinton, Mr. Lee defended his government's corporal punishment approach as an effective way to stem crime.

Lee characterizes American society as an overly permissive society that has lost its ethical and moral underpinnings. He asserts that the United States should not try to impose its model of government elsewhere, especially on Eastern nations whose cultures do not lend themselves to a democratic approach.

Since retiring as prime minister in 1990, Lee continues to serve the country in the newly created position of "senior minister." Former President Nixon was one of his many admirers, writing that if he had lived in a different time and place, Lee might have "attained the world stature of a Churchill, a Disraeli or a Gladstone."

Rosenbach and Taylor (1993) suggest another lens through which to view power. They break power down into three components:

1. Power over—the traditional view of power as domination
2. Power to—enhance other people's power or power as empowerment
3. Power from—being able to resist the power of others' unwanted demands

Finally, Etzioni (1993) describes three types of organizational power—coercive, utilitarian, and normative (see Figure 6–4).

Coercive power, as we have noted, compels certain behavior with threats or fear. **Utilitarian power** is exercised through providing rewards. Those with **normative power** can influence members of an organization to act in certain ways by arguing that something is the "right" thing to do. According to Etzioni, organizations fall within three types:

1. **alienative**—those whose members are primarily unhappy, negative, and don't want to be part of the organization
2. **calculative**—those whose members are constantly assessing the tradeoffs of belonging and ceasing to belong
3. **moral**—those whose members make sacrifices to further the larger cause

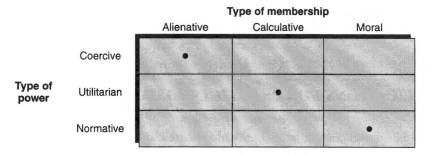

Figure 6–4   Etzioni's Power Analysis

EVALUATING INFLUENCE TACTICS

The Ethical Perspective

Managers and leaders of all sorts must make constant decisions about the influence tactics they choose to use. Blanchard and Pearl (1980) suggest several questions we should ask ourselves before seeking to influence others:

Is it legal?

Is it balanced?

How will it make me feel about myself?

Mohandas Gandhi, one of the twentieth century's most influential leaders, proposed an equally humane form of evaluation:

Whenever you are in doubt, or when the self becomes too much with you, recall the case of the poorest and weakest man who you may have seen, and ask yourself if the step you contemplate is going to be any use to him. Will he gain anything by it? Will it restore him control over his own life and destiny? Will it lead to swaraj, that is, self-government for the hungry and spiritually starving millions? Then, you will find your doubts and self melting away. (Nair, 1994)

Although most tactics can be used in a manipulative manner, DuBrin (1995) offers a framework for the ethical exercise of influence:

- Leading by example
- Using rational persuasion
- Developing a reputation as a subject-matter expert
- Exchanging favors and bargaining
- Legitimizing a request
- Making an inspirational appeal and showing emotion
- Consulting with others before making a decision

- Forming coalitions
- Being a good team player

Do the Means Justify the Ends?

DuBrin also devised a list of dishonest and unethical influence tactics:

- Deliberate Machiavellianism by advocating the ruthless manipulation of others for one's own ends
- "Gentle" manipulation by falsifying statements or arguing that everybody else has already followed the request
- Coercion via threats, criticism, excessive demands
- Debasing or demeaning oneself to control others
- Upward appeal, going over a person's head to influence his or her actions
- Passive control by sulking, ignoring, or otherwise giving someone the "silent treatment"
- Ingratiation and charm
- Joking and kidding (which can be either ethical or manipulative, depending on tone, tact, and situation)

Most of us have witnessed first hand the negative and positive uses of power. McClelland (1975) describes a different type of positive use of power, which he calls **social power** and defines as the positive expression of power unleashed by achieving group goals. According to McClelland, managers are most successful when they combine a high need for social power with a relatively low affiliation need. These leaders, he says, exhibit four characteristics regarding power:

1. They believe in the validity of the authority system from which they draw their power. They are comfortable with influencing others and being influenced. They believe in the organization.
2. They enjoy their work and bring to it a sense of order. They value work beyond its income-producing ability.
3. They are altruistic, believing that their well-being is linked with the corporation. They put the company first.
4. They believe in seeking justice above all else and that justice should extend to the workplace.

HOW DO INDIVIDUALS ACQUIRE AND LOSE POWER?

The balance of power between individuals and among individuals in organizations rarely remains static. Several leading theories help us understand how people obtain, maintain, and lose power in organizations. These are the **vertical dyad linkage** and the **social exchange theory.**

Vertical Dyad Linkage

In certain instances, a leader and a small group of followers share a high degree of mutual attraction and influence. These select few people, the *in-group*, are typically quite loyal, committed, and highly trusting of the leader. These leaders most often exercise reward, legitimate, and coercive power to influence their followers.

What are the implications for leadership in such situations? Effective leaders are those who avoid creating groups of insiders and outsiders because such a cleavage is divisive and reduces overall group performance. Some leaders find that the best way to improve group performance is to make everybody feel a part of the in-group. In fact, charismatic leaders (those with referent power) have a striking ability to do so.

Social Exchange Theory

According to this theory, leadership is a transaction between leaders and followers, both of whom benefit in the process. The benefits may include status, praise, identity, money, or other types of rewards. When the benefits each receives are close to equivalent, the relationship between leader and followers is most effective. According to this line of reasoning, members of a group can stockpile "points" by demonstrating loyalty, problem solving, and so forth. Leaders may emerge from a leaderless group based on how many of these types of points they have earned.

Once leaders have power, why would they give it away? Ironically, you will acquire more power by sharing the power you have with others. When followers increase their power, they perform better, thus raising the overall productivity of the group. This practice of sharing power also is known as *empowerment.* For examples of how managers view empowerment differently than leaders, see Table 6–1.

TABLE 6–1   Differences in the Empowering Process as a Function of Role: Leaders Compared with Managers

Empowering Process	Leader Activities	Manager Activities
Providing direction for followers/subordinates	Via ideals, vision, a higher purpose, superordinate goals	Via involvement of subordinates in determining the paths toward goal accomplishment
Stimulating followers/ subordinates	With ideas	With actions; things to accomplish
Rewarding followers/ subordinates	Informal; personal recognition	Formal; incentive systems
Developing followers/ subordinates	By inspiring them to do more than they thought they could do	By involving them in important decision-making activities and providing feedback for potential learning by giving them training
Appealing to follower/ subordinate needs	Appeal to needs of follower-ship and dependency	Appeal to needs for autonomy and independence

Source: Burke, W. Warner. "Leadership as Empowering Others," Table 4, p. 73, adapted as submitted. In S. Strivasta and Associates, *Executive Power.* Copyright 1986 by Jossey-Bass, Inc. Publishers.

Leaders can empower followers/subordinates through a variety of methods, including:

- Rewarding and encouraging followers in visible ways, such as certificates, worker-of-the-month recognition, membership in certain clubs, etc.
- Creating a positive work environment because confident and comfortable workers are willing to take on more challenges.
- Showing confidence. Empowering leaders tell their followers verbally and nonverbally that they have confidence in their abilities.
- Promoting initiative and increasing responsibility with appropriate rewards.
- Starting small and taking on larger changes one step at a time.
- Praising initiative, even when results fall short.

PRESIDENTIAL LEADERSHIP IN THE UNITED STATES

When political scientists in the United States study leadership (please note that in this section, for purposes of brevity, we are focusing our examination only on presidential leadership in the United States—other countries have different presidential histories and traditions), they often focus on presidential leadership and its implications for democracy. Naturally, the modern presidency differs greatly from the presidency as conceived of by the founders and described in the Constitution. Even though much has changed during the course of our history, the past is prologue. Presidents remain constrained by constitutional limits on their authority, even as extraconstitutional powers have come to play a larger role in the exercise of presidential power. Having thrown off the shackles of monarchy and the trappings of aristocracy, the founders were concerned most with the potential abuses of concentrated power as they set out to forge our national government.

From 1781–1788, the Articles of Confederation governed the new United States. Remember that the Articles lacked an executive office and reserved many rights to coequal state governments. The weaknesses of the national government under the Articles propelled our founders toward an uneasy compromise between the excessive power of monarchy and the national power void of the Articles. Indeed, concerns about tyrannical power resulted in the divided and representative system of government that we still have today. States share power with the national government and the national government itself is divided into three branches with separate but overlapping powers (checks and balances). The U.S. president operates under a Constitution ratified more than 200 years ago yet leads a country in a world vastly different from that of the men who wrote the document.

Sources of Presidential Power

Delegates to the Constitutional Convention grappled with many difficult and complex matters, such as how much power to give to the national government, how much should remain with the states, and how best to balance power between the executive, judicial, and legislative branches of government. Debates about the executive prompted some of the greatest controversy. At the beginning, everything about the form and function of an executive officer was open for discussion. Many at the convention opposed the idea of an executive officer because they feared the president would be nothing but a king in plain clothes. Others, Alexander Hamilton chief among them, argued that a strong executive officer would be necessary to safeguard the republican system. After all, only a unitary figure with certain powers can act quickly during crises to protect the nation, and a president with republican virtues would be able to rise above the more parochial concerns of Congress—especially those of the House of Representatives, whose members each represent small fragments of the total population—to represent the national interest. In particular, delegates "wanted an executive that was strong enough to check a runaway legislature, but not so strong as to become despotic" (Milkis and Nelson, 1999).

Under the Constitution, the president received several specific powers, including the power to:

- Act as commander in chief of the military
- Serve as head of state
- Veto acts of Congress
- Convene Congress
- Appoint executive branch officials
- Make treaties
- Grant pardons

From the start, however, our nation has debated what constitutes the proper exercise of presidential power. Hamilton, for instance, believed that the president had the authority to act where the Constitution was silent. In other words, he believed the president wasn't limited to the specific powers outlined in the Constitution but had the latitude to expand presidential authority where necessary to better serve the nation.

Gradually the powers of the presidency have expanded to include many powers not specifically listed in the Constitution. Presidents George Washington and Thomas Jefferson—despite Jefferson's belief in a more limited executive—began augmenting the powers of the presidency from the beginning and today presidents regularly exercise powers neither envisioned by the founders nor spelled out by the Constitution. These **extraconstitutional** powers include but are not limited to:

- Congressional grants of power
- Executive orders
- Prestige and material resources of the office
- Going public
- Use of information, especially in the areas of military and foreign policy

Although early presidents began expanding presidential power in new ways, presidents throughout the nineteenth and into the early twentieth centuries typically played a more traditional, limited role in the American political system. Indeed, during much of the nineteenth century, for instance, Congress took the lead in determining public policy for the nation. As a result, members of Congress—Daniel Webster and John Calhoun, for instance—remain better known than certain nineteenth century presidents (think of Millard Filmore, for example). However, the gradual expansion of presidential powers, coupled with the trauma of the Great Depression and World War II, reshaped the American presidency.

During the presidency of Franklin Delano Roosevelt the traditional model of the presidency gave way and the modern presidency emerged. To meet the challenges of the Depression, FDR enhanced the powers of the presidency exponentially. The breadth and scope of the federal government grew during this period as well, as the *alphabet soup* of New Deal programs—the WPA, TVA, SEC, and many more—emerged to help the country recover. In addition, FDR changed the executive office of the president through the Executive Reorganization Act of 1939, which institutionalized the presidency by increasing the number of staff and offices that directly report to the president and by expanding presidential control over existing government departments and agencies.

Today, as Theodore White has written, the moment a new president takes over constitutes "the most awesome transfer of power in the world—the power to marshal and mobilize, the power to send men to kill or be killed, the power to tax and destroy, the power to create and the responsibility to do so, the power to guide and the responsibility to heal—all committed in the hands of one man."

FRANKLIN DELANO ROOSEVELT: THE MAN BEHIND THE NEW DEAL

Born into a wealthy Hudson Valley, New York, family in January 1882, Franklin Roosevelt enjoyed all the privileges money could offer along with the love of his two devoted parents. He attended high school at Groton and moved from there to Harvard University, where he became editor of the *Crimson*. How did a man from such a background become a champion of downtrodden Americans and the most progressive U.S. President? How did FDR come to sympathize with Americans from all walks of life, and especially the third of a nation left "ill-housed, ill-clothed, and ill-fed" in the wake of the Depression?

It took more than the sense of noblesse oblige he inherited to transform FDR into the leader he became. In his twenties, Roosevelt spent a few years in the business world before quickly moving into the political career that would fill the rest of his life and, ultimately, would change the nation and even the world. As a young man not long out of Harvard, Franklin married his distant cousin, Eleanor Roosevelt, whose uncle, Theodore Roosevelt, gave her away at her wedding. FDR in many ways modeled his political career on TR's, though FDR was a Democrat and TR a Republican. Like Teddy Roosevelt, FDR first served in the New York state legislature (1910–1913), then as assistant secretary of the navy under Woodrow Wilson (1913–1920), and governor of New York (1928–1932) before finally being elected president in 1932. But TR and FDR shared more than just a career trajectory. They both stand out as two of the leading progressive presidents in U.S. history. Franklin Roosevelt, however, carved out his own path, leaving a legacy that has outdistanced that of TR.

His family and educational emphasis on social responsibility help explain why he embarked on a career in public service and why he exhibited reformist leanings as a young man. However, many point to his battle with polio as a turning point in his life. He contracted polio in 1921 at his boyhood summer home on Campobello Island located off the coast of Maine. Before polio he was known as a capable man but not as an intellectual and certainly not as a man destined to transform the nation. The famous quote of Justice Oliver Wendell Holmes seems to reflect what many thought about FDR, that he had a "second-class intellect. But a first-class temperament." Although the country never knew the extent of his paralysis, FDR in fact became a paraplegic, never regaining the use of his legs despite years of effort. He spent much of the 1920s adapting to his condition by building his upper body strength so that he could appear to walk. While he focused on recovery, Eleanor became his eyes and legs, giving speeches and keeping Roosevelt's name current in Democratic circles. Elected four times to the presidency and in office for 13 years before his death on April 12, 1945, FDR was able to keep the extent of his disability from most Americans.

Many biographers have noted that his experiences with polio left an indelible mark on FDR, perhaps explaining in part how a man of wealth developed empathy for those in need and how a nation in need found a kindred spirit in a man who never had to work to earn his way. As the noted scholar Robert Dallek has written, "Afflicted by a crippling Depression, Americans took psychological hope from a president who, after losing the use of his legs, had surmounted his handicap to become governor of New York and president of the United States."

In addition, Roosevelt's quest for a cure brought him to Warm Springs, Georgia, where he spent many months recuperating and where he vacationed during his years as president. His time there brought him into contact with a rural poverty he might otherwise never have witnessed, and which may have prompted some of his anti-poverty programs.

Despite his inability to walk, FDR never considered retiring to his family's country estate, as his mother assumed he would. Instead, he rose to the challenge, revealing many of the personality traits that make him one of our nation's greatest presidents. During weeks of pain following his initial bout and through years of stubborn and grueling exercise, FDR revealed a raw courage that impressed those around him. Just as he refused to believe he would be unable to reenter politics, he never doubted that the country would recover from the Depression's devastation and that the Allies would prevail in World War II. As he told the American people, "The only thing we have to fear is fear itself." More than anything else, FDR gave Americans hope.

Indicative of the leadership flare and forceful personality he demonstrated throughout his presidency, Roosevelt broke precedent by flying to Chicago in 1932 to accept the Democratic Party's nomination in person. After assuming the presidency in March 1933, Roosevelt acted swiftly to deliver his "new deal" to the American people. He continued to break new ground as president, creating the modern presidency and remaking the federal government.

During our nation's darkest hour, FDR showed Americans only confidence and optimism. His famous Fireside Chats carried his resonant voice into living rooms across the country, signaling to the American people that recovery was on the way. And so it was as FDR ushered in numerous programs to confront the Depression head-on during his First Hundred Days—the single most active period of American government—and throughout his 12 years in office.

Exercising Presidential Leadership

An examination of the presidency begs many of the same questions as an examination of leadership in general. For instance, are great men born or made? FDR and other modern presidents shifted power back to the president and away from Congress (especially compared to the balance of power typical of the nineteenth century), giving presidents center stage in our political system. Of course, some modern presidents have been stronger than others—Jimmy Carter ranks as a particularly ineffectual president while Ronald Reagan (profiled in Chapter 4) used his skills as the Great Communicator to remold American governance. What explains the difference? Do men make history or does history make men? The *great-man theory* of history fuels the idea that Americans expect greatness from presidents, as history is moved forward and shaped by great men. As we evaluate the American presidency, we must also consider whether the office itself limits or facilitates presidential leadership.

In his book, *Presidential Power and the Modern Presidents*, Richard E. Neustadt (1990) develops an understanding of presidential leadership modeled after FDR, whom he upholds as the ideal U.S. president. Neustadt, and others, were struck by the incongruity between what we expect of our presidents and the constitutional powers of the president, which he considers to be limited in nature. What explains the exception of Roosevelt and what does that suggest about the nature of presidential leadership? Neustadt argues that the power of the presidency is the power to persuade and to influence, particularly through bargaining. His book endorsed the extraconstitutional powers that FDR used so effectively and which Neustadt considers so important given the weakness of the president's actual legal powers. Neustadt explains that the Constitution does not give presidents the powers they need to be strong leaders, but the Constitution's system of separation of powers requires a strong executive to unify the government.

The essence of presidential power, he says, is the power to persuade, which depends on both a president's professional reputation and his public approval ratings. In other words, "The power to persuade is the power to bargain. Status and authority yield bargaining advantages" (Neustadt, 1990). The president's responsibility is to maintain his potential to exert influence through the decisions he makes because his power is a function of those decisions. Because FDR used his power so effectively, Neustadt holds him up as a model of an ideal president.

While Neustadt specifically addresses the power of presidents, many of his lessons apply to broader questions of leadership. As he explained, "The purpose here is to explore the power problem of the man inside the White House. This is the classic problem of the man on top in any political system: how to be on top in fact as well as in name. It is a problem common to prime ministers and premiers, and to dictators, however styled, and to those kings who rule as well as reign. It is a problem also for the heads of private "governments"—for corporation presidents, trade union leaders, and churchmen."

If Neustadt's ideas are correct, then much of a president's effectiveness as a leader depends on his abilities, such as what type of public and private communicator he (or, someday, she) is. What other factors might affect presidential leadership?

Whether liberal, conservative, or independent, the public in general expects a president to have a vision and to adhere to that agenda diligently. It makes sense, therefore, that presidents with forceful and charismatic personalities tend to be popular. Such individuals are most likely to harness the persuasive forces of the presidency and lead the country down the road of progress. Are the paths presidents take predetermined by their personalities, the historical moment in which they serve, or something else? Do presidents, as some suggest, remain true to their personality types and so act in predictable ways, or is presidential leadership more a function of a president's ability to break free of such constraints? What else might influence presidential leadership? What if Roosevelt had served during another historical time? Would he still be considered one of the few irrefutably great U.S. presidents or would another time have proved limiting? Without a Depression to confront or a war to wage, how would Roosevelt have accomplished what he did?

While most of us don't want to cede control of our destiny to historical forces, it is difficult to imagine FDR president during another era. In *The Politics Presidents Make,* Stephen Skowronek (1993) argues that the historical times in which a president serves are paramount. He examines the institution of the presidency in terms of historical times, asking several questions, including what presidents past and present have in common, what conditions of leadership they share, and what they do to succeed or fail. Skowronek looks for historical patterns to enhance our understanding of the presidency. Power for him centers on the idea of repudiation, by which he means a president's ability to carve out his own path by repudiating that of his predecessor: "The power to recreate order hinges on the authority to repudiate it." **Presidential authority,** according to Skowronek, is the legitimacy of a president to do what he wants.

Types of Presidential Authority in the United States

There are four types of presidential authority: the reconstructionist, the disjunction, the articulation, and the preemptive. Presidents, in Skowronek's view, are most effective when they can negate what has come before and so offer a new vision of their own. The personality of presidents, understandably, turns out to "reflect characteristics of the office under different circumstances" rather than characteristics of the individual. Skowronek says that an examination of the institution from a historical perspective reveals certain patterns that are much more than coincidental. He concludes that various times call for various responses from the president. What becomes known as a president's personality and/or character thus derives from the period in which he serves. Presidents are likely to heed the clarion call of history and march to its beat. Presidential power is, hence, delineated by forces largely out of the hands of individual presidents, and what they can achieve is, to an extent, predetermined. So, while Neustadt says modern presidents should model themselves after FDR, Skowronek disagrees. "Roosevelt succeeded magnificently, but it does not follow that if we could just get more people like Roosevelt into the office, the problems and dangers the presidency poses would recede."

In this view, individuals are captives of history to a certain extent. Do you agree? Can you reconcile this idea with the notion that great men and women shape great events and are, therefore, the forces that move history forward? Is leadership derivative of individuals in positions of power, or does the process of leadership transcend the character of individual leaders? How much should leaders, presidents or not, heed the times in which they serve? Can you think of leaders who have defied the limits of their historical times, thereby, perhaps, remaking history? Can effective leaders create moments ripe for leadership? Or, is it the right combination of personality and historical opportunity that provides for presidential greatness? (See the summary of *Presidential Greatness* in Appendix II for further discussion.)

Evaluating Presidential Leadership

In a recent *Presidential Studies Quarterly* (2000) article, presidential scholar Fred Greenstein describes qualities associated with presidential success. He sets forth six types of skills that particularly influence presidential effectiveness. These are a president's:

1. Skills as a public communicator

2. Organizational capacity, which is defined as the "ability to rally colleagues and structure their activities effectively"

3. Political skill

4. Vision, meaning a president's ability to organize the administration around a clear set of public-policy goals

5. Cognitive style, which is the way in which presidents process all the information they receive

6. Emotional intelligence, meaning "the extent to which the president is able to manage his emotions and turn them to constructive purposes rather than be dominated by them to undermine his public performance" (Greenstein, p. 180)

In the wake of former President Clinton's impeachment and his rather scandal-laden presidency, it is not surprising to consider how significant a president's emotional intelligence may be. Nixon stands out as perhaps the most emotionally compromised U.S. president, but as Greenstein points out, Lyndon B. Johnson, Carter, and Clinton all lacked a certain amount of emotional stability. "The vesuvian LBJ was subject to mood swings of clinical proportions. Jimmy Carter evinced a rigidity that impeded his White House performance. The lack of self-discipline of Bill Clinton led him into actions that resulted in his impeachment."

Should we do a better job screening presidential candidates with some degree of emotional instability, or are there benefits to having had such individuals as president? Clearly communication skills were key to the success of Ronald Reagan. Is it good or bad that a president can compensate for less than exceptional skills in other areas by being an effective speaker? Of course, George H. W. Bush's problem with the "vision thing," as he called it, proved problematic in his 1992 campaign against Bill Clinton. Keeping in mind that leaders of all sorts wield power, how do these traits that Greenstein identifies translate into other arenas? Can the head of a company or a manager be effective without emotional intelligence? Vision is important for obvious reasons for presidents, but what about for managers and leaders of smaller groups? Will people be motivated to follow somebody who lacks a cohesive vision for the future?

SUMMARY

In this chapter, we've explored the link between political science and leadership. As we know, leadership requires the exercise of power and political science studies the distribution and use of power. We've reviewed the influence tactics individuals in power use and the sources and types of power exercised by those in positions of authority. Finally, we've examined presidential leadership as a means of analyzing how leaders exercise power once they have it and the dilemmas associated with the exercise of power in a democracy.

CREATE YOUR OWN THEORY

This chapter has focused on the importance of understanding power and its many forms and dimensions. Which types of power do you exhibit and which do you respect and/or fear? Have there been times where you have seen power used unethically? What forms of unethical power usage disturb you the most and how can you best use your talents to challenge this unethical behavior?

Also heavily emphasized in this chapter was presidential leadership. Which skills do you think are most important for a president to have? Can a president in today's world get by with poor skills in any of the above areas? What, in your view, is the most serious deficiency a president could have? How important is vision to leadership? What does the experience of George H. W. Bush reveal about vision and the public's understanding of the presidency? What does his son seem to have learned from George the Elder?

Do great brains make great presidents? How important is exceptional cognitive ability to presidential leadership? How did high intelligence shape Carter's presidency? Has Clinton's high I.Q. been an advantage or a hindrance? How does the media affect our perception of presidents?

What characteristics would your ideal president exhibit? Think back to our opening Leadership Moment. If you were president of the university, how would you handle a tenured professor who was misusing his positional power? If you were a student at this school, how might you challenge this abuse of power, or would you?

KEY TERMS

power
influence
influence tactics
expert power
referent power
legitimate power
reward power
coercive power
position power
personal power

utilitarian power
normative power
alienative organizations
calculative organizations
moral organizations
social power
vertical dyad linkage
social exchange theory
extraconstitutional powers
presidential authority

QUESTIONS FOR DISCUSSION AND REVIEW

1. What types of leaders are most effective? Why?
2. What are some of the ways leaders seek to influence followers?
3. What are different sources of power and which types are more associated with effective leadership?
4. How do you define personal power?
5. How important is it for leaders to be ethical?
6. Define empowerment and its place in leadership.
7. What is the difference between constitutional and extraconstitutional powers?
8. What is the cornerstone of presidential leadership, according to Neustadt?

ONLINE SELF-ASSESSMENT TOOL

To learn more about how your points of view on leadership match up with the strengths and weaknesses of a host of modern leaders, visit http://www.humanmetrics.com/rot/politicalsuccess/HPSSQ.asp.

CHAPTER 7

Military Leadership— The Art of Command

LEADERSHIP MOMENT

Looking to enhance performance, your office has decided to recruit more heavily from the armed services when hiring new personnel. One of the more recent hires, Sgt. Tina Smith, a 20-year army vet who served in the Persian Gulf, has been assigned to your workgroup. The news of this hire is being met with decidedly mixed feelings by other group members. Some feel that hiring from the military is a very positive step and are excited to be working with somebody who has served her country and has a sense of discipline. Others worry that Smith will order everybody around (or want to be ordered around by somebody else) and won't know how to work in the "real world" of corporate America. Still others think that her military background is irrelevant. Today is Sgt. Smith's first day and you have been assigned to orient her to her new work environment and to introduce her to her new work team.

1. *What would you do?*
2. *What characteristics would you expect somebody from a military background to bring to your group?*
3. *How would you address the assumptions being made by your peers about Sgt. Smith's strengths and weaknesses?*

Wars may be fought with weapons, but they are won by men. It is the spirit of the men who follow and of the man who leads that gains the victory.—Gen. George S. Patton

Recently a group of military officers was asked to define leadership. After reciting some of the more traditional definitions, they concluded that it would be easier to determine how many angels would fit on the head of a pin than to come up with a commonly agreed-upon definition. As one Marine Corps Colonel put it: "It's a little like obscenity—I can't define it, but I sure know it when I see it."

Even if someone were to possess all possible leadership characteristics and abilities, success is not guaranteed. What works in one instance may fail in another. Leadership is not determined by age, gender, race, religion, or ethnic group. Part art and part science, leadership is the one constant in every successful organization.

THE STUDY OF MILITARY LEADERSHIP: WHAT'S IN IT FOR ME?

There are no bad regiments, only bad Colonels.—Napoleon

Because leadership involves the most basic of all human behaviors, emotions, and motivations, it lends itself to examination in almost any organizational setting. The military environment, however, offers the greatest opportunity to examine and understand leadership's true nature, analyze its various elements, and emulate the behaviors of some of our nation's most successful commanders. As Lt. Gen. Walter F. Ulmer Jr. USA (ret) put it, "Military operations tend to highlight success or failure, confirm courage or hesitation, validate selflessness or ego, assess empathy or callousness, and take measure of the integration of the behavioral and management sciences."

One might ask, Why should civilians study military leadership? What's in it for me if I am not in the service—or even if I am? Here are a few benefits. At some point in their career, most people will work for, with, or lead at least one former service member, so it's helpful to be familiar with their leadership background, values, and beliefs. In addition, many of the most admired corporations in America seek out and offer hiring preferences to former service members. Corporations such as General Electric, Procter & Gamble, MCI Worldcom, Allied Signal, and Bank of America, to name but a few, have concluded that former service members have the requisite traits of integrity, hard work, dedication, and loyalty to succeed.

When motivational speaker Zig Ziglar studied Fortune 500 CEOs to discover the common traits that had advanced their rise to the pinnacle of Corporate America, a staggering 270—more than half—identified their military service as a significant factor in their success.

Increasingly, our military forces are committed to distant corners of the globe to support our country's political and foreign policy initiatives. As citizens we exercise the responsibility to elect government officials who will decide when and where to commit American youth to protect our vital political and economic interests. A basic understanding of the military system and way of thinking is a valuable asset for an informed citizenry.

The nation that will insist on drawing a broad line of demarcation between the fighting man and the thinking man is liable to find its fighting done by fools and its thinking done by cowards.— Sir William F. Butler

BOARDROOM TO BATTLEFIELD: COMPARISON AND CONTRAST

Military leaders must have a strong sense of the great responsibility of their office: the resources they expend in war are human lives.—FMFM 1

The test of character is not "hanging in there" when you expect the light at the end of the tunnel, but performance of duty and persistence of example when you know that no light is coming.—James Stockdale

Life in the military services is unlike any other existence in the world. The differences in culture, pay, people, organizational structure, mission, and even laws are so distinct and so vast as to represent entirely different cultural systems. In recent years much fanfare and a great deal of hoopla has been paid to the perceived widening cultural gap between those who serve and those whom they protect and obey. While the warrior class has always seen itself as different from society at large, the military must draw its members from the large, diverse pool of citizens. And despite its much-publicized gender shortcomings, the military is probably far more diverse than any other organization in modern America. No other organization includes such a wide representation of demographic groups.

Even though each branch of service has its challenges and opportunities, people who want to advance their leadership skills and thinking may still find similarities among the branches which offer ample opportunity for thought, reflection, and personal growth. See Figure 7–1.

Figure 7–1 provides some of the primary similarities between military and nonmilitary organizations and will serve as a framework for our discussion. One of the most obvious differences between the military and all other organizations is its reason for being—its mission. The five branches of the military exist for a number of reasons: most notably to win our country's wars, defend the Constitution against all forces foreign and domestic, protect our sovereign interests, and continue our country's political objectives by other means. In a nutshell, the military's mission is the management of violence. As John Lehman, former Secretary of the Navy, noted, "The mission of our armed forces is to fight wars. To deliver violence and

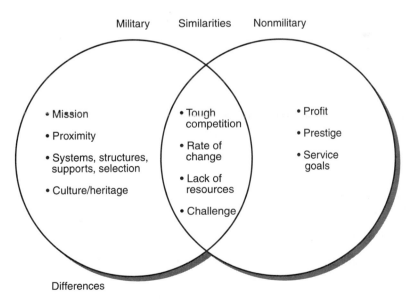

Figure 7–1   Similarities and Differences between Military and Nonmilitary Organizations

destruction on our enemies when our security demands it."[1] The military doesn't decide who, what, and when to fight—that decision rests within the National Command Authority (NCA), elected civilians who decide where and when our vital national interests must be protected. Our military is charged with fighting and winning those battles within the parameters dictated by its civilian overseers. Although the military serves a particularly vital role in preserving our way of life, every organization in the world has a unique and specific mission. **Mission** dictates what authority its leaders can exercise over the resources (people, capital, and machines) furnished to them.

Another obvious distinction between military and civilian worlds is the personal proximity people experience in pursuit of their organization's stated mission. Very few civilian occupations require the type of closeness—both physical and emotional—that people experience in the military. This may help explain why military relationships, particularly those of individuals who have shared the hardships of combat, tend to last well beyond their time in service. What most service members experience on a daily basis most civilian employees and employers would consider intolerable by modern standards.

Every organization offers its leaders a unique combination of support services in the role of human resources or staff functions: recruiting, legal, training and development, benefits, payroll, systems, MIS, audit, and so on. Competing for the same scarce budgetary resources necessary to function, these functions tend to be understaffed, underfunded, and frequently not given the support or respect they deserve. The military has always viewed the systems, support, structure, and selection business as one of its top priorities, as evidenced by the fact that one of the most prestigious jobs for senior-ranking officers is that of selecting, training, and educating other service members. Frequently referred to as the "tooth-to-tail relationships, " these vital areas have always received a great deal of attention from the military's top ranks and those who oversee the day-to-day administrative functioning of the military in Washington.

It's worthwhile to consider selection (recruiting, screening, and selection) and legal areas. The average selection period for military officers as represented by the time they spend at Officer Candidate School is about 10 weeks: 7 days a week, 24 hours a day of evaluation, testing, physical training, peer evaluations, and command screenings, all designed to evaluate a future officer's leadership potential. In effect, it's a 1300-hour interview. Even at that total, many people would characterize it as a ridiculously *short* period of time to spend evaluating a prospective leader who will be eventually entrusted with the lives of our nation's youth.

The civilian and military legal systems are also distinct. The **Uniform Code of Military Justice (UCMJ)** governs *every* facet of a service member's life, including attire, speech, grooming, conduct (on and off the job), and other personal and professional elements.

One of the most vital distinctions between the military and the rest of society lies at its very core—the military's unique heritage and culture. In this age of

---

[1]John Lehman, "Our Military Condition," in *Military Leadership: In Pursuit of Excellence* (3rd ed.), edited by R. L. Taylor and W. E. Rosenbach, Westview Press, 1996.

12-month-old e-businesses with IPOs and here-today-gone-tomorrow merger mania, the U.S. military traces its roots back more than 220 years. Perhaps no organization in the world takes greater pride or devotes more time and resources to preserving and communicating its culture and heritage than the U.S. military. **Cultural indoctrination and transformation** form the foundation of all initial military training. The stories of great battles fought and won, of freedom preserved and evil overcome, of individual acts of heroism and courage help to inoculate recruits, hoping to make them better soldiers, sailors, aviators, and Marines. Eventually, when their time in the service is finished and they return to the civilian community, the stories help to make them better citizens, as well.

In recent years the military, academia, the scientific community, government, and Corporate America have all come together to share ideas, best practices, and even personnel. One significant common venture includes new, nontraditional forms of competition. Competition is a major battlefield, as when large corporations face pricing pressures from smaller and more nimble companies using the Internet as a marketing and distribution medium or when military forces must check the spread of weapons of mass destruction or engage in peacemaking and nation building in places like Kosovo, Panama, and Haiti.

Another area in which the military and others have found a common challenge involves the rate and pace of change. Every organization is faced with the challenge of effectively integrating technology. Numerous examples show how technological advances have changed the way warfare is waged. Just as the invention of the repeating rifle made line-and-column tactics obsolete and the machine gun, tank, and airplane relegated trench warfare to the annals of history, technological advances require leaders to develop bold new approaches to solving age-old problems.

Many leaders can relate to the saying, "If you're short of everything but enemy, you must be in a combat zone." Precious resources—whether people, equipment, or money—must often be rationed, thereby creating scarcity and shortage.

The similarities between military and civilian organizations include challenges of fierce competition, rapid unprecedented change, scarcity of precious resources, and increasingly demanding business environments. This common ground offers novice and veteran leaders the opportunity to learn from each other as they share ideas, resources, and experience, and in the process strengthen their organizations and improve their own leadership abilities.

FOUNDATIONS OF MILITARY LEADERSHIP

Success in battle is not a function of how many show up, but who they are.—Gen. Robert H. Borrow

In war the chief incalculable is the human will.—B. H. Liddell Hart

Clearly, one leadership model or style will not work well in every situation. Differences in people, resources, and environment demand different sets of skills and abilities from the competent leader. What works in the boardroom of large

Corporate America would most certainly not work in an emerging e-commerce startup or in a not-for-profit organization dedicated to feeding the hungry or raising money for the arts. Even though every leadership challenge is unique, a number of leadership fundamentals and foundations exist that can help even the most novice volunteer or guide the thoughts and decisions of the most experienced corporate executive.

Over the years the military has refined what many believe to be the essential foundations of leadership. Although every branch of the military service has developed unique sets of core values tailored to its own beliefs, the leadership traits and principles taught to all service members are nearly identical. The 14 leadership traits and 11 leadership principles in the lists that follow form the foundation from which all of the demands and challenges of leadership can be met. Every newly minted lieutenant, ensign, cadet, midshipman, and NCO will have committed these core values to memory in an effort to ensure that the very best people lead our young men and women in the armed services.

> Like blocks in an arch, each depends on the other to provide support. With core values serving as the keystone, they all serve to buttress the structure which leaders may draw upon. Just as builders must use every block in the arch to support it, so too must leaders use every element of our leadership foundation at their disposal. But just as every arch is different, requiring different shapes of building blocks, every leadership challenge is different, requiring a different use and blend of the leadership foundations.[2]

Fourteen Leadership Traits

1. **Dependability:** The certainty of proper performance
2. **Bearing:** Creating a favorable impression in carriage, appearance, and personal conduct
3. **Courage:** The mental quality that recognizes fear of danger or criticism but enables an individual to proceed with calmness and firmness
4. **Decisiveness:** The ability to make good decisions promptly
5. **Endurance:** The mental and physical ability to withstand stress, hardship, fatigue, and pain
6. **Enthusiasm:** The display of sincere interest and exuberance
7. **Initiative:** Taking action in the absence of orders
8. **Integrity:** Uprightness of character and soundness of moral principles; includes truthfulness and honesty
9. **Judgment:** The ability to weigh facts and possible solutions on which to base sound decisions
10. **Justice:** The ability to administer a system of rewards and discipline impartially and consistently

---

[2]*Leading Marines* FMFM 1-0

11. **Knowledge:** The range of one's information and understanding

12. **Tact:** The ability to deal with others without creating offense

13. **Unselfishness:** Avoiding providing for one's own personal well-being at the expense of others

14. **Loyalty:** The quality of faithfulness

Often, military students ponder which of the above fourteen leadership traits is most important. Despite the lively discussions about the merits of each one, eventually the students almost always conclude that without integrity, nothing else really matters. Do you agree? Which of these fourteen leadership traits do you find most important?

Eleven Leadership Principles

1. *Know yourself and seek self-improvement.* Leaders are in fact five or more separate people. They are who they are, who they think they are, who their boss thinks they are, who their subordinates think they are, and finally who their peers think they are. The real leader is somewhere in the middle. Leaders who work hard to know themselves and seek feedback from a variety of honest sources are better able to capitalize on their own strengths, protect (or better yet, grow out of) their weaknesses, and learn from the past.

2. *Be technically proficient.* Leaders who can demonstrate technical proficiency or command of the task at hand will earn subordinates' respect.

3. *Develop a sense of responsibility among your subordinates.* Give them new opportunities and challenges that they can handle with some degree of difficulty. By expanding their boundaries and developing their own solutions, they gain confidence and valuable experience. Encourage initiative among your subordinates and in the end you will be rewarded with employees who can run the show even in your absence.

4. *Make sound and timely decisions.* Nothing instills confidence in subordinates like a decisive leader. The ability and willingness to make tough decisions in an expeditious manner are hallmarks of good leadership. A combat pearl of wisdom advises, "A good decision executed now is better than the perfect solution executed too late."

5. *Lead by example.* This is the *most* important leadership principle of all. Just as the parent who says "Do as I say, not as I do" is doomed to hypocrisy, so too are leaders who can't stomach their own medicine doomed to face their subordinates' contempt and resentment. Leaders frequently underestimate the messages their behaviors send to subordinates.

6. *Keep your people and look out for their welfare.* All great leaders develop a sincere interest in their subordinates' well being. This principle is demonstrated in Marine Corps officers eating last, after all the troops have been fed. The attitude that "rank has its privilege" (RHIP) often interferes with this most basic leadership principle.

7. *Keep your people informed.* When you are communicating twice as much as you think you should be, you probably have it about right. In the absence of good communication people will make up the information they lack. Communicating is one of the hardest tasks for good leaders (see Chapter 4), and the one most susceptible to failure.

8. *Seek and take responsibility for your actions.* The adage states that, "Leaders are responsible for everything their unit does or doesn't do," and Gen. Norman Schwarzkopf used to say, "When in charge take command." One of the best ways to develop new skills and abilities is to seek opportunities to perform outside your normal comfort zone.

9. *Make sure that assigned tasks are understood, supervised, and accomplished.* The key words here are **expectations** and **desired-end-state.** Leaders and followers need to share and understand each other's expectations and hold clear understandings of the desired outcomes or end-states. This leadership principle is the antithesis of micromanagement, a practice far too common in Corporate America that destroys morale more quickly than almost any other leadership shortcoming.

10. *Train your people as a team.* Approximately 85 percent of all military training is accomplished in a team or unit format as opposed to less than 5 percent in the civilian world. Team training allows the organization to more rapidly develop the critical mass necessary to move the organization to the next level of performance.

11. *Employ your unit in accordance with its capabilities.* Even the best units/organizations in the world have limitations and shortcomings. Complete leaders know, analyze, and understand their organization's strengths and weaknesses. Asking an individual or group to attempt a task too far beyond their competencies without proper support or training is playing against the odds and risking unit morale and confidence.

> *Yours is the profession of arms, the will to win, the sure knowledge that in war there is no substitute for victory, that if you lose, the nation will be destroyed, that the very obsession of your public service must be duty, honor, country.*—Douglas MacArthur

MILITARY TOOLS TO AID THE BUSY LEADER

> *Everything in war is simple, but the simplest thing is difficult. The difficulties accumulate and end by producing a kind of friction that is inconceivable unless one has experienced war.*—Carl von Clausewitz

There's a great deal of truth in the saying, "Show me a pilot who sits on his checklist, and I'll show you a pilot who flies by the seat of his pants." Good leaders have at their disposal a vast array of tools, techniques, and systems that help in the day-to-day operation of an organization, no matter how large or small. Wise leaders use these weapons or tools to augment their own abilities and increase the organization's

LEADERSHIP SKILLS FOR THE TWENTY-FIRST CENTURY

DECENTRALIZATION: THE RULE OF THREE

Many organizations have sought to improve efficiency and streamline operations by flattening their organizational structures and removing several layers of management. The effort often leaves managers or small unit leaders with a dozen or more direct reports. They feel overwhelmed, understaffed, and without the ability to properly supervise or support their direct reports.

The military has adopted an entirely different model that moves decision making authority to the lowest appropriate level, yet retains a simple organizational structure designed to keep everyone's job manageable. Structurally, everyone has three (four at the most) people or things to worry about. Lieutenants who command an infantry platoon have three squads led by three squad leaders (sergeants); squad leaders have three fire-teams led by three corporals who, in turn, lead three others. Many people might view this organizational structure as overly narrow and laborious, but when the need arises these layers disappear to streamline communications and reduce decision-making time.

Major General Perry M. Smith USAF (ret) stated, "The best leaders understand that leadership is the liberation of talent: hence they gain power not only by giving it away, but also by not grabbing it back." [3] The functional version of the **Rule of Three** dictates that people should limit their attention to three tasks or objectives. When used as a decision-making discipline, the rule requires leaders to distill an infinite number of possibilities to three potential courses of action (COAs). This streamlining enables leaders to evaluate relatively quickly the best, worst, and most likely scenarios prior to implementation.

effectiveness and efficiency. These aids let leaders make better, quicker, and more effective decisions in a fast moving, chaotic environment.

The **fog of war** refers to a leader's inability to deal with all of the variables and uncertainties in a combat environment. Napoleon called it **friction**—the force or action that inhibits an individual or unit's ability to carry out the task at hand. In many organizations friction may manifest itself in bureaucratic delays, senior-level indecision, lack of support or resources, turf battles, office politics, and so on. This section sets forth some time-tested tools found widely throughout the U.S. military that help leaders at all levels reduce the friction or fog that clouds good decision making.

---

[3]Maj. Gen. Perry M. Smith, Learning to lead, *Marine Corps Gazette,* Jan. 1997.

Improved Feedback Loops: Seeing with Your Ears

Leaders who are serious about improving their organizations as well as their own performance seek feedback from a variety of qualified sources. All of us—even organizations—have blind spots, which if undetected limit our ability to perform at our peak. On an organizational level this means reviewing every organizational event or activity, down to individual actions and behaviors. One reason our military enjoys air superiority over almost every theater of operations is that our pilots receive detailed reviews of their individual and their section's performance after every training mission. Such debriefings and hot-washes are so vital to continuous improvement that special systems, programs, and units are dedicated to providing our warfighters with the best possible feedback on their performance.

One of the most useful tools leaders have found recently is the Multirater or 360-degree performance reviews. These feedback tools are invaluable in helping individuals and organizations identify strengths, weaknesses, and blind spots. Whether used as a performance development tool or tied to performance measurement and compensation, Multirater feedback can be a very powerful aid in improving constructive feedback loops.

Checklists and Standard Operating Procedures (SOPs)

Even though every leadership situation is unique, leaders frequently encounter situations that repeat certain patterns, such as hiring and firing employees, selecting external vendors or consultants, performing large functions or operations, and dealing with the media and regulatory authorities. Recurring patterns in these situations allow small unit leaders to develop checklists or SOPs. Just as pilots refer to checklists prior to takeoffs and landings and during emergencies, so too should small unit leaders begin to develop their own checklists to help in decision making.

Mission Orders and Commander's Intent

Several years ago the services adopted a process of communicating orders to operational forces that vastly reduced the time needed to relay instructions and improved the clarity of the message. In the past, commanders and their staffs would painstakingly construct detailed plans and instructions which, when completed, often required significant amounts of time to write, disseminate, and brief to operational units. On today's battlefield speed and tempo of operations help our forces maintain the advantage, ultimately overcoming our enemies' will to resist. Today commanders have drastically streamlined their instructions so they can provide operational forces with the essential elements for mission success:

> There are two parts to any mission: the task to be accomplished and the reason or intent behind it. **Commander's Intent** is a device designed to help subordinates understand the larger context of their actions. The purpose of providing intent is to allow subordinates to exercise judgment and initiative—to depart from the original plan when the

unforeseen occurs—in a way that is consistent with higher commanders' aims. The task describes the action to be taken and intent describes its purpose. The task denotes what, sometimes when and where; the intent explains why. Of the two, intent is predominant. The situation may change, making the task obsolete, but the intent is more lasting and continues to guide our actions. Understanding intent allows operational units to exercise initiative in harmony with the commanders' desires.[4]

Never tell people how to do things. Tell them what to do, and they will surprise you with their ingenuity.—Gen. George S. Patton

OODA Loops

Not some kind of new breakfast cereal for kids, this is a decision-making tool developed by Gen. Charles G. Boyd USAF (ret) during the Vietnam war to help leaders, particularly fighter pilots, make decisions better and (more importantly) more quickly than the enemy. **OODA Loops** notes that the essence of decision making boils down to four interrelated functions: *observation, orientation, decision making,* and *action.* The warfighter who can accomplish these four functions the quickest gains the advantage. Much as in a Wild West gunfight, the person who observes, orients, decides, and acts quickest is able to dictate the tempo of the fight. The goal is to get inside your opponents' OODA loop (making better and quicker decisions).

Speed is the essence of war. Take advantage of the enemy's unpreparedness; travel by unexpected routes and strike where he has taken no precautions.—Sun Tzu

Personnel Evaluations: Proficiency and Conduct Marks

What manager or employee hasn't dreaded the thought of the annual ritual known as the performance review? In many organizations both parties view this most vital of all administrative leadership functions with all of the enthusiasm and gusto of a root canal. That's unfortunate, because when accomplished with thought, reflection, and broad input from others, the performance review allows the leader and employee to do more than simply document past performance. It offers a chance to chart the course for individual employee development plans, discuss long-term career goals, review strengths and weaknesses, and assess an individual's overall contribution to the organization. The military performance evaluation system has traditionally consisted of two broad categories: *proficiency* (performance) and *conduct* (sharing of corporate values or behavior). By examining an individual's overall contribution to the organization within these two parameters, leaders can more effectively and efficiently document an employee's capacity for additional responsibility and growth. All things being equal, a leader would favor high conduct over performance. By demonstrating shared organizational values or behaviors, many leaders believe that performance issues will resolve themselves through experience, supervision, and

[4]*Marine Corps Doctrinal Publication* (MCDP) 1.

counseling. Good leaders rarely miss an opportunity to counsel people about their performance and take advantage of the infinite number of teachable moments that occur each day. See Figure 7–2.

BECOMING A BETTER LEADER

Make the most of yourself, for that is all there is to you.—Ralph Waldo Emerson

Obviously there is no magic formula for developing leadership skills. It takes hard work, practice, discipline, and dedication. What serves leaders well in one situation may fail them in another. Yet in the same way that anyone who studies music can be a better musician, with a select few capable of truly extraordinary performances, so too it is with leadership. Anyone can be a better leader with practice, persistence, and experience. As the great military thinker S.L.A. Marshall wrote in *Leaders and Leadership*, "Great military leaders of the past possessed a certain set of qualities. These were inner qualities rather than outward marks of greatness." Although very few enjoyed acclaim in their early years, "The most successful are molded by the influences around them and have the average person's faults and vices."[5]

Here are some key points to take from this chapter:

1. *Live the leadership traits and principles.* Review and reflect on them frequently. Focus on one or two leadership elements daily for a week to 10 days. Keep this up for three to six months and you will have developed a more full and complete understanding of these most important leadership foundations.

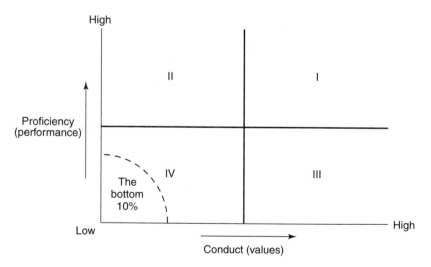

Figure 7–2   Values vs. Performance

[5]S.L.A. Marshall, in *Military Leadership: In Pursuit of Excellence* (3rd ed.), edited by R. L. Taylor and W. E. Rosenbach, Westview Press, 1996.

2. *Always keep the three C's in your mind: Character, Courage, and Competence* [6]

3. *Read widely and wisely as many leadership biographies as possible.*

4. *Be yourself!* Use the leadership tools at your disposal and develop a style that fits your personality and mission.

5. *Remember your team*—the people who made you successful. Every individual life is equally precious and everyone has a contribution to make.

6. *Reward success, not failure.* Be sure you reward the right behaviors.

7. *Develop mental toughness.* Be brutally honest with yourself; if you make a mistake, don't hesitate to make things right. For further elaboration on this subject, see the summary of Joe D. Batten's *Tough-Minded Leadership* in Appendix II.

8. *Develop a strong, diverse network or brain trust.* [7]

9. *Take good care of yourself.* Be physically fit. The time you invest in yourself is invaluable.

10. *Avoid the cowardice of silence.* You get paid for your opinion, so make sure to voice it. [8]

There is less a line between the leader and the led than a bond.—*Leading Marines* FMFM 1-0

The following Leadership Profiles highlight the background and accomplishments of three individuals who reflect these ideals.

RIGOBERTA MENCHU: THE GUATEMALAN PEASANT WHO WON THE NOBEL PRIZE

A 37-year-old Mayan Indian woman leveraged the power of language to help rally the world behind the cause of the mistreated indigenous peoples of Guatemala. One of the first Indian activists to learn Spanish, the language of the wealthy landowners and military men running the government, Rigoberta Menchu clearly understood the importance of communicating with the "enemy."

In a similar way, she understood the importance of her fellow Indians keeping their own languages—upwards of 20 Indian dialects are spoken in Guatemala—to preserve their own culture. Once she mastered Spanish, Menchu began defending Indians' rights against the government that all too often viewed Indians as easy prey. In addition, she also learned three of the principal Indian dialects.

[6]Gen. Matthew B. Ridgway, in *Military Leadership: In Pursuit of Excellence* (3rd ed.), edited by R. L. Taylor and W. E. Rosenbach, Westview Press, 1996.
[7]Maj. Gen. Perry M. Smith, "Learning to lead," *Marine Corps Gazette*, Jan. 1997.
[8]Ibid.

Although Indians comprise 60 to 80 percent of Guatemala's 10 million people, they have repeatedly been subjugated by colonial powers and their descendants since the Spaniards' sixteenth-century conquest of Central America. Menchu believed that part of their vulnerability came from their cultural and linguistic isolation.

Descendants of the advanced Mayan civilization, today's Mayans reside on the mountaintops of Guatemala, living simple lives centered on respect for the land and close community ties. They frequently work on the coffee plantations of wealthy landowners.

Rigoberta Menchu learned to organize from her father, with whom she frequently traveled to villages across the country as a young child. She learned that the source of the government's terror against the Indians came from a concern over owning the land. She taught other villages to master the art of "trapping" government soldiers through a carefully rehearsed plan of hiding and surprising them, making the soldiers think they were armed.

After her father had been killed in an unsuccessful occupation of the Spanish embassy in Guatemala City and her brother and mother were tortured and killed, Menchu vowed to keep organizing the peasants. At a fraction over five feet tall, this powerful leader mobilized peasants, students, and workers in a series of strikes and demonstrations. As death threats escalated, she escaped to Mexico.

Her insistence on nonviolence despite the government's atrocities that included the deaths of her family members attracted the world's attention. Her efforts to bring peace and justice to Guatemala prompted two Nobel laureates, Argentina's Adolfo Perez Esquivel and South Africa's Bishop Desmond Tutu, to nominate her for the Nobel Peace Prize. The nomination itself was controversial, coming as it did amid the celebrations of the 500th anniversary of Columbus's "discovery" of the Americas. She was awarded the Nobel Peace Prize in 1992. She insists that the objective of the movement she heads is not to retaliate against the government's cruelty, but rather to assure the basic human rights of the people of Guatemala who have no recourse.

She accepted the Nobel Prize in 1992 in Oslo. As the chairman of the Norwegian Nobel Committee said, "By maintaining a disarming humanity in a brutal world, Rigoberta Menchu appeals to the best in us. She stands as a uniquely potent symbol of a just struggle."

One of her primary strategies as leader has been to teach other compañeros to read and write Spanish so that Indians could learn to speak for themselves and understand what the government was really saying.

Her award was criticized by the Guatemalan government as well as by some in the United States who saw her victory as a win for feminist, socialist, and violent causes.

With the $1.2 million award money from the prize, she has established a foundation for the human rights of indigenous peoples in Guatemala and throughout the Americas.

In 1993, the United Nations nominated her as Goodwill Ambassador for the International Year of the Indigenous Peoples. She was also appointed personal advisor to the general director of the United Nations Educational, Scientific and Cultural Organization. She also presides over the Indigenous Initiative for Peace.

GENERAL COLIN L. POWELL: PROBLEM SOLVER

When General Colin Powell's book, *My American Journey,* was published in 1995, he began a book-signing tour that drew throngs of people at sites across the nation. What was the attraction?

In part, it may have been the fact that he was the first African American ever to hold the prestigious positions in the U.S. government of Chairman of the Joint Chiefs of Staff and National Security Advisor. Later, he became Secretary of State and his name has also been raised as a possible candidate for president and vice president. Powell's hold on the American public, however, is founded on his integrity and the leadership he showed during conflict.

Born of Jamaican parents, Powell grew up amid a mix of Jews, Poles, Hispanics, Irish, and Italians in the South Bronx. An indifferent student, he remembered feeling a lack of direction until he entered ROTC (Reserve Officers Training Corps) at City College. There, he says in his autobiography, he felt for the first time a sense of belonging. His admission to the selective Pershing Rifles group deepened his closeness to the military and to other young men with whom he has maintained contact throughout his career.

After accepting a commission as a second lieutenant in the infantry at Fort Benning, Georgia, Powell served as platoon leader and executive officer in West Germany. As he began ascending the military career ladder, he learned that to lead one had to make decisions, often unpopular ones. A quotation he kept on his desk reminded him: "Being responsible sometimes means pissing people off."

His years within the military—which he contends is the most democratic institution in the country—were relatively free of discrimination and prejudice. Outside the service, however, he was saddened to see so much hatred and distrust among the races. At the dedication of the memorial for the Buffalo Soldiers, black soldiers who had fought courageously for the Union during the Civil War but who had received little recognition, Powell noted the injustice these brave soldiers encountered:

> I know where I came from . . . . All of us need to know where we came from so our young people will know where they are going. . . . I am deeply mindful of the debt I owe to those who went before me. I climbed on their backs. . . . I challenge every young person here today: don't forget their service and their sacrifice; and don't forget our service and sacrifice, and climb on our backs. Be eagles!

Powell learned in his first eight weeks these essential guidelines about the military:

> "Take charge of this post and all government property in view"—the Army's first general order.
>
> The mission is primary, followed by taking care of your soldiers.
>
> Don't stand there. Do something!

Lead by example.

"No excuse, sir."

Officers always eat last.

Never forget, you are an American infantryman, the best.

And never be without a watch, a pencil and a notepad.

(*My American Journey*, p. 41)

An early assignment, prosecuting three soldiers whose car crash killed several Germans, had shown him that he was skilled in taking in a large amount of information, shaping it, and conveying it competently and persuasively. Much of his future accomplishments serving presidents and commanding troops called on and refined this ability.

Powell's take on leadership is straightforward: "Leadership is solving problems. The day soldiers stop bringing you their problems is the day you have stopped leading them. They have either lost confidence that you can help them or concluded you do not care. Either case is a failure of leadership." (p. 52)

His combat service included two tours of Vietnam where he earned the Purple Heart and the Soldier's Medal for rescuing his colleagues from a helicopter crash.

He completed his Masters degree in business administration at George Washington University and was selected as a White House fellow during the Nixon administration. Powell chose to serve in the Office of Management and Budget, obtaining invaluable experience about budgetary matters that would help him enormously in his later career.

During his time serving presidents and troops, Powell learned to get along with all types of people. He also learned the importance of acknowledging everyone's effort. In fact, "share the credit" is one of the 13 rules he kept on his desk. He valued teamwork and cherished the existence of a sense of family in the military, of each one looking out for the other.

In many tense situations, including during the Gulf War, Powell resisted others' insistence on quick military reaction. He stressed, instead, the importance of not letting himself be stampeded into an action until he had analyzed it in depth. He vowed to take no action until a clear objective had been established.

Upon Powell's retirement from the Joint Chiefs of Staff, President Clinton had this to say of the General: "He clearly has the warrior spirit and the judgment to know when it should be applied in the nation's benefit. . . . I speak for the families who entrusted you with their sons and daughters . . . you did well by them, as you did well by America."

General Powell counted himself fortunate in many ways: "I had found something to do with my life that was honorable and useful, that I could do well, and that I loved doing. That is rare good fortune in anyone's life. My only regret is that I could not do it all over again."

MAO ZEDONG (MAO TSE TUNG): REVOLUTIONARY AND POET

Born in a rural village 60 miles from the capital of the Hunan Province, Mao endured the privations of poverty as well as the punishments of his harsh father, whom Mao later dubbed "the Ruling Power." Even as a young boy, he hungered for knowledge of China and the outside world. He became an avid reader, sacrificing much to attend school where he was ridiculed for his backcountry ways. He excelled in debate, however, and learned early that it was possible to defy arbitrary authority.

Mao was 18 before he ever saw a map of the world. Rather than attend school at this age, he stayed in the school library from opening until its closing, taking only enough time to eat his ration of two rice cakes for lunch. Instead he devoured books, reveling in the folk tales and history of his native country and also in the biographies of world leaders such as Napoleon, Peter the Great, and Americans such as Abraham Lincoln and George Washington. He later compared himself to Washington leading a rebel army against an entrenched power. He also loved to write poetry, often glorying in the delights of the natural world.

As he saturated himself with the proud history of his country, however, he also became by turns saddened and enraged at its domination by foreign powers. He was thrilled by newspaper stories of uprisings against feudal landlords across the country Stirred by Sun Yat Sen's victory over the Manchu Dynasty, Mao signed up for the revolutionary army, but was later disillusioned when Sun was overtaken by the military and the country broke into warring factions.

Mao tossed about for a future, joining and quitting police, soap-making, and law and business schools. He finally decided on teaching. His remarkable entrance scores earned him free tuition and board for the next four years as he increased his debating skills and continued to rebel against arbitrary authority. He continued reading stories about how sheer willpower could overcome any obstacle, a belief that remained central to his life. He also entered a period of rugged conditioning, eating little and pushing his physical endurance to the limit. His prodigious physical ability stood him well in the years to come.

After reading about the Bolshevik revolution in Russia in 1917, Mao formed communist study groups in China. He disagreed with the Marxists that the revolution would depend on the working class; instead, Mao stressed the role that the peasants would play in overthrowing the government in China.

While fighting the Nationalist Chinese led by Chiang Kaishek, Mao was captured one day and designated for beheading. He managed to evade his captors and hide, stealing back to his headquarters.

In the newly developing Red Army, Mao had set up a very different organization from traditional armies. Officers (including himself) had no special privileges: they were called *leaders* but wore no outward designation of rank and ate the same food as the others. Mao insisted that the soldiers show kindness and helpfulness to the peasants, helping them in whatever way they could. He told them that they must be servants of the people. This passion for serving the peasants created a love for the Red Army among the villagers, who often helped in significant ways. In addition, Mao sought to enlist women and young people in the great effort of liberating China.

Chiang encircled the Red Army, gradually tightening the stranglehold. After long deliberation, Mao convinced his soldiers that the only way to escape was through the treacherous mountains to the north. This began the Long March, a trek of nearly 7,500 miles through rugged territory, often circling back and changing directions to confuse the Nationalists. The journey was exceedingly difficult and resulted in massive numbers of deaths. The Reds also took the opportunity to talk about land reform and other issues to the peasants along the way, building strong support for Mao's revolutionary ideas. Out of the 100,000 troops who began the trip, only 20,000 finished it alive. Often compared with Hannibal crossing the Alps, the amazing feat helped solidify Mao's growing idolization among the people of China.

Following World War II, an out-and-out battle for control of the leadership of China erupted into civil war. Finally Chiang was defeated, moving his enclave to Formosa (Taiwan) in 1949. Mao announced the founding of the People's Republic of China.

During the next three decades Mao showed himself as an astute strategist, a militarist who enjoyed provoking the major world powers, and a polemicist trying to overturn the cultural practices of Confucianism in China. He instigated the Cultural Revolution, asserting that artists and intellectuals needed to come down from their ivory towers to work alongside the peasants. He who had been such a voracious reader now denigrated the need to read anything more than his little blue book, *Quotations from Chairman Mao*. He closed all the universities, turning high school and college students into impassioned members of the Red Guard.

Little else was available to read beyond Mao's works and his likeness loomed everywhere. He delighted in surprising the world, as when he sent a Chinese team to the World Ping Pong championships in Japan and then allowed the U.S. team to play in China. The remarkable meeting between U.S. President Nixon and Mao was another in a long line of unexpected events. It was the first time any U.S. president had set foot on Chinese soil and signaled a thaw in the U.S.-China relationship. During Nixon's visit in 1972, however, Mao was in very poor health, and the country was in suspense about who would take over after his death, which came on September 9, 1977 when Mao was 82.

Summarizing Mao's life, Rebecca Steffof writes in *Mao Zedong:*

> Mao has been viewed as both a hero and a tyrant. His patriotism is undeniable; he fought valiantly to defend China against the Japanese. . . . He was a visionary who dreamed of a new China and had the force of will to reshape the world to fit his dream. Yet sometimes visionaries are dangerous. Sometimes they cannot tolerate the existence of anything or anyone outside their own narrow field of vision. Mao Zedong was an idealist who gave the Chinese people freedoms they had never known. He was also a tyrant, who ruthlessly crushed anyone who dared to dream of freedoms beyond those he offered. He may be both a savior and a villain, but one thing is certain: In shaping the lives of one fifth of the world's population, Mao Zedong had a greater impact on the destiny of the Chinese people than any other single person, except perhaps the emperor who first united China 2,200 years ago.

SUMMARY

The study of military leadership in the United States should not be an exercise undertaken only by those in the military, but rather provides lessons for all aspiring leaders. Current and former military men and women hold influential positions in all segments of society. While each individual is different, there are several specific core values emphasized by the U.S. military which all servicemen and women have been exposed to. This chapter highlights these core values and provides examples of their application in leadership both within and beyond the military.

CREATE YOUR OWN THEORY

The U.S. military has some very distinct and clear core values as related to leadership. Looking back over the 14 leadership traits and 11 core leadership principles described earlier in this chapter, are there other ideas you would add to this list? Do you believe that these core values work best within a military climate or do they translate to other areas of life? Which of these do you find to be most powerful and/or relevant to your own view of leadership?

Now think back to our opening Leadership Moment. If you do not have a military background and learn that you will be working closely with somebody who does, what assumptions would you make about that person? Do you see military experience as an asset or a liability? If you have a military background, how has your experience shaped the way that you view leadership?

KEY TERMS

mission
Uniform Code of Military Justice (UCMJ)
cultural indoctrination and transformation
dependability
bearing
courage
decisiveness
endurance
enthusiasm
initiative
integrity

judgment
justice
knowledge
tact
unselfishness
loyalty
expectations and desired end-state
fog of war or friction
Rule of Three
commanders' intent
OODA loops

QUESTIONS FOR DISCUSSION AND REVIEW

1. How does the description of military leadership put forth in the chapter overlap with conceptions of leadership expressed by other disciplines represented in this book?

2. What are the primary missions of the U.S. Armed Forces?

3. What are some similarities and differences between military and civilian life? How might these impact on an individual's personal theory of leadership?

4. Of the 14 leadership traits listed in this chapter, what is the one that most military students agree is the most important? Do you agree with this assessment? Why or why not?

5. What is the *fog of war?* Does this concept apply only to military settings? Describe a time when you felt like you were in the fog of war.

6. What is the *Rule of Three?*

7. Which do you feel is more important when communicating to others that you are depending on, task or intent? Why?

8. Why are performance reviews important?

ADDITIONAL RESOURCES ON MILITARY LEADERSHIP

You are the same today that you are going to be five years from now except for two things: the people with whom you associate, and the books you read.—Charles Jones

Most chapters in this text provide information about online self-assessment tools readers can utilize to further develop their knowledge base and self-awareness. Unfortunately, the leading self-assessment tools utilized by the military are not accessible online. As an alternative, this reading list was compiled for those who wish to learn more about military leadership.

Military Leadership: In Pursuit of Excellence, third ed., edited by Robert L. Taylor and William E. Rosenbach, Westview Press, 1996.

Rules & Tools for Leaders—A Down-to-Earth Guide to Effective Managing by Maj. Gen. Perry M. Smith USAF (Ret) and Norman Augustine, Avery Publishing Group, August 1998.

The Mask of Command by John Keegan, New York: Penguin USA, 1989.

The Enchiridon by Epictetus, George Long (translator), New York: Promethean Press, 1955.

Leadership Secrets of the Rogue Warrior: A Commando's Guide to Success by Richard Marcinko, New York: Pocket Books, 1997.

The Moral Compass: Stories for a Life's Journey, by William J. Bennett, New York: Touchstone Books, 1996.

Nineteen Stars: A Study in Military Character and Leadership by Edgar F. Puryear Jr., Presidio Press, 1997.

Military Leadership FM 22-100, Department of Army Publication.

Leading Marines FMFM 1-0,

Warfighting MCDP 1, Department of the Navy.

Killer Angels by Michael Shaara, New York: Ballantine Books, 1993.

CHAPTER 8

Practicing Leadership in a Multicultural Society

LEADERSHIP MOMENT

You are a product manager for a leading consumer goods manufacturer. For ten years, you've reported to the head of the North American division. Last year, however, your company reorganized, creating "global teams" for each brand. Now, as the brand manager for Sparkle Shampoo, you have your main production plant in South America, distribution centers throughout Asia, and sales representatives throughout Europe. Needless to say, team meetings have become quite a challenge! First, you face the logistical dilemmas of video conferencing and time zone differences. Then, even when your team members travel to meet in person, the communication and decision making is more complicated than ever. You agree with the company's decision that managing brands globally can have the greatest financial return by quickly reapplying business success principles to markets across the globe. Now if you could only figure out how to make it work.

1. *What would you do?*

2. *What cultural challenges would you anticipate in attempting to coordinate the efforts of individuals working in different parts of the globe?*

3. *What opportunities does going global offer for potential leaders?*

Whether you are the leader of a multinational conglomerate or a not-for-profit organization based in the Midwestern United States, you are undoubtedly a part of an increasingly interconnected global economy and multicultural society. Companies strategize about how they will compete in international markets; government agencies debate over how they will serve minority and immigrant populations; hospitals and health organizations consider the patient care implications of different religious beliefs and practices; and Baby Boomers and Gen-Xers each struggle to understand what motivates the other. Whether the cultures are domestic or international, how leaders prepare themselves to be effective in a multicultural world will greatly determine their effectiveness in this century. As Peter Drucker, the renowned management consultant, advises business leaders: "Tomorrow's challenges are less technical than they are cultural. Culture must be managed just like any other business phenomenon."

As you've learned in other chapters, it is the constituencies surrounding leaders who literally constitute their power and influence. Knowing whom one is leading and how that population may be changing has become an absolute imperative for the twenty-first century. This chapter takes a look at the leadership implications of a changing multicultural society within the United States and considers the enormous challenges and opportunities that accompany being a leader of a global business or organization.

IMPORTANCE OF MULTICULTURAL LEADERSHIP

You may be a business manager who is sent to Asia for an international assignment. You may be an advertising executive who is developing new commercials to appeal to the growing Hispanic population in the United States. Perhaps you are a hospital administrator who is considering redesigning the chapel to reflect the faiths of Islam and Hindu, as well as Christian, patients and doctors. Each of these situations calls for insight and knowledge about a culture other than one's own in order to exercise leadership effectively. Yet, "Our scarcest resource is globally literate leaders," warns Alfred Zeien, chairman and CEO of Gillette, one of the most global companies in the United States.

Multicultural leadership allows you to respond to diverse cultures by increasing your insights into each population's needs and world view, equipping you to best mobilize the entire group. Building multicultural insights and skills can place a taxing demand on a leader; yet, hardly any other competency will be as critical. Let's take a closer look at some of the many reasons why multicultural leadership is so important.

U.S. Demographic Changes

Not only are we connected to other cultures through an interdependent global economy, we also face tremendous cultural differences within the diverse U.S. population. If a U.S. organization considers all of its internal and external stakeholders—shareholders, clients, patients, suppliers, customers, and so on—the combination of personalities, cultures, and backgrounds would paint a colorful mosaic. Immigration, an aging population, changes in cultural and social norms, and civil rights legislation have all contributed to a more diverse workforce. While we've seen these trends at the entry levels of organizations for nearly 20 years, companies are now reaping the benefits of multicultural leaders who have progressed through the organizational ranks. A boardroom filled entirely with white men over 40 of Northern European heritage may have typified Corporate America in the 1950s and 1960s, but now we witness women breaking the glass ceiling, 24-year-old Internet entrepreneurs, and people of color occupying increasingly senior management positions. See Figure 8–1.

U.S. Population in 2000	U.S. Population in 2050 (projected)
72.5% Caucasian/White	52.8% Caucasian/White
12.1% African American	24.5% Hispanic/Latino(a)
11.0% Hispanic/Latino(a)	13.6% African American
3.7% Asian/Pacific Islander	8.2% Asian/Pacific Islander
0.7% Native American	0.9% Native American
Total Population: 270.0 million	Total Population: 393.9 million

Source: U.S. Census Bureau.

Figure 8–1   Changing U.S. Demographics

Global Economy

Most companies' financial health cannot depend on U.S. markets alone. Increasingly, corporations see the benefits of tapping into one of the ten biggest international markets: China, Indonesia, India, South Korea, Turkey, South Africa, Poland, Argentina, Brazil, and Mexico. One study of 1,250 manufacturers showed that businesses that built on a broad base of international operations were more profitable and faster growing. In their report, "The Necessity of Being Global," authors Charles Taylor and Gail Fosler report that "Corporations—in all size categories and industries—that had global activities grew at significantly faster rates; sales figures for those companies without foreign activities grew at half the survey average." Even organizations that do not operate internationally are still connected to an economy that operates across borders and an electronic media system that makes it as easy to contact a customer in Taiwan as one in Chicago. For a description of other important global trends, see Figure 8–2.

Virtual Technology

Many argue that our global economy and sense of global connectedness would be impossible if not for the revolutionary technological explosion of the past 20 years. Just as television began to bring images from around the world into the average American's living room in the 1950s and 1960s, e-mail and the Internet now expose us to myriad new causes, organizations, and individuals. Accessible, widespread electronic communications open markets around the globe with a click of a mouse. E-commerce, video conferencing, e-mail, and other modern modes of communication allow global teams to be connected without constant physical contact. For the leader, dramatic new avenues for connecting others and communicating a common vision have emerged or are emerging.

How we choose to lead is dramatically altered by the technological options available to us. Critical functions of leadership, such as organizing, communicating, and networking, are greatly enhanced through electronic communication. More important for the multicultural leader, however, is the diversity of individuals and groups

Globalizing Growth	The globalization of companies and brands makes it difficult, if not impossible, to determine the home country of many corporations.
International Megamergers	Global mergers create giant multinational corporations that are larger, richer, and more powerful than many countries.
Regional Economic Power	Strong regional trade associations, such as the European Union, NAFTA, ASEAN, and Mercosur, will enhance economic bases around the world.
Economic Interdependence	Strong global monetary and regulatory agencies will be required to handle severe volatility in the international financial system.
Privatizing Power	The privatization of state-run enterprises and the diminished economic decision-making power of nation-states will continue if there is not major worldwide depression.
Identity Problems	In an increasingly interconnected world, people will be torn between being global cosmopolitans, regional traders, national cheerleaders, ethnic personalities, and local citizens.
American Backlash	Defensiveness against ubiquitous American culture, democracy, military might, and free-market capitalism will counter the continuing strength of the United States as the primary world power.
European Integration	The economic integration of Europe and its euro, with the seemingly inevitable political integration to follow, will further solidify that continent's influence of the world stage.
Asian Rebound	The hardworking nature of Asians and their social and family networks, combined with their commitment to education, form a strong foundation for their economies to rebound—and sooner rather than later.
China, Inc.	If China holds together as one nation and if its economic development continues, this will become the largest, most important market in the world.
Haves and Have-Nots	The gap between the haves and have-nots, both within and among countries, will continue to widen unless more-developed countries make a stronger commitment to wealth creation and wealth distribution in less-developed nations.
Ethnic Conflicts	The number and intensity of ethnic conflicts will increase worldwide, as will terrorism driven by these ethnic and religious differences.
Economics versus Environmentalism	As economic development expands globally, pollution and global warming will accelerate, creating political and economic conflicts in all countries, with all parties culpable.
Demographic Dilemmas	The swelling population of young people in the developing world and the need to create jobs for them—combined with the growth of the elderly population in the developed world and the need to take care of them—will create economic and political challenges for all.

Source: Rosen (2000) Global Literacies.

Figure 8–2   Global Trends Affecting Multicultural Leaders

that one may now reach. Technology solves many logistical problems, but the human beings on the receiving end still have unique perspectives and needs based on their cultural identities. Multicultural leaders must find ways to use technology to connect individuals, rather than increase the cultural divides between them.

DOMESTIC AND INTERNATIONAL VIEWS OF MULTICULTURALISM

Multicultural is a term that evolved during the latter part of the twentieth century and that assumes different meanings depending on the context. **Culture** itself is a complex concept, referring to a system of beliefs, behavioral norms, customs, and values of a group with a shared identity and history. For multicultural leaders, becoming adept at discerning the explicit (attributes that are visible) and implicit (attributes that are invisible) elements of the cultures of their constituencies is a journey full of surprises, obstacles, and great learning.

Recognizing Cultural Differences

Although culture may be the most defining characteristic of an individual or group, we are often unaware of its power and influence, particularly when we are surrounded by individuals most like ourselves. In these cases, culture is almost invisible, just as the familiar phrase suggests: "A fish can't see the water in which it swims." Although culture is reflected in every aspect of our daily lives—through the clothes we wear, the accent with which we speak, the way we go to school or to work—these elements are usually taken for granted. They simply represent the millions of habits, decisions, and behavior patterns that fill our daily lives.

Even though being surrounded by others like us can lead us to forget about central characteristics of the cultures to which we belong, traveling to another country or being introduced to individuals far different from us can instantly raise our attention. A Caucasian woman in the United States may hardly think about her white skin color until she walks into a neighborhood of mostly African Americans, and then the fact that she is white may be the dominant thought in her mind. Someone who grew up in a family that practiced Christianity may not recognize how that faith has shaped his values and beliefs until visiting a Hindu or Jewish household and noticing differences in how the family eats together, worships, or dresses. Just as a painting with sharp contrasts draws attention to the differences in color and form, so does a multicultural society lead us to notice the aspects of culture which most dramatically make up our identity and social practices.

The Diversity Kaleidoscope

We often think of culture in terms of nationality and ethnicity. In this framework, *multicultural* refers to a group that is comprised of individuals from more than one country or ethnic group. But culture could also refer to other dimensions of our social identity, including characteristics such as gender, religion, region of the country in which we live, or political affiliation. You are part of a generational culture based on the year you were born (such as the Baby Boomer or Generation-X cultures). You are also part of a culture based on your gender—as every society has differences in the ways males and females are socialized. A leader aspiring to be effective in a multicultural environment must develop an awareness of the different dimensions of culture that may be most central to different constituencies of followers.

Gardenswartz and Rowe provide an excellent tool for illustrating the multiple dimensions of diversity that make up each of us as individuals. The first circle in the **diversity kaleidoscope** represents our personality—the internal aspects of our character and temperament that uniquely define us. The second circle on the kaleidoscope represents our physical attributes, such as age, gender, race, and ethnicity, which are largely visible to others. The third circle represents our social characteristics such as marital status, economic status, religion, and geography. Finally, the outer circle represents the organizational aspects of who we are—our position within a work system, our tenure, formal authority, and work group. Just as each turn of a kaleidoscope creates an entirely different pattern, so does each individual possess a complex, multicultural identity based on each of the four circles. For anyone who thinks that diversity has nothing to do with white men, consider a group of white men identifying their personal attributes by all aspects of the four circles. Thousands of diverse possibilities exist! See Figure 8–3.

The diversity kaleidoscope can remind a multicultural leader that even if his constituencies look physically similar, they may very well represent diverse cultures, even within the United States. Understanding how dimensions of diversity at each level affect attitudes, behaviors, and motivations can be a tremendous asset when trying to bridge a cultural divide. Wise multicultural leaders know to be aware of how their own cultures shape their view of the world, while nurturing a curious and open attitude toward other cultural views.

The Iceberg View of Culture

Just as some aspects of an individual's diversity are visible to others and some are not, entire cultures also have internal and external dimensions. Cultural psychologists and sociologists offer a metaphor that can be extremely helpful in conceptualizing the more obvious, and more hidden, aspects of culture. Viewing another's culture as an **iceberg,** with only a small portion of a massive entity in sight, is in many ways similar to our experience of interpreting other cultures in a multicultural society. See Figure 8–4.

Imagine that you are a leader for a Red Cross relief organization, and you are traveling to a country you've never visited before to learn about the Red Cross's operations there. When you first arrive, many visual clues will tell you that you are no longer at home. Cars drive on the opposite side of the street (in relationship to what you are used to); women's and men's attire may be more colorful or formal; street signs may be written in a language other than English. In terms of our culture iceberg, you are observing the part of the culture that is "above water"—characteristics that are visually noticeable to others. But as every seafarer knows, what lies below the tip of the iceberg is a massive foundation.

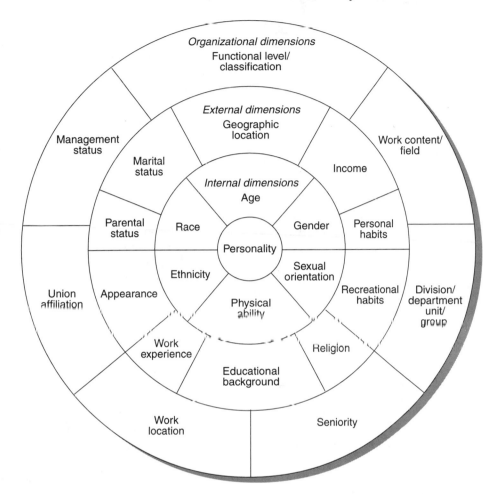

Figure 8–3   Dimensions of Diversity
Source: Gardenswartz, L., and A. Rowe (1994)

Not surprisingly, it is the elements of culture that lie below the metaphorical waters that typically create the most confusion and misunderstanding. To begin to conceptualize what lies outside of our view, the leader must ask, "What are the values, beliefs, and assumptions that this population holds that manifest themselves in the visible artifacts that I can observe? What is the political and religious history of this culture that shapes its world view?" Through this type of inquiry, a leader can begin to understand the cultural influences that shape a person's or group's motivation, work behaviors, reward preferences, and communication styles.

As an amateur cultural anthropologist, you may begin to ask those *why* questions as you start to form relationships with members of cultures other than your own. You may start to do so on an overseas mission with the Red Cross or while trying to understand the hidden influences that shape the behaviors, appearance, and

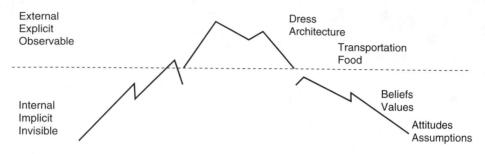

Figure 8–4   The Culture Iceberg

clothes choices of your parents' generation. Whether you are considering international cultures or social cultures (such as gender, age, religious affiliation), recognizing how much is below the line of sight, or beyond our current understanding, can
motivate a multicultural leader to carry on a continuous learning journey.

One famous athlete who was often misunderstood due to the cultural bias of
many who observed him was the great Roberto Clemente, the subject of our next
Leadership Profile.

ROBERTO CLEMENTE: CHAMPION, HUMANITARIAN

This Hall of Fame baseball player started his career in the major leagues unappreci-
ated and misunderstood, largely because of his cultural and language differences.
When sportswriters mocked his English, he retorted by telling them to come to
Puerto Rico and see how good their Spanish was.

Baseball wasn't used to someone who was so sure of his ability—they saw him as
cocky—or so forthright and honest. When he didn't feel good, he said so: a bad back
nearly forced him to quit several times. Sportswriters and managers called him a
hypochondriac, claiming that he would talk about his aches and pains in the dugout
but then go on to play superbly. They didn't understand that his back did hurt, but
he couldn't give any less than 100 percent on the field. Long-time Pittsburgh manager Danny Murtaugh acknowledged that Clemente "was such a truthful man, it
backfired on him sometimes. If you asked him if his shoulder hurt, he'd say, 'Yes, it
does.' Then he'd go out and throw a guy out at the plate. That's how he got the
hypochondriac label."

And, in 1954, baseball was still very much afraid of race. True, Jackie Robinson
had broken the color barrier, but many players and managers were hostile to nonwhite
players. Even the Dodgers, who had the most black players on the roster, had an un-
spoken agreement never to have a majority of black players on the field at one time.

In Pittsburgh, the fans loved watching Clemente's dazzling plays, but for most of
his career he was called "Bobby," a name he never liked for himself, insisting that
Roberto was his real name.

After he won the MVP award in 1966, Clemente took up the cause of the Latin players in the major leagues, asserting that he was happy to be an example for Latin kids to follow.

Yet still his actions could be misunderstood. When he broke Pie Traynor's team record for Runs Batted In in 1973, he refused to acknowledge the fans' standing ovation. Only later did he explain, "The man whose record I broke was a great ballplayer, a great fellow. And he just died here a few months ago. That's why I didn't tip my cap."

His teammates looked to him for inspiration. Teammate Willy Stargell wrote about the 1971 World Series, in which Clemente racked up a staggering .414 batting average: "Each one of us wanted to be like Roberto. He taught us to take pride in ourselves, our team, and our profession."

Clemente's off-season actions were marked by service to others. When an earthquake devastated Nicaragua in 1973, he personally supervised gathering supplies in Puerto Rico and then insisted on accompanying the shipment so that the people, not the ruling dictator, obtained the help. The plane went down, and Roberto's body was never found.

At his death, contributions poured into his dream—Ciudad Deportiva, Sports City, a sports facility where Puerto Rican children and young adults could learn the value of teamwork and sacrificing for the common good.

CULTURAL VARIATIONS IN THE DEMONSTRATION OF LEADERSHIP

Consider what makes a leader effective. One person may answer, "Because he speaks in a loud, commanding voice and looks you straight in the eye!" Another may respond, "Because she is efficiently working behind the scenes to coordinate every aspect of a project, and no one even realizes it!" One person may say, "Because he comes up with all the good answers!" while another replies, "She comes up with all the good questions!"

If we begin to dissect the actual behaviors, facial expressions, use of language, and interpersonal gestures that indicate to another individual "what a leader is," we quickly realize that there is little agreement about what techniques are universally effective. Once we consider various cultural perspectives, we realize that what we consider to be effective leadership varies depending on our cultural lens. This section explores some of the cultural variation in the demonstration of leadership and introduces the concept that effective leadership may not look identical in all cultures—either around the world or within the United States.

Leadership as Emotional Intelligence

Daniel Goleman coined the term **emotional intelligence,** which has become synonymous with social skill, intuitive savvy, and interpersonal acumen in the realm of leadership and management. In fact, Goleman's research shows that emotional intelligence has much greater influence in determining leadership potential than does a person's IQ, test scores, or college performance. Far more than fast talking or displaying artificial sympathy, emotional intelligence requires five vital characteristics that are integral to practicing leadership: self-awareness, self-regulation, motivation, empathy, and social skill. Importantly, leaders with high emotional intelligence are able to connect genuinely with others, conveying an authentic sense of concern, interest, and enthusiasm.

Although the outcomes of emotional intelligence may be universal (such as respecting others, being trustworthy, managing one's moods and emotions), the demonstration and interpretation of those attributes may vary widely by culture. For example, looking others straight in the eyes while speaking to them is a sign of confidence and focus in the United States; in many Asian countries, focusing one's eyes slightly below the other person's (especially if the other is a superior or elder member of the community) is a welcomed sign of deference and respect. Many Caucasian sales managers view calling a customer by his or her first name as a sign of friendliness and comfort. However, many African Americans prefer being addressed by their surname (Miss, Mrs., or Mr.) and may take offense at what they perceive as inappropriate familiarity if addressed on a first-name basis by a salesperson. For one culture, a particular behavior facilitates a positive relationship; in another it is a barrier to building rapport, trust, and open communication.

MULTICULTURAL CHALLENGE FOR LEADERS

In a study that surveyed more than 2,500 individuals, Kouzes and Posner found that great leaders tend to emerge during times of extreme stress and change. Routine, predictable, and uneventful periods of an organization's history don't offer much opportunity for a leader to envision a new path, mobilize others, or confront tough challenges. Just as the Chinese symbol for *change* is a combination of *danger* and *opportunity,* so too do the challenges that surround multicultural leadership provide the most promising opportunities for growth and progress. We'll consider some of the double-edge swords of multicultural leadership, highlighting common dilemmas that can be turned into great opportunities.

Building on Common Ground While Honoring Differences

Regardless of the setting, every leader must find a way to mobilize others effectively to achieve a common goal. When everyone agrees on every aspect of the problem, the solutions, and the way to get there, there is little hard work for a leader. As we know, this is seldom the case. In multicultural leadership, leaders must consider the very real differences that may divide subcultures within a given population (for example, Republicans who favor one policy and Democrats who favor another). There they face a precarious balancing act—figuring out how to acknowledge and respect the distinct needs of each group while finding a common value that can motivate them to work collaboratively.

Often, leaders are tempted to acknowledge only one side of the equation. In other words, a leader may assume that one or more groups have to disavow their attitudes or position in order for compromise to occur. Compromise is usually necessary, but effective multicultural leaders find ways to honor difference while at the same time forging collaboration. Thinking that a solution must be either/or, or that only one group can be right is actually a cultural phenomenon itself, called **dichotomous thinking.** In many Western nations whose philosophy has been influenced by the work of Descartes—who envisioned a clear split between mind and body—either/or thinking is a way of life. Another way of viewing a tough decision, however, is with both/and, or **diunital thinking.** Most indicative of Eastern religious and philosophical tenets, both/and thinking recognizes that multiple realities exist simultaneously and resist an all-or-none approach, often leaving room for novel solutions to emerge.

Supporting Global Teams

Tapping into the talents and perspectives of an international workforce is one of the most powerful skills a multicultural leader can have. Having human resources in different regions of the world, however, is only advantageous if the multicultural leader can adequately and creatively connect those resources and mobilize them collectively. Physical distance, time zone differences, travel expenses, and other logistical challenges are formidable. Even when the logistics of a globally dispersed team are overcome, the cultural and regional differences of team members may seriously challenge communication and decision-making.

Multicultural leaders can support global teams in numerous ways. First, a greater portion of a team's travel budget should be spent earlier in the project life cycle, when a team is building interpersonal connections and group norms. Many global consultants recommend that global teams spend an entire week in the same location, using their in-person time to set clear project goals, success criteria, and processes for making decisions and resolving conflict.

As another strategy, a multicultural leader can provide guidance in explicitly identifying some of the cultural differences that may exist among team members. Once some initial trust is established, exploring how each culture represented within the team prefers to express gratitude, receive feedback, address dissent, and celebrate success may produce long-lasting benefits. If done early in the team's history, the cross-cultural dialogue can provide interpersonal guidelines for how this diverse body can best operate.

Finally, multicultural leaders can support global teams by identifying conflicts in reward structures or bureaucratic procedures between the different regions or countries. If a team member in South America is being evaluated on completely different criteria from those of her teammate in the Philippines, misunderstanding and costly resentments may occur. A multicultural leader should challenge the organizational structures that create those international discrepancies to foster greater team morale and cohesiveness among members.

Supporting Women as Global Managers

Although U.S. businesses have made great strides in creating environments that recognize and reward women's leadership contributions, we do not see the same results internationally. Women hold 37 percent of managerial positions in the United States but only 3 percent of business leadership positions around the globe. Nancy Adler, a leading scholar on women and leadership, claims that the situation is not a result of women declining international offers. In fact, studies of recent MBA graduates reveal that women desire international placements as much as their male counterparts. With the demand for competent, insightful global managers so great, why are so few women chosen for the job?

Terence Brake, an international management consultant and author, describes common myths that perpetuate erroneous views of women's ability to fill international leadership positions successfully. Many assume that women will decline international assignments because of a spouse's job or children's schooling. However, studies show that support systems such as job relocation services for spouses and strong family preparation for entering a foreign culture can dispel these concerns, for both male and female managers. Brake points out that some companies may have limiting beliefs such as, "I don't think a woman would have the stamina to survive in the tropics," or "We shouldn't send a single woman into that part of the world," or even, "She'll face too much sexual prejudice abroad." These attitudes, whether conscious or unconscious, can limit a woman's global opportunities before she's even had a chance to decide to accept an international assignment.

Understanding gender differences is as important for a culturally sensitive leader as is knowledge about different regions of the world and different ethnic groups within the United States. Recognizing the stereotypes and prejudices that both genders may face, based on the socializing rules that accompany being a man or a woman in a particular culture, is critical if a multicultural leader wants to be an advocate for everybody.

WHAT DISTINGUISHES GREAT MULTICULTURAL LEADERS?

So what characteristics and behaviors make a multicultural leader effective? Jimmy Carter has had a distinguished career as an international diplomat after his term as president. He is able to win trust and confidence from leaders around the world, even during tense situations of conflict and political disagreement. Anita Roderick, the founder of The Body Shop, spends much of her time traveling internationally, dedicated to environmental causes and to helping indigenous peoples around the world. Colin Powell, the U.S. military hero of the Gulf War and later Secretary of State (see profile in Chapter 7), can effectively motivate all soldiers and military personnel regardless of their race, gender, or ethnicity because of his strong example and excellent communication skills. In each case, these leaders have transcended their own cultural limitations to make a lasting impact on multicultural constituencies. Here is a closer look at some of the skills they have cultivated.

Ability to Generate Social Capital Across Cultures

Social capital is a term used by economists and sociologists to refer to the value of interpersonal connections in solidifying a relationship, organizational culture, or business deal. Financial capital is a term that may sound more familiar, referring to the monetary backing that an individual or business has that increases net worth and the ability to pursue wealth-expanding endeavors. Social capital captures the notion that strong relationships, in terms of emotional connection, communication, and trust, have a tremendous value on which one cannot put a dollar amount. It can be thought of as *the value of goodwill.* Think of a close mentoring relationship you may have had. The value you receive from the relationship is social capital and will most likely benefit you as much as a graduate degree or official certification in pursuing your dreams.

Great multicultural leaders are able to generate this goodwill across cultures. Bill Clinton can enter an African-American church and fully participate in their lively, animated services because his southern upbringing and Baptist faith allow him to connect authentically with that group of people. In this way he developed social capital among African-American constituents. Bonnie Blair, the Olympic gold medallist in speed skating, is as comfortable on the ice rink as she is among youth in a community outreach program. Her fame as an athlete, along with her example of great discipline and optimistic personality, give her social capital among the young girls she speaks to and motivates. Great multicultural leaders are able to inspire strong interpersonal relationships not only between people very much like themselves but also among people who may be quite different from themselves.

Demonstration of Multicultural Literacy

Robert Rosen, author of the book *Global Literacies,* states that learning how to lead effectively in a multicultural world is a process much like learning to read. It doesn't come all at once, and may be difficult and slow going in the beginning, but ultimately, those skills will open up worlds and opportunities that one can hardly imagine. **Multicultural literacy** is comprised of the skills, insights, and attitudes that allow one to learn from diverse individuals and places continuously. It can be thought of as a *backpack of tools* that accompanies you on any multicultural journey.

For example, the first step in becoming multiculturally literate is to increase your recognition of your own cultural influences and biases. Like the fish that is oblivious to the water around it, someone who has not taken inventory of the culture that makes up his social lifeline is bound to run into trouble if he travels to a different shore. By acknowledging the customs, attitudes, and values that our own culture promotes, we can more easily accept different cultures' central characteristics. You can remain comfortable in your own culture, while still being able to fully engage with cultures different from your own. As with becoming literate in a new language, you do not forget or diminish the knowledge you have of your first language. Becoming literate in another culture simply enhances your overall appreciation and mastery of what makes each of us human.

Creating and Sustaining a Rich Teaching and Learning Environment

Finally, great multicultural leaders are able to create environments where everyone around them is supported and nurtured in his or her own multicultural journey. Not content to invest only in their own learning, multicultural leaders take the time and effort to encourage teaching and learning around them. Because every individual has a unique cultural background, we can all be teachers helping others learn. And because no one can have complete knowledge, we must all remain students, constantly learning and reflecting upon our new knowledge.

Multicultural leaders assist others on a one-on-one basis, but they also consider the organizational structures, policies, and practices that would enhance the overall organizational culture. A manager may advocate to provide foreign language lessons to his work team, if they are willing to take the time to study another language. She may recognize cultural holidays that are not traditionally celebrated in the workplace and use that celebration as an opportunity to learn about the foods, customs, and beliefs that are honored by that day. Multicultural leaders consider the impact of organizational culture and make sure that their work environment upholds teaching and learning from one another as a central value.

PRACTICING MULTICULTURAL LEADERSHIP

As you prepare your toolkit of effective leadership practices, it is essential that guidelines for multicultural leadership are included for any journey! Here are some suggestions for increasing your insight and skill as a leader of multicultural groups.

Practice the Platinum Rule

Regardless of their religious upbringing, most individuals could recite from childhood the **Golden Rule**—"Do unto others as you would have them do unto you." Although this admonition may have been helpful on the playground or even at one time in the workplace, a multicultural society calls us to question the assumptions that lie behind the Golden Rule. For example, treating others the way you would want to be treated assumes that the other individual wants exactly what you want, or likes to be rewarded in the same way that you prefer to be recognized. When dealing with others who are very similar to you, this may be helpful advice. But for a multicultural leader, it is inadequate.

Effective multicultural leaders recognize that different cultures, and certainly different individuals, are motivated by different things, in different ways. A 40-year-old woman may want a pay raise as an expression of a job well done. A 24-year-old male may choose flexible time or a longer vacation as a reward. Effective multicultural leaders learn to practice a principle that transcends the Golden Rule: the **Platinum Rule.** The Platinum Rule states that a multicultural leader is best served by following the principle, "Do unto others as they would like for you to do unto them." In other words, ask what their preferences are instead of assuming that they are the same as your own.

"How do you like to be rewarded?" and "How do you like to be shown respect?" may be the most important questions multicultural leaders can ask when first forming a team or new work group. The Platinum Rule reminds us that our own cultural preferences for interpersonal interaction and personal motivation are just that—our own preferences. Other individuals from other cultures may have an equally valid, but very different, manner of expressing the same sentiment. Asking the question of how another person would like to be treated introduces an opportunity to talk explicitly about culturally driven behaviors. It also shows the person or group that you are sincerely interested in finding out how you can best serve them as a leader. Such attention seldom goes unnoticed or unappreciated.

Distinguish Between Stereotypes and Generalizations

Many cultural offenses are committed by making the assumption that every person of a particular culture shares an identical feature. We've all heard comments that unfairly place every member of a culture in one group: "All men are violent," "All women are emotional," "All Asians are smart." These universal statements are typically negative, even when based on a kernel of accurate information. They are damaging to productive working relationships because they are **stereotypes.**

At the same time, we do know that cultural groups share common characteristics, as a group. Thus **generalization** about cultural groups can help you increase your multicultural knowledge. For example, if you were leading an organization with a large Hispanic population, it would be helpful to know that, in general, many Hispanics grew up practicing the Catholic faith, and thus may have a special reverence for family celebrations and worship. You may also want to know differences in gender roles that are common among Hispanics, or the kinds of music or food they typically enjoy. Making these generalizations does not mean you are stereotyping. There are certainly Hispanic individuals who do not like Latin music or who did not grow up Catholic. However, these generalizations may help you understand the unique attributes of Hispanic culture that differentiate them from other groups of Americans.

Recognize That Your Intent May Not Match Your Effect

Because multicultural leadership is an ongoing journey, we must accept that we will make mistakes along the way. Often, even when our intentions are the best, we make cultural mistakes due to our lack of understanding or limited knowledge. A male manager may continue to use sports analogies exclusively around a woman who reports to him because he "just wants her to feel like one of the guys." Although his **intent** is to be inclusive, his **effect** may be the exact opposite. Although he feels he's being a great mentor, she may be thinking, "If he uses one more football story I'm going to go crazy!"

Have you ever found yourself speaking very loudly to an individual who was sight impaired or physically disabled? Your intent may simply have been to communicate clearly, but your effect could have been offensive—after all, there was nothing wrong with the individual's hearing! In order to realize that our intent has produced an unwanted effect, multicultural leaders must be open to feedback, even if it at first sounds critical.

Understanding the principle of intent and effect means realizing that communication is a two-way channel. Both the speaker and the receiver must share the intended meaning for the communication to have been successful. Sometimes, a multicultural leader's best strategy is to simply share her intention: "I meant to communicate that I was interested in you being on this project team. Is that what came across?" Being willing to make mistakes is part of the multicultural leader's journey, and receiving feedback is part of the process.

This chapter closes with a profile of Marian Wright Edelman, a multicultural leader who has worked tirelessly within Washington and elsewhere to mobilize others and advocate for social change.

MARIAN WRIGHT EDELMAN: WORKING FOR A GOOD AND JUST SOCIETY

The daughter of a Baptist minister, Marian Wright Edelman grew up in racially segregated Bennetsville, South Carolina. Her parents were intensely involved in improving conditions for African Americans in the community, and those values became second nature to Marian.

"I was taught that the world had a lot of problems; that I could struggle and change them; that intellectual and material gifts brought the privilege and responsibility of sharing with others less fortunate; and that service is the rent each of us pays for living," she said.

Although she had a secure and happy family life, she witnessed the results of prejudice and discrimination time and time again, as when a childhood friend stepped on a nail and died after he couldn't get proper medical care because he was black and poor.

In 1954, her father suffered a heart attack, and among his final words to Marian in the ambulance were that she could do anything, be anything; that she must not let anything interfere with getting an education and being everything she could be.

As a senior at Spelman College in Atlanta, she took a stand in support of the black students picketing at the lunch counter in Greensboro, North Carolina. She was arrested for picketing the Atlanta City Hall cafeteria in a demonstration she had planned.

Her plans to go into foreign service (she had earlier traveled and studied in Europe and Russia) changed after volunteering at a local NAACP branch where she witnessed the numbers of poor and black people who could not get legal help for the discrimination they faced.

After receiving a fellowship to Yale Law School, she worked with groups such as the Student Non-Violent Coordinating Committee to promote voter registration in Mississippi. While there, she and a group of other activists seen as "outsiders" were attacked by the local police department's German shepherd police dogs. She became more resolved than ever to finish her studies and promote the civil rights of blacks.

After graduating, she became one of the first interns in the NAACP's Legal Defense and Education Fund in Jackson, Mississippi. There she faced threats of violence against herself and her clients. She passed the Mississippi bar, becoming the first black female to practice law in Mississippi.

She grew increasingly concerned about the effects of poverty, especially on young children. When Mississippi refused to accept federal funds for children as part of President Johnson's War Against Poverty, Marian helped form an organization that would seek federal funds for the children of Mississippi. She served as general counsel for the group, which provided educational programs for children throughout the state.

During Senate subcommittee hearings on hunger, she caught the attention of Senator Robert F. Kennedy, who joined her in an effort to do something about hunger. She met and eventually married Peter Edelman, a lawyer on Kennedy's staff. Their wedding marked the first interracial marriage in Virginia since the Supreme Court struck down state laws that made such marriages illegal.

After helping draft a major piece of legislation that offered health and education aid to preschool children, she was devastated by then-President Richard Nixon's veto. Marian had nevertheless found a direction for her energy: to look at children and their needs as a way to build a coalition for social change.

In 1973, she founded the Children's Defense Fund, an organization that identifies the problems facing children and then lobbies for legislation and programs to respond to those problems. In later years, the organization expanded its focus to include preventing teenage pregnancy, an increasing factor in the cycle of poverty, malnutrition, and neglect.

Although praised by many politicians (Senator Edward Kennedy called her the 101st senator of children's issues and noted that she uses the real power she has brilliantly), Marian claims that it all comes down to perseverance and commitment: "I'm a good pest is what I am," she says.

SUMMARY

A leader's effectiveness depends primarily on his or her ability to mobilize others, setting a vision and directing a group to work toward a common goal. To do that, a leader must authentically understand the needs, attitudes, and desires of those he or she is leading. When someone is leading others very much like herself, this may be a fairly natural and effortless process. But when she is leading others who differ from her in many ways, her ability to understand those differences is paramount. This is both the challenge and opportunity of multicultural leadership.

CREATE YOUR OWN THEORY

Chose a leader in your community or school whom you admire. Thinking about all of the constituencies that person must consider, identify what cultures are represented. Don't limit your list to ethnic, regional, or national cultures. Consider also gender, age, education, religion, and economic status, among others. What approach would you recommend this leader take in preparing himself or herself to provide the best leadership to the entire group? What reasons for striving to become a multicultural leader would you give him or her? What strategies do you have for yourself for increasing your multicultural literacy as a leader?

Now think back to our opening Leadership Moment. How might you approach this situation? What characterizes your ideal global leader and which of these characteristics do you possess? Where do your global skills fall short and how can you address this?

KEY TERMS

multicultural leadership	social capital
culture	multicultural literacy
diversity kaleidoscope	Golden Rule
cultural iceberg	Platinum Rule
emotional intelligence	stereotype
dichotomous thinking	generalization
diunital thinking	intent and effect

QUESTIONS FOR DISCUSSION AND REVIEW

1. Why is multicultural leadership even more critical today than it was 10 years ago? What conditions do you think will perpetuate the need for effective multicultural leadership?

2. What is the difference between a stereotype and a generalization? What are the dangers of using stereotypes rather than generalizations?

3. What are some of the explicit (visible) characteristics of your own culture? Name some of the implicit characteristics.

4. Describe the logic of the Platinum Rule.

5. Give an example of a situation where someone's intent produced a different effect, based on cultural misunderstanding.

6. What are Goleman's five components of emotional intelligence? Choose one of the components and give an example of how its demonstration may look different in one country versus another.

ONLINE SELF-ASSESSMENT TOOL

Test your knowledge of the laws and dynamics surrounding sexual harassment by taking the quiz at http://www.capstn.com.

CHAPTER 9

Modern Leadership Theories

LEADERSHIP MOMENT

You are the newly hired principal of Roosevelt High School. Among the leading complaints about your predecessor is that she played favorites. As a result, you have inherited a staff that mostly views you with suspicion. In reviewing the backgrounds of the school professionals, you notice that there is a wide range of experience and skills. There are 20 teachers aged 24 or younger, yet there are also 34 who have been at the school for more than 20 years. There are also an increasing number of "specialists" (speech therapists, psychologists) who report to you that they felt slighted by the previous principal, who they feel worked to keep them isolated from the "real school workers" (i.e., teachers). The students generally ignore you—they only really saw the previous principal when they were in trouble. As for the community, your school's standardized test scores are declining and they expect a turnaround—fast.

1. *What would you do?*
2. *How would you attempt to understand and manage the diverse backgrounds and perspectives of school personnel?*
3. *What might some of your first steps be in this process?*
4. *To whom would you look for guidance in this process? Who are potential allies?*

$\mathbf{N}$ow that we've seen what the related disciplines have contributed to leadership theory, this chapter looks at the various theories that are or have been popular in leadership literature. We'll touch on trait theory, behavioral management approaches, and situational approaches. It is fitting that our discussion begins with the seminal work of John Gardner, the former U.S. Secretary of Health, Education, and Welfare, and current professor at Stanford University. His book, *On Leadership* (1989), lists ten functions of leadership:

1. Envisioning goals
2. Affirming and regenerating important group values
3. Motivating others toward collective goals

4. Managing the processes through which collective goals can be reached
5. Achieving unity of effort within a context of pluralism and diversity
6. Creating an atmosphere of mutual trust
7. Explaining and teaching
8. Serving as a symbol of the group's identity
9. Representing the group's interests to outside parties
10. Renewing and adapting the organization to a changing world

These functions describe an ideal state that can be used as a benchmark to measure the effectiveness of any leader.

This list should be examined in terms of another well-known leadership theorist, Warren Bennis, former president of the University of Cincinnati. Bennis (1985) proposed his own list of competencies for leaders, based on a five-year project that studied 90 effective, successful leaders in corporations and the public sector.

He concluded that there are four major competencies:

1. Management of attention—the ability to attract others, not only through a compelling vision, but also through communicating commitment
2. Management of meaning—to make dreams apparent to others
3. Management of trust—to let others believe in one's constancy and focus
4. Management of self—understanding one's skills and using them well

TRAIT THEORY

Trait theory was very popular during the second part of the twentieth century. Simply stated, this theory suggests that the traits of successful leaders should be studied and emulated. The enormity of the challenge is daunting. How can people who seek to practice leadership gain the needed "traits"?

One answer can be seen in Gardner's 14 leadership attributes, which he says "seem to be linked with higher probabilities that a leader in one situation could also lead in another." They are

1. Physical vitality and stamina
2. Intelligence and action-oriented judgment
3. Eagerness to accept responsibility
4. Task competence
5. Understanding of followers and their needs
6. Skill in dealing with people
7. Need for achievement
8. Capacity to motivate people
9. Courage and resolution
10. Trustworthiness

11. Decisiveness

12. Self-confidence

13. Assertiveness

14. Adaptability/flexibility

Rather than merely compiling this list from his own thoughts and experiences, Gardner worked from a five-year field study of organizations and interviews with hundreds of leaders. To what end do leaders employ these traits? Gardner asserts that leaders should focus on building and rebuilding community—on working for the common good. And their primary renewal task, he says, is "the release of human energy and talent."

In studying and questioning great leaders, Gardner and Bennis have returned to the trait theory approach (see Chapter 4). They looked at the person and tried to figure out how he or she practiced leadership. A sports analogy is reviewing video from the game and breaking down the component parts to analyze a power swing, for example.

James M. Kouzes and Barry Z. Posner also made a major contribution to trait theory in their book, *The Leadership Challenge*. In the early 1980s, more than 1,500 managers responded to their survey, in which they asked, "What values do you look for in your superiors?" Of the 225 values, characteristics, and attitudes compiled from the answers, the top four listed were being honest, forward looking, inspiring, and competent. They called these four characteristics being credible. Please also see their essay in Chapter 5 and a summary of their book *Credibility* in Appendix II for more information about Kouzes and Posner's theory.

Many others have composed lists of leadership characteristics, typically including such traits as energy level, height, general cognitive ability, and, to a lesser extent, particular technical skills and knowledge about a group's task. See Table 9–1 for a summary of effective physical, social, and personal leadership characteristics.

BEHAVIORAL THEORIES OF LEADERSHIP

The behavioral approach to studying leadership assumes that leader behaviors rather than personality characteristics are the elements exerting the most effect on followers. Significant research on this perspective was conducted at Ohio State University and the University of Michigan.

The Ohio State Studies

The **Ohio State studies** examined the effects of two dimensions of leader behavior: *consideration* and *initiating structure*. Consideration refers to the leader's awareness of and sensitivity to subordinates' interests, feelings, and ideas. Leaders high in consideration are typically friendly, prefer open communications, focus on teamwork, and are concerned with the other person's welfare.

Initiating structure, on the other hand, is a leader behavior marked by attention to task and goals. Leaders who are high in initiating structure typically present instructions and provide detailed, explicit timelines for task completion.

TABLE 9–1   **Personal Characteristics of Leaders**

Physical:	Active
	Energetic
Personality:	Alert
	Creative
	Ethical
Social:	Skilled interpersonally
	Can enlist others in goal
	Sociable
	Cooperative
Intelligence:	Good judgment
	Fluent in speaking
	Knowledgeable
Work-related traits:	Task-oriented
	Tactful
	Driven to excel
	Responsible
	Ethical

Since the two behaviors are independent of each other, researchers tested the effectiveness of four combinations of leader behaviors: high initiating structure–low consideration (HIS–LC), low initiating structure–high consideration (LIS–HC), high initiating structure–high consideration (HIS–HC), and low initiating structure–low consideration (LIS–LC). The high initiating structure–high consideration style was associated with the best performance and greatest satisfaction. These leaders both met the needs of their subordinates and were effective in accomplishing their task and/or goals.

University of Michigan Studies

Similarly, in the late 1950s, researchers including Rensis Likert looked at the behavior of effective and ineffective supervisors. The **University of Michigan studies** concluded that supervisory behavior could be analyzed in terms of *employee-centered* and *job-centered behavior*. Employee-centered supervisors were found most effective. To these researchers, supervisors exhibited either one or the other of these patterns; there was no middle ground, no combination of centers.

The Leadership Grid

Robert Blake and Jane Mouton developed the concept of the **Leadership Grid** (see Figure 9–1), which graphically depicts the characteristics of leaders based on some of the dimensions examined in the Ohio State and University of Michigan studies. Questionnaire responses were used to rate managers on a scale from one to nine for

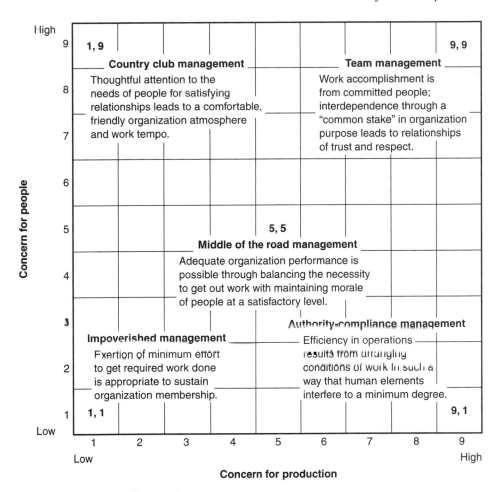

Figure 9–1 The Leadership Grid® Leadership Styles
Source: Leadership Dilemmas—Grid Solutions. p. 29, by Robert R. Blake, Ph.D. and Anne Adams
McCanse. Copyright © 1991, by Robert R. Blake and the Estate of Jane S. Mouton, Austin, Texas. The
Grid® designation is property of Scientific Methods, Inc. Gulf Publishing Company, Houston, Texas.
Used with permission. All rights reserved.

two dimensions: concern for people and concern for production. An individual's
scores on these two dimensions were then plotted, with a score of (9,9) equaling the
ideal leader ("team" style). See Chapter 10 for a more detailed discussion of this
leadership style and also see the Online Self-Assessment Tool later in this chapter
for a link to an online quiz where you can learn where you stand on this grid.

Based on a person's location on the grid, Blake and Mouton (1964) identified
four other distinct management styles. Most managers fall near the (5,5) point on
the grid, indicating a "middle of the road style." These managers rate in the middle
range on the concern for people scale and in the middle range on the concern for
production scale. Those scoring high on concern for people and low on concern for

production scales demonstrate a "country club" style. Finally, managers scoring very low on both scales are said to have an "impoverished" style.

While Blake and Mouton concluded that managers perform best when working under a (9,9) "team" style, there is little substantive evidence to support this claim; some question whether a (9,9) is even possible, since often a leader is forced to make a decision that favors either people or production.

SITUATIONAL APPROACHES TO LEADERSHIP

Leaders can lead in many ways depending on their style—the situation as shown in Figure 9–2. This section reviews major situational theories about leadership. Situational leadership looks at three elements: the leader, the follower (we prefer the term *collaborator*), and the situation itself. Situational theories, then, look at one behavioral aspect of leadership. The **Path–Goal** theory, for example, centers on motivation and its relationship to the leader, follower, and situation.

Path–Goal Theory

Path–Goal theory simply states that a leader must motivate followers: leaders are successful if they can successfully motivate their followers as shown in Figure 9–3.

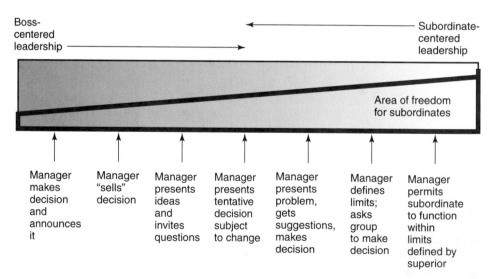

Figure 9–2   Continuum of Leadership Behavior
Source: J. Donnelly, J. Gibson, J. Ivancevich, *Fundamentals of Management,* 9th edition, 1995. Irwin Professional. Used with permission.

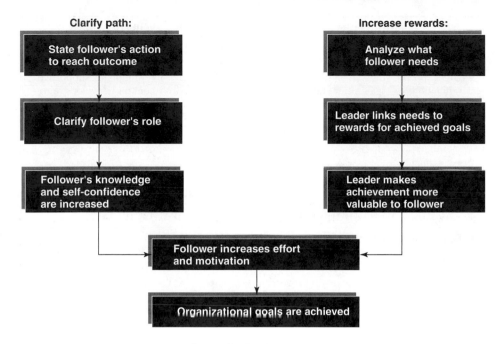

Figure 9–3 Leader's Role in the Path–Goal Model

In order to utilize the Path–Goal theory effectively, House demonstrates the need to select the leadership style that best fits the situation (see Figure 9–4). Directive, supportive, achievement-oriented, and participative approaches are all appropriate for different situations.

The expectancy factors the leader must consider in assessing followers are

1. Followers' valences (a valence is one's perspective about what is important). Leaders can help followers identify and pursue an outcome that is under the leader's control.

2. Followers' instrumentalities. Leaders can make sure that high performance means satisfying outcomes.

3. Followers' expectancies. Leaders can reduce followers' frustration by overcoming barriers.

4. Equity of rewards. Leaders raise the levels and types of rewards available for good performance.

5. Accuracy of role perceptions. Leaders specify clearly the routes for effective performance.

Exercise 9–1 is helpful in bringing these concepts to life.

DIRECTIVE	SUPPORTIVE
• Emphasizes management functions such as planning, organizing, and controlling • Gives specific guidelines, rules, and regulations to organization members • Clearly spells out expectations for group members • Typically improves performance when tasks are unclear or organization unstable	• Emphasizes concern for well-being of group members • Establishes an emotionally supportive work environment and develops mutually satisfying relationships among group members • Group members who are unsure of themselves prefer this style • Typically improves performance where tasks are dissatisfying, stressful, or frustrating
ACHIEVEMENT-ORIENTED	PARTICIPATIVE
• Emphasizes setting challenging goals and high expectations for performance • Continually pushes for work improvement • Group members expected to assume significant responsibility • Typically improves performance with achievement-oriented team members and with those working on ambiguous and nonrepetitive tasks	• Emphasizes consultation with group members and takes their suggestions seriously when making decisions • Typically improves performance of well-motivated employees who perform nonrepetitive tasks

Figure 9–4   House's Path–Goal Theory: Leadership Style

A Continuum of Leader Behavior

In considering the appropriate leadership style, some leaders use the continuum of leadership behavior (see Figure 9–2), choosing either a directive, supportive, participative, or achievement-oriented approach (see Figure 9–4) based on the leadership of the expectancy factors that fit the situation.

> **Directive:** Authoritarian. Collaborators know precisely what is expected and when, but have no say in decision-making.
>
> **Supportive:** A directive leader who nonetheless shows concern and interest in collaborators.
>
> **Participative:** A leader who enlists and accepts others' ideas, but still makes the decision.
>
> **Achievement-oriented:** A leader who establishes challenging but possible goals for collaborators and fully expects their achievement.

With the five expectancy variables, the four leadership styles, and the knowledge that situational and follower factors also affect the process, the Path–Goal theory can become very complicated. As you might expect, wise individuals select a leadership style based on elements of the task, the situation, or the subordinates. They may fluctuate, too, between leadership styles, depending on which one promises the best results in a given situation.

For example, *participative leadership* produces satisfaction in situations in which the task is not routine and the collaborators are themselves not authoritarian. *Directive leadership* results in high satisfaction and performance only when collaborators have great needs for clarity. *Supportive leadership* produces satisfaction among collaborators only when the task is highly structured, and *achievement-oriented leadership* yields improved performance only when collaborators express commitment to goals.

Chart Summary: Path–Goal Theory

Centers on:

Expectancy theory, which suggests that people calculate the advantages of different levels of effort (e.g., if I practice the piano for eight hours, how likely is it that I will do well at the recital?); performance (e.g., If I do well at the recital, how likely is it that I will get a record contract?), and values (e.g., how much do I want a performing career?)

Useful for:

Predicting to which tasks people will devote their energy

Understanding the complexity of the factors involved in practicing leadership

IMPLICATIONS FOR PRACTICING LEADERSHIP

Effective leaders make sure appropriate rewards are available for followers (the goal) and then help them find the best way to achieve it (the path). Practicing leadership involves helping others see that the more effort and energy they put into a task, the greater the chance of accomplishing it. *Plus*, leaders must make sure that achieving the task will have valuable consequences.

Leadership skills needed:

Ability to identify and communicate with others

Ability to use motivation to encourage activity

Ability to accurately assess the situation and the collaborators

Flexibility in determining when to use which of the four styles

Most effective when:

Research (Mitchell, Smyser, and Weed, 1975) shows that others' satisfaction with a leader depends not only on the leader's style, but on certain variables of the follower. For example, some studies showed that not everyone was satisfied with participatory leadership approaches. In fact, those who were happiest with participating in decisions were people with an internal locus of control—who thought that outcomes were directly related to their behavior. Conversely, those with an external locus of control—who felt that the outcomes depended on factors outside their control—were more satisfied with a directive leader.

Another collaborator variable that affects leader style is the collaborators' perception of their own abilities to perform the tasks.

Situational factors:

The task—is it in itself motivating? Routine?

The authority system—are there standards for performing the task?

The primary work group—is there an accepted way of performing the task?

The Path–Goal model is very comprehensive. It sees leadership within organizations as helping members clarify their goals and identify the best ways to achieve those goals.

Normative Decision Model

Vroom and Yetton (1973) and Vroom and Yago (1988) contend that leaders can improve group performance by selecting the most appropriate amount of participation in decision making. Thus, they developed a model designed to assess the amount of input group members should contribute to the decision-making process (Figure 9–6).

Their investigation of decision-making processes in groups led them to propose a continuum of decision processes ranging from autocratic to consultative to group process. Two criteria, they suggest, can be used to evaluate decisions: decision quality and decision acceptance. Quality decisions, for example, would affect profit, cost-saving, or level of service, all measurable objectives. For a decision to be accepted, subordinates/group members would come to consider the decision one they "buy into" and feel comfortable with, not one that they are compelled to obey.

Whether at one extreme managers make the decision or at the other extreme subordinates make the decision, each has its advantages and costs.

LOUELLA THOMPSON, FOUNDER OF "FEED THE HUNGRY"

Since 1987, Louella Thompson has been working on an all-consuming assignment. That year, the Middletown, Ohio, hairdresser says God told her, "Open the door and feed whoever comes. Don't ask any questions."

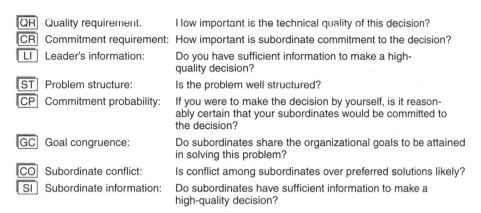

QR	Quality requirement.	How important is the technical quality of this decision?
CR	Commitment requirement:	How important is subordinate commitment to the decision?
LI	Leader's information:	Do you have sufficient information to make a high-quality decision?
ST	Problem structure:	Is the problem well structured?
CP	Commitment probability:	If you were to make the decision by yourself, is it reasonably certain that your subordinates would be committed to the decision?
GC	Goal congruence:	Do subordinates share the organizational goals to be attained in solving this problem?
CO	Subordinate conflict:	Is conflict among subordinates over preferred solutions likely?
SI	Subordinate information:	Do subordinates have sufficient information to make a high-quality decision?

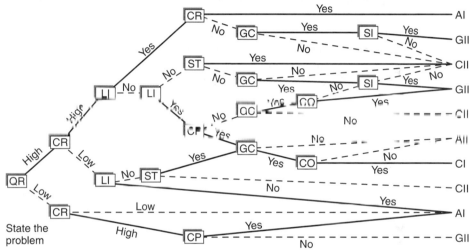

Figure 9–5   The Vroom-Yetton-Yago Model

Source: J. Donnelly, J. Gibson, and J. Ivancevich, *Fundamentals of Management,* 9th edition, 1995. Irwin Professional. Used with permission.

For the past eight years that's exactly what the 70-year-old has done, fixing hot meals for free carryout or delivery for an average of 600 people a month. (That doesn't count the donuts, juice, and coffee she hands out to a steady stream of children and adults each morning.) She chose the fourth Saturday of the month for the hot meals because by that time, many people's budgets were stretched to the breaking point.

Thompson supervises volunteers from all over the area, and graciously accepts donations of food, money, clothing, and old roasting units (her crowded kitchen now has five electric units in addition to her original stove). There are "five or six" freezers scattered throughout her combination house/office/soup kitchen.

For six years she was a regular presence at county commissioner meetings, promoting the Feed the Hungry project. Her mission of feeding and not asking questions has captured the city's attention, bringing donations and volunteer help from groups and individuals. Community groups, including adults on probation and mentally retarded young people, schedule weekly sessions to help out with bagging food or peeling apples or helping in some other specific way. Thompson welcomes all contributions—of time, service, and money. "I'm not hard to please," she says. "Whatever people want to do to help feed the hungry, that's all right with me."

Her biggest project sits on the lot next to her house: a partially completed two-story community kitchen, which she envisions serving not only the nutritional needs of the community but also its spiritual needs by providing meeting areas for drug and alcohol recovery groups.

The building would have been completed long ago, she acknowledges, if she had accepted government money. "But to do that, I would have to ask the people I feed questions about their work, etc. I won't do that."

As a result, the building has been five long years in the making. Currently, the shell is up and the walls are framed, but there is little progress beyond that. She's waiting, patiently, for the electrician who volunteers his time to complete the blueprints so that the city can approve them.

Thompson shies from being called a leader. "God is the leader," she asserts. "I just do what He tells me to." Rev. Martin Luther King Jr. exemplifies leadership for her. "He was humble. People tried to use him, but he kept on doing what he had to do," she says.

For her, that meant visiting the presidents of the local banks—not to ask for money, but to inform them of her plans. "I wouldn't see anyone else but the presidents. I had no fear," she says, smiling at the memory of marching into those executive offices and waiting for an appointment.

Her rewards for leading this effort against hunger? "I just enjoy seeing people happy. It makes me happy to see people eating good food." Her generosity is contagious. Often, people drop off food, saying they were returning the favor of eating there. "They know how it feels to be hungry and get a good meal," she says. "I feel real good to see them giving to someone else."

On a larger scale, her efforts have inspired several other food programs in the community. "I'm glad to see them popping up in other places, because the times are hard. And they're going to get harder before they get better," she says, noting that she meditates each day to find the guidance and energy to persist. Asked how she maintains her vigorous schedule, she admits to getting tired sometimes, especially after staying up the entire night to help prepare the community meal. "I just work it," she says with a shrug.

She maintains a confidence in people's willingness to help. "I just love that I don't have to call people to help. They just do it. That way, I don't feel like I'm making them do it. I feel if I leave it open, they'll do it for themselves, not to please me."

Her advice to younger people: "Search yourself. Let your mind tell you what to do."

The LPC Model: Least Preferred Coworker

Compared to the Path–Goal Model, which sees the leader as being able to change styles of behavior to suit the situation and the group, the **LPC model** is very precise and it assumes that leaders possess broad, general orientations that are unlikely to change. Fred Fiedler (1989) suggested that leaders behave with either a task orientation or a relationship orientation. He derived his model from analysis of scores on the LPC checklist shown in Exercise 9–2 at the end of this chapter.

The LPC checklist, while seeming to provide information about coworkers, actually says something about the leader. Categorized as either high or low LPC, leaders are grouped according to their motivation hierarchy.

Fiedler suggested that relationship-oriented leaders are most effective in situations that are moderately favorable and task-oriented leaders are most effective in situations that are either extremely favorable or extremely unfavorable (Figure 9–6).

Hughes, Ginnett, and Curphy (1993) draw some helpful corollaries with Maslow's hierarchy of needs. Just as Maslow postulated that lower-level needs must be met first, so high LPC leaders will emphasize task accomplishments after they have established favorable relationships with their followers. Similarly, low LPC leaders will proceed to relationship deepening only after they believe the task is being adequately addressed.

What about those leaders whose scores lie somewhere in the middle? Kennedy (1982) suggests that these people may be able to switch between orientations more easily than those scoring at either extreme.

Situation Favorability

Beyond leader orientation, Fiedler linked situational factors with leadership success. He equated situation favorability with the amount of control a leader held over collaborators. Within situation favorability, he further broke down the elements into the strongest variable, *leader-member relations;* the second most powerful variable, task structure; and the weakest element of the three, *position power.* (See Figure 9–6.)

	Very favorable				Intermediate			Very unfavorable
Leader–member relations	Good	Good	Good	Good	Poor	Poor	Poor	Poor
Task structure	High		Low		High		Low	
Leader position power	Strong	Weak	Strong	Weak	Strong	Weak	Strong	Weak
Situations	I	II	III	IV	V	VI	VII	VIII
	Best							Worst

Figure 9–6   Fiedler's Classification of Situation Favorableness
Source: Fred E. Fiedler, "The Effects of Leadership Training and Experience: A Contingency Model Interpretation," *Administrative Science Quarterly* 17 (1972), 455. Reprinted by permission of *Administrative Science Quarterly.*

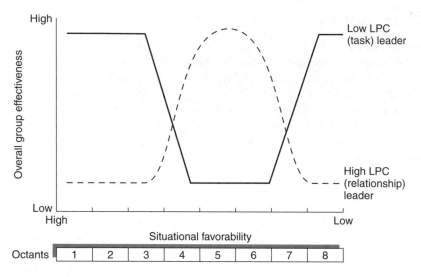

Figure 9–7   Leader Effectiveness Based on the Contingency Between Leader LPC Score and Situation Favorability

Source: From Richard L. Hughes, Robert C. Ginnett, and Gordon J. Curphy. *Leadership: Enhancing the Lessons of Experience,* 1996. Irwin, Inc. Used with permission.

He proposed that adding the relative weights of these three elements creates a continuum of situational favorability.

Leader–member relationship is assessed by the degree of cooperation and friendliness or antagonism and difficulty in the leader–collaborator relationship. A high number on this element indicates a generally positive relationship.

Task structure depends on the level of specificity about work products, processes, or objective work evaluations. Here, too, high numbers represent a high level of structure in the task. Position power, according to Fiedler, refers to the title, authority, or rank of the leader.

Using this continuum, you can see that the highest degree of situation favorability occurs when leaders and members enjoy a positive relationship, the task is structured, and the leader has legitimate authority. Conversely, the situation is least favorable when the leader and member have a poor relationship, the task is unstructured, and the leader has no position of power.

Fiedler has further refined his theory with research on which type of leader (high or low LPC) is more effective on different levels of situation favorability. As Table 9–2 shows, high LPC (relationship-oriented) leaders do best with moderate situational favorability. Task-oriented, or low LPC, leaders do best at the extremes.

Chart Summary: Fiedler's LPC Model

Centers on:

Situational variables that affect group performance (and by extension, leader's effectiveness).

Useful for:

Examining the orientation of the leader

DOCTORS WITHOUT BORDERS: HEALING HUMANITY

What has more than 4,000 legs and appears in the wake of natural and man-made disasters across the world?

The answer: Doctors Without Borders, an organization of more than 2,000 medical professionals who serve people in all manner of crises across the globe.

Begun in France in 1971, the organization offers health care to people who have no access otherwise. The members witness atrocities but take no sides in the political disputes that may have brought the disasters about.

Because they send representatives into trouble spots even before being asked, their presence has caused some diplomatic and political tension. But that hasn't kept them from showing up and helping out.

Typically, the group sends a team of people to an area to lay the groundwork for the actual medical care. This advance team asks refugees what kinds of medical care they need the most, then works with local authorities to set up more permanent solutions.

For its humanitarian work in such locales as Uganda, Kosovo, China, the Philippines, and Sri Lanka—80 locales at last count—Doctors Without Borders won the 1999 Nobel Peace Prize. "As entire families are chased from their homes in East Timor and as thousands more are targeted in conflicts around the world,...the Nobel Prize is an important confirmation of the fundamental right of ordinary people to humanitarian assistance and protection," said the group's spokesman, James Orbinski.

THE HERO'S JOURNEY—BY GORDON BARNHART

The heroic journey is the story of the change process in its healthiest form. The classic heroic journey begins with crossing a threshold, leaving a known world or comfort zone. After crossing that threshold, we face tests and trials that usually require new or altered ways of perceiving, thinking, and acting. As Alice found in *Alice in Wonderland,* things often aren't what they seem. What worked before is no longer effective, and can even be counterproductive or dangerous.

Many journeys are failures because we never really leave the known world. Because we never truly let go, we can never really discover the new truths and the revelations that are possible. Our trials may be physical, intellectual, emotional, or spiritual, and consequently, our changes may be in those

TABLE 9–2 Situational Leadership Applied to Eight Situations

Situation	Leader-Member Relations	Task Structure	Position Power	Most Effective Leadership	Reason(s) for Effectiveness
1. First-line supervisor at Ford Motor Company	Good	High	Strong	Task oriented	Employees respect task expertise, recognize power, and permit supervisor to lead.
2. Chairperson of college department	Good	High	Weak	Task oriented	Faculty member elected because she possesses group values. Understands what the group needs to do and pushes for task completion.
3. Sales manager at Procter & Gamble	Good	Low	Strong	Task oriented	Manager has formal authority and power, but salespeople work all over territory. They must have some autonomy because of unstructured nature of job.
4. Committee chairperson	Good	Low	Weak	About equally task and relationship oriented	Chair has little power and must rely on both types of leadership to accomplish job.

5. Middle-level manager at IBM	Poor	High	Strong	Relationship oriented	Manager is not well liked but has power to motivate. Can accomplish more if relationship approach is used.
6. Supervisor at General Mills	Poor	High	Weak	Relationship oriented	Employees know what they're supposed to accomplish. Is unpopular and has little say-so. More effective to use relationship style instead of creating more hostility.
7. Operating-room nurse supervisor at Massachusetts General Hospital	Poor	Low	Strong	Almost equally task and relationship oriented	Difficult to control unstructured activities through use of power. Because person is unpopular, it is best to use relationship orientation when appropriate and task orientation if necessary.
8. Detective in charge of other detectives working on a case in Washington, D.C.	Poor	Low	Weak	Task oriented	Detective has little power, is not well liked, and case is unstructured. Concentrate on solving the case.

Source: From J. Donnelly, J. Gibson, and J. Ivancevich, *Fundamentals of Management*, 9th edition, 1995. Irwin Professional. Used with permission.

same areas. We may face tests in dealing with mistakes and failures; avoiding the seductive lures of taking the easy way out; dealing with uncertainty, doubt, and perhaps despair; and finding sources of energy and renewal along the way.

Few, if any, of the heroes who do cross the threshold must face the trials and tests alone, even though the heroic journey is ultimately an individual one. Almost every journey features helpers of various sorts who can provide direction, tools, nourishment, encouragement, and coaching in coping in the new environment.

Healers will also be present to help overcome the inevitable injuries that befall us on our journeys. As the tests, the help and healing may take the form of physical, emotional, intellectual, or spiritual help. Although the roles of helpers and healers may vary, they will almost always be present in some form. Our challenge is to see them and use their help on the journey.

We may also find companions for part of the journey, just as we're likely to encounter other characters, including tricksters, jokers, allies, enemies, and opponents.

Those of us who successfully meet the challenges of the journey will arrive at the final phase, which is some form of return or completion. We "return" with the gifts that we have discovered, whether they are new truths, new abilities, new technologies, or new opportunities.

The return may be the most difficult part of all because a hero's return may evoke changes that the rest of the "kingdom" does not appreciate. The hero's changes will alter relationships, requiring changes in others that may ripple in many directions and for long distances. The gifts of the hero can easily threaten the status quo.

Sometimes heroes are welcomed and celebrated; sometimes they are ignored. Sometimes they are shunned, reviled, or attacked (even crucified). The reactions hold true in families, organizations, corporations, or communities—regardless of size.

We face major challenges in beginning the journey and crossing the threshold, traversing the unknown and facing the trials and tests found there, and in dealing with the impact of our return.

The hero's journey requires three forms of courage, each more challenging than it first appears:

The courage to see and speak the truth,

The courage to create and affirm a vision of the desired state, and

The courage to persevere, to "hold the course."

ROSA PARKS: A TIME TO SIT

Rosa McCauley Parks was 42 that afternoon in Montgomery, Alabama. The soft-spoken woman took the bus every day to her job as a seamstress. She fumed with the injustice and indignity of the bus company and its drivers. Once before, bus driver

James Blake had tested her spirit; he let her enter the front door to pay, but then insisted she follow the custom in which blacks then got off and reentered through the back door to claim a seat. This time, when she had paid and moved outside to the rear door, he pulled away before she could reenter. It was an insult that black people faced all the time in Montgomery.

On the next occasion, she was ready for Mr. Blake. He ordered her to leave her seat so a white person could sit, but Parks calmly said no. He insisted, in louder and louder terms. "No," came her reply, just as firmly. It wasn't simply that she was tired. Yes, she was weary from working, but she was more tired of the treatment she and her fellow blacks had to put up with.

What many people don't know is that Rosa Parks was sophisticated about her rights. For twelve years she had been secretary of the local NAACP, watching and learning as the group took on ever more ambitious goals. In addition, shortly before her famous act of resistance, she had participated in a training session at the High-lander School in Tennessee, where blacks and whites met to encourage each other and learn how to organize opposition to injustice. She was much more than a symbol of resistance and protest; but she was an awfully dignified symbol.

Throughout the 11-month bus boycott that Parks's resistance prompted, she and her husband endured hate calls, death threats, and eventually, the loss of both of their jobs before segregation in public transportation was struck down by the U.S. Supreme Court in 1956. The Parks moved to Detroit, where Rosa took care of her ailing mother and husband.

Rosa Parks has continued to be active in civil rights, resisting many people's attempts to see her only as a symbol and not as a woman with definite views and convictions. In addition to winning a seat on the board of the Detroit NAACP, she founded the Institute for Self Development, to encourage young people to work for change and to grow as people.

LEADERSHIP SKILLS FOR THE TWENTY-FIRST CENTURY

The effectiveness of training in changing leader behavior is questioned in Fiedler's model, as he asserted that a leader's task or relationship orientation was the product of years of experience and not amenable to swift change. He suggests, instead, reengineering the situations to fit the leader's dominant style. This approach has been called the Leader-Match training program.

Leadership skills needed:

Ability to analyze situation's favorability

Ability to identify personal leadership orientation

Most effective in:

A complex work setting involving many people

> ### Situational factors:
>
> Analyze the task: how complex or self-rewarding is it?
>
> Analyze the leader's style.
>
> Analyze the sophistication of the work group.
>
> ### Advantages:
>
> Fiedler's theory prompted an examination of the complexity of leadership factors, and served to introduce the situational approach to leadership.

Despite extensive laboratory and field research using Fiedler's model, the results are equivocal. Nevertheless, as Hughes et al. (1996) note, the fact that Fiedler's theories have prompted so much research speaks highly for the initial work. Fiedler has proceeded to answer some of the criticisms of his model, and he has also gone on to develop another situational model, the **Cognitive Resources theory.**

Cognitive Resources Theory

In this theory, Fiedler and his colleagues (Fiedler, 1986; Fiedler & Garcia, 1987) focus on the impact of the leader's intelligence and experience as these two cognitive traits affect group performance. Naturally, the theory is more complicated than that simple summary. The cognitive traits interact with leader behavior (directive, nondirective) and with elements of the situation (interpersonal stress and the nature of the group's task).

A fairly recent theory, the Cognitive Resources theory has not been as yet the subject of much research to validate its assumptions. Yukl (1995) points out methodological problems and weaknesses in the theory. The Cognitive Resources theory is useful, however, because it focuses on the ability of the leader and collaborator, a component that few other models explore.

According to Cognitive Resources theory, directiveness (giving specific instructions) is most effective when leaders are competent, relaxed, and supported. Because the group is prepared, a directive style is the clearest way to communicate with them. However, when leaders experience stress, experience becomes more important than ability. Low support means the group is less receptive and the leader will have lower effectiveness. A nondirective leader (who does not give specific instructions) with high group support makes group member ability more critical. Weak support, however, gives more power to variables outside the leader or the group members.

Multiple Linkage Theory

Yukl (1995) looked at the interaction of "managerial" behavior and situational factors on the performance of the manager's work group. He recognizes the importance of six intervening variables that are aspects of member motivation and ability.

These intervening variables interact singly or in combination with situational variables comparable to Kerr and Jermier's (1978) "substitutes" and "neutralizers." Yukl offers two major propositions for the **Multiple Linkage theory:**

1. In the short term, unit effectiveness is greater when the leader acts to correct any deficiencies in the intervening variables.

2. In the longer term, unit effectiveness is greater when the leader acts to make the situation more favorable. After extinguishing fires, in other words, leaders should focus on the situation rather than directly on the intervening variables.

Among the long-term actions he cites are

*   Cultivating better relationships with suppliers, finding alternative sources, and reducing dependence on unreliable sources
*   Undertaking long-term improvement programs to upgrade personnel, equipment, and facilities
*   Modifying the work unit's formal structure to solve chronic problems and reduce demands on the leader to perform troubleshooting (Yukl, 1994)

Life Cycle Model

In an interesting turnabout, Paul Hersey and Kenneth Blanchard (1969) envision that the effectiveness of leaders' styles depends largely on their collaborators' job experience and emotional maturity. This is the **Life Cycle model.** Maturity is defined as the ability to perform a job independently, the tendency to assume additional responsibility and the desire to achieve success.

Hersey and Blanchard outline four types of leader behaviors:

1. Telling (best for group members with low levels of maturity)
2. Selling (effective with members at moderately low maturity levels)
3. Participating (effective with moderately high levels of maturity)
4. Delegating (best with those at the very highest maturity levels)

The model posits two basic decision styles: task orientation and relationship orientation.

As group members become more "ready" (mature), leaders should change their behaviors to reflect this increased maturity. Increased maturity is defined as an increase in collaborator readiness and ability. As collaborators mature, leaders should begin to focus on supportive behavior and less on task behavior until followers reach the highest phase of maturity, a stage Hersey and Blanchard termed *high readiness*.

At this stage, followers have become skilled, confident, and self-sufficient. When followers reach this stage, the task of the leader is to delegate and thus serve as a low-task, low-relationship leader.

Leadership skills needed:

Ability to identify followers' maturity for specific tasks

Ability to diagnose demands of situations

Ability to choose the appropriate decision style to match task and follower requirements

The model has been well received by leadership practitioners, perhaps in part because it is intuitive and focuses on the followers' feelings of competence as well as on their behaviors.

Leader–Member Exchange (LMX) Model

The **Leader–Member Exchange model,** developed by George Graen (1975), operates on the premise that all subordinates are not treated equally. Because of a combination of time constraints and human nature, the model assumes that leaders tend to spend disproportionate amounts of time with a select group of subordinates who are, thus, the *in-group.* Those in the in-group tend to perform at a higher level than subordinates who fall in the *out-group.*

Graen says that early on in the relationship, a leader determines whether another person will be part of the in-group. Precise criteria for making this determination are unclear, but some suggest that the decision is affected by three characteristics of the subordinates/collaborators:

1. Characteristics similar to the leader's
2. A higher degree of competence than members of the out-group
3. Higher levels of extraversion than out-group members

Research on the LMX theory is still preliminary and questions exist about the ways in which leaders make the determinations of in- versus out-groups. What is clear, however, is that leaders invariably devote more time to certain employees and that the selection process is not a random one.

THREE ROLES OF THE LEADER

DR. STEPHEN R. COVEY

The leader of the future, of the next millennium, will be one who creates a culture or a value system centered upon principles. Creating such a culture in a business, government, school, hospital, nonprofit organization, family, or other organization will be a tremendous and exciting challenge in this new era and will only be achieved by leaders, be they emerging or seasoned, who have the vision, courage and humility to constantly learn and grow. Those people and organizations who have a passion for learning—learning through listening, seeing emerging trends, sensing and anticipating needs in the marketplace, evaluating past successes and mistakes, and absorbing the lessons that conscience and principles teach us, to mention just a few ways—will have enduring influence. Such learning leaders will not resist change; they will embrace it.

A White-Water World

The world has changed in a very profound way. This change continues to happen all around us, all the time. It is a white-water world. The consumer revolution has accelerated enormously. People are so much more enlightened and aware. There are so many more dynamic, competitive forces operating. The quality standards have raised to the point, particularly in the global marketplace, that there is simply no way to fake it. You may be able to survive in a local marketplace without meeting these standards, perhaps even in a regional marketplace, but certainly not in a global marketplace.

In all sectors—business, government, healthcare, social, nonprofit, etc.—the marketplace is demanding that organizations transform themselves. They must be able to produce services and goods and deliver them in a fast, friendly, and flexible way, and on a consistent basis that serves the needs of both internal and external customers. This requires a workforce that is not only allowed, but is enabled, encouraged, and rewarded by giving of its full creativity and talent. Even though tens of thousands of organizations are deeply involved in quality initiatives designed to produce those very results, transformation is still being demanded. The fundamental reason why most quality initiatives do not work is because there is a lack of trust in the culture—in the relationships between people. Just as you cannot fake world-class quality, so also is it impossible to fake high trust. It has to come out of trustworthiness.

I put more faith, however, in what the global economy is doing to drive quality than in any other factor. It is teaching us that principles such as empowerment, trust, and trustworthiness ultimately control the effective results we seek.

The most effective leaders are first *models* of what I call principle-centered leadership. They have come to realize that we're all subject to natural laws or governing principles, which operate regardless of our awareness of them or our obedience to them. Our effectiveness is predicated upon alignment with these inviolate principles—natural laws in the human dimension that are just as real, just as unchanging, as laws such as gravity are in the physical dimension. These principles are woven into the fabric of every civilized society and constitute the roots of every organization that has endured.

To the degree that we recognize and live in harmony with such basic principles as fairness, service, equity, justice, integrity, honesty, and trust, we move toward either survival and stability on the one hand or disintegration and destruction on the other. Principles are self-evident, self-validating natural laws. In fact, the best way to know they are self-evident is by trying to imagine a world, or for that matter, *any* effective, enduring society, organization or family based upon its opposite.

Correct principles are like compasses: they are always pointing the way. They don't change or shift, and if we know how to read them, we won't get lost, confused, or fooled by conflicting voices and values. They provide true north direction to our lives as we navigate the "streams" of our environments. Thus we see that a changeless, principle-centered core is the key to having the confidence, security, power, guidance, and wisdom to change the way we address the changing needs and opportunities around us.

So the first role of the leader is to be a model of principle-centered leadership. Whenever a person or an organization is principle-centered, that person or organization becomes a model—an example—to other people and organizations. It is that kind of modeling, that kind of character, competence, and action that produces the trust among the people, causing them to identify with this modeling and be influenced by it. Modeling, then, is a combination of character (who you are as a person) and competence (what you can do). These two qualities represent your potential. But when you actually *do* it—when you put action together with character—you've got modeling.

Three Roles of a Leader

What is it, then, that the principle-centered leader models? I suggest that you can break leadership into three basic functions or activities: pathfinding, aligning, empowering. Let's explore each one in turn.

Pathfinding   The essence and power of *pathfinding* are found in a compelling vision and mission. Pathfinding deals with the larger sense of the future. It gets the culture imbued and excited about a tremendous, transcendent purpose. But in relation to what?—to meeting the needs of your customers and other stakeholders. Pathfinding, then, ties together your value system and vision with the needs of customers and other stakeholders through a strategic plan. I call this the strategic pathway.

Aligning   The second activity of a leader is *aligning*. It consists of ensuring that your organizational structure, systems and operational processes all contribute to achieving your mission and vision of meeting the needs of customer and other stakeholders. They don't interfere with it, they don't compete with it, and they don't dominate it. They're only there for one purpose—to contribute to it. Far and away the greatest leverage of the principle of alignment comes when your people are in alignment with your mission, vision and strategy. When your people are filled with true understanding of the needs, when they share a powerful commitment to accomplishing the vision, when they are invited to create and continually improve the structures and systems that will meet the needs, then you have alignment. Without these human conditions, you cannot have world-class quality; all you have is brittle programs. Ultimately, we must learn that programs and systems are vital, but that *people* are the programmers.

Empowering   The third activity of a leader is *empowering*. What does that mean? People have enormous talent, ingenuity, intelligence, creativity. Most of it lies dormant. When you get true alignment toward a common vision, a common mission, you begin to co-mission with those people. Individual purpose and mission is commingled with the mission of the organization. When these purposes overlap, great synergy is created. A fire is ignited within people that unleashes their latent talent, ingenuity, and creativity to do whatever is necessary and consistent with the principles agreed upon to accomplish their common values, vision and mission in serving customers and other stakeholders. This is what we mean by empowerment.

But then you have to study what happens. What are the results? Are we really meeting the needs of the customers and the other stakeholders? Data and information that indicates whether the needs are truly being met must be fed back to these empowered people and teams inside the culture so that they can use it to make the necessary course corrections and improvements, and continue to do whatever it takes to fulfill the mission and to serve the needs.

A New Paradigm of Leadership

These roles of modeling principle-centered leadership—pathfinding, aligning, and empowering—represent a paradigm that is different in kind from traditional management thinking. There is a very significant difference between management and leadership. Both are vital functions, and because they are, it's critical to understand how they are different so one isn't mistaken for the other. Leadership focuses on doing the right things; management focuses on doing things right. Leadership makes sure the ladders we are climbing are leaning against the right wall; management makes sure we are climbing the ladders in the most efficient ways possible. Most managers and executives operate within existing paradigms or ways of thinking, but leaders have the courage to bring those paradigms to the surface, identify the underlying assumptions and motivations, and challenge them by asking, "Does this still hold water?"

For example:

- In healthcare, new leaders might challenge the assumption that medicine should focus upon the diagnosis and treatment of disease. Some medical schools today don't even teach nutrition, even though one-third of all cancers are nutrition-related and two-thirds of all diseases are tied to lifestyle. Still, the medical community heads down the path of diagnosis and treatment of disease. They claim that they deal with the whole package—the health and welfare of people—but they have a treatment paradigm. Fortunately, new leaders are creating more preventive-medicine alternatives.

- In law, new leaders might challenge the assumption that law is best practiced in courtrooms using confrontational, win-lose litigation. They might move toward the use of synergy and win-win thinking to prevent and settle disputes. Alternative dispute resolution usually results in compromise. New leaders will seek "win-win or no deal" options that lead to synergy. Synergy is more than cooperation; it's creating better solutions. It requires empathetic listening and courage in expressing one's views and opinions in ways that show respect for the other person's view. Out of genuine interaction come synergistic insights.

- In business, new leaders will challenge the assumption that "total customer satisfaction" represents the ultimate service ethic. They will move toward total stakeholder satisfaction, caring for everyone who has a stake in the success of the operation and making decisions that benefit all stakeholders. To bring about this new mindset, leaders must develop a new skill-set of synergy. Synergy comes naturally from the quality of the relationship—the friendship, trust, and love that unites people.

If you can put the new skill-set of synergy together with the new mind-set of interdependence, you have the perfect one-two punch for achieving competitive advantage. When you have the mind-set and the skill-set, you create effective structures, systems, and processes that are aligned with your vision and mission. Every organization is perfectly designed and aligned to get the results it gets. If you want different results, you need a new mind-set and a new skill-set to create synergistic solutions. Because we are so interdependent, it's only enlightened self-interest to keep all stakeholders in mind when making decisions.

Who Is the Leader of the Future?

In many cases, the leader of the future will be the same as the leader of the present. There will be no change in personnel, but rather an internal change: the person becomes the leader of the future by an inside-out transformation. What drives leaders to change, to become more centered on principles?

I think the main source of *personal* change is pain; this pain may come from disappointment, failure, death, troubled or broken relationships with family or friends, violated trust, personal weakness, discouragement, boredom, dissatisfaction, poor health, the consequences of poor decisions, loneliness, mediocrity, fear, financial stress, job insecurity, or life imbalance. If you aren't feeling pain, there is rarely enough motivation or humility to change. Most often there just isn't a felt need. Without personal pain, people tend to be too deeply invested in themselves and their world to rise above their own interests or the politics of running things, both at work and at home. When people are experiencing personal pain, they tend to be more open to a new model of living in which the common elements of humility and personal sacrifice lead to inside-out, principle-centered change.

The primary driving force of organizational change is the global economy. The standard of quality is now so high that unless you have an empowered work force and the spirit of partnership with all stakeholders, you can't compete, whether you work in the private sector, public sector, or social sector. When you're facing competitors who think more ecologically and interdependently, eventually the force of circumstances drives you to be humble. That's what is driving the quest for quality, learning, process re-engineering, and other initiatives. But many of these initiatives don't go far enough. The mindshift is not great enough. The interests of all stakeholders must be dealt with in an orchestrated way.

We either are forced by circumstance to be humble or can choose to be humble out of a recognition that principles ultimately govern. To be humble is good, regardless of the reason. But it's better to be humbled by conscience rather than by circumstance.

The Leader of the Future—A Family Within

The leader of the future has the humility to accept principles and the courage to align with them, which takes great personal sacrifice. Out of this humility, courage, and sacrifice comes the person of integrity. In fact, I like to think of this kind of leader as having an entire family within him or her: humility and courage the parents, and integrity the child.

Humility and Courage the Parents   Humility says, "I am not in control; principles ultimately govern and control." It understands that the key to long-term success is learning to align with the "true north" principles. That takes humility because the traditional mind-set is "I am in control; my destiny lies in my hands." This mind-set leads to arrogance—the sort of pride that comes before the fall.

Leaders of the future will have the courage to align with principles and go against the grain of old assumptions or paradigms. It takes tremendous courage and stamina to say, "I'm going to align my personal value system, my lifestyle, my direction, and my habits with timeless principles." Courage is the quality of every principle at its highest testing point. Every virtue is ultimately tested at the highest level. That's where courage comes into play. When you confront an old approach directly, you experience the fear of ripping out an old habit and replacing it with something new.

Integrity the Child   Out of the marriage of humility and courage is born the child of integrity. We all want to be known and remembered as men and women of integrity. Having integrity means integrating ourselves with principles. The leaders of the future must be men and women of integrity who internalize these principles. They grow in wisdom and cultivate an abundance mind-set—a sense that there are opportunities for all. If you have integrity, you are not caught up in a constant state of comparison with others. Nor do you feel the need to play political games, because your security comes from within. As soon as you change the source of your security, everything else flows from it. Your security, power, wisdom, and guidance increase, because you constantly draw upon the strength of these principles as you apply them.

A Final Note

We are becoming increasingly and painfully aware of the perilous weakening of our social structure. Drugs, gangs, illiteracy, poverty, crime, violence, breakdown of the familiy, these all continue in a downward spiral. Leaders of the present are beginning to recognize that such social problems put at risk *every* aspect of society. The leaders of the future realize that the solutions to these problems are far beyond the ability of the sectors that have traditionally been expected to deal with them— namely, the government and social sectors. My intent is not to criticize these sectors. In fact, I believe that they would be the first to admit that they are bound to fail without a broader network of helping hands.

The problem is that, on the whole, there has been a marked weakening of the sense of responsibilty that neighborhoods, communities, churches, families and individuals feel toward volunteering. It has become too easy to absolve ourselves from this responsiblity to our communities. I believe that is a family responsibility and that everyone should have a sense of stewardship about the community—every man, every woman, and every child. There should be some real sense of stewardship around service on the part of young people, particularly those who are at the most idealistic age, the late teens and early twenties.

The leader of the future will be a leader in every area of life, especially family life. The enormous needs and opportunities in society call for a greater responsibility toward service. There is no place where this spirit of service can be cultivated like the home. The spirit of the home, and also of the school, is that they prepare young people to go forth and serve. People are supposed to serve. Life is a mission, not a career. The whole spirit of this philosophy should pervade our society. I also think that it is a source of happiness, because you don't get happiness directly. It only comes as a by-product of service. You can get pleasure directly, but it is fleeting.

How, then, do we influence our children toward the spirit of service and meaningful contribution? First, we must look inward and ask, "Am I a model of this principle of service myself? Does my family see me dedicating my time and abilitites to serving them and the community?" Second, "Have I taken time to immerse myself and my family in the needs of others in order to create a sense of vision about how our family and each of us as individuals can make unique and meaningful contributions to meet those needs (pathfinding)?" Third, "Have I, as a leader in my home, aligned the priorities and structures of our life so that this desire to serve is supported, not undermined?" Finally, "Have I created conditions and opportunities in the home that will empower my children to serve? Do I encourage and support the development of their minds and talents? Do I organize service opportunities for the entire family and do all I can to create a fun environment around those activities?" Even if the answer to every one of these questions is "No," we all still have the capacity to decide what our lives will be about from today on.

This inherent capacity to choose, to develop a new vision for ourselves, to re-script our life, to begin a new habit or let go of an old one, to forgive someone, to apologize, to make a promise and then keep it, in any area of life, is, always has been, and always will be a moment of truth for every true leader.

© 1995 Covey Leadership Center. Used by permission.

SUMMARY

This chapter begins with a review of trait theories of leadership, featuring the work of such prominent leadership experts as John Gardner, Warren Bennis, James Kouzes, and Barry Posner. Behavioral theories are also addressed, beginning with the Ohio State and University of Michigan studies. A section on situational approaches includes reviews of Path–Goal theory, Continuum of Leader Behavior, Normative Decision model, Least Preferred Coworker theory, Cognitive Resources theory, Multiple Linkage theory, Life Cycle model, and Leader–Member Exchange model.

CREATE YOUR OWN THEORY

In this chapter you have been exposed to a broad range of major leadership theories, from trait to behavioral to situational. Did you find yourself nodding to yourself more when reading about a particular approach? If so, which approaches fit best with your own view on leadership? Can you imagine situations in which a behavioral approach would be most effective and other situations in which a situational perspective would be more effective?

Now let's revisit our opening Leadership Moment. What factors must leaders of large systems, such as school principals, consider when attempting to bring about change? What tack would you take were you in this principal's shoes and what are the strengths and pitfalls of such an approach?

KEY TERMS

Ohio State studies
University of Michigan studies
Leadership Grid
Path–Goal theory
Directive leadership
Supportive leadership
Participative leadership

Achievement-oriented leadership
LPC model
Cognitive Resources theory
Multiple Linkage theory
Life Cycle model
LMX model

QUESTIONS FOR DISCUSSION AND REVIEW

1. According to Gardner, what should be the primary aims and tasks of leaders?

2. What are some of the historical assumptions behind the characteristics of "great leaders"?

3. What were the primary similarities and differences between the University of Michigan studies and the Ohio State studies?

4. Select five leaders. Where would their leadership style fall on the Leadership Grid, and why?

5. In what situations do you feel a directive leadership style would be most appropriate? A supportive style? Participative style? Achievement-oriented style?

6. In which situations would a relationship-oriented leader be most effective? A task-oriented leader?

7. Of the numerous leadership theories proposed, which speaks to you most, and why?

8. How are the leadership theories in this chapter reflective of American culture? How might other cultures view these approaches?

9. Do you think that there are any universal attributes of leaders, or are leadership traits always culturally and/or situationally bound?

ONLINE SELF-ASSESSMENT TOOL

Are you more task oriented or people oriented? To see where you fall on Blake and Mouton's Leadership Grid, take their online quiz at: http://www.nwlink.com/~donclark/leader/bm_model.html.

EXERCISES

Exercise 9–1   Using Path–Goal Theory to Select a Leadership Strategy

Directions: Think of a group of which you are or have been a member. This can be a student organization (SGA, activities board, sorority/fraternity, etc.), a team (sports, debate, chess, etc.), an institution (church, Boy/Girl Scouts, college, etc.), or a workplace. Use what you have learned about Path–Goal theory to select an appropriate leadership style for that particular organization.

Name of group/organization:
Evaluating two sets of contingency factors—types of subordinates and types of work. Rate each factor by circling the appropriate indicator below.

Factor #1—*Locus of Control:*	In this organization, members feel like it is: High..........Medium..........Low
Factor #2—*Prediction of Positive Performance:*	In this organization, members think that they: Will Be May Be Probably Will Successful......Successful......Not Be Successful
Factor #3—*Members' Tasks:*	In this organization, they are: Repetitive......Combination......Nonrepetitive
Factor #4—*Authority Within the Organization:*	In this organization, the authority system is: Authoritarian........Mixed........Democratic
Factor #5—*Work Group:*	In this organization, there are: High Morale Low Morale and and Satisfying Unsatisfying Relationships...Mixed...Relationships

Based on your analysis of the organization's contingency factors, which of House's four leadership styles would be best suited? Circle the most appropriate leadership style.

Directive   Supportive   Participative   Achievement-Oriented

Answer Key

Using the key on page 199, how well did your analysis of the five contingency factors match the selection of the most appropriate leadership style?

Directive Style:

Factor #1—Low
Factor #2—Maybe → Probably Not
Factor #3—Ambiguous
Factor #4—Authoritarian
Factor #5—Low Morale

Supportive Style:

Factor #1—Low
Factor #2—Maybe → Probably Not
Factor #3—Combination
Factor #4—Mixed → Democratic
Factor #5—Low Morale

Participative Style:

Factor #1—Medium → High
Factor #2—Will Be Successful
Factor #3—Nonrepetitive
Factor #4—Mixed → Democratic
Factor #5—High Morale

Achievement-Oriented Style:

Factor #1—High
Factor #2—Will Be Successful
Factor #3—Nonrepetitive
Factor #4—Mixed → Democratic
Factor #5—Mixed → High Morale

Exercise 9–2 Using Fiedler's Contingency Theory: Analyzing a Company or Organization

The purpose of this exercise is to utilize Fiedler's contingency theory in order to analyze the match between a particular leader in a specific situation.

Step One: Select a business, company, or organization with which you are familiar. Name of Organization:

Step Two: Use the Least Preferred Coworker (LPC) scale to measure whether the leader is task motivated or relationship motivated. Ask the leader to fill out the LPC assessment as shown on the following page.

The Least Preferred Coworker (LPC) Scale for Measuring Leadership Style

Throughout your life you will have worked in many groups with a wide variety of people—on your job, in social groups, in church organizations, in volunteer groups, on athletic teams, and in many other situations. Some of your coworkers may have been very easy to work with in attaining the group's goals, while others were less so.

Think of all the people with whom you have ever worked, and then think of the person with whom you could work *least well.* He or she may be someone with whom you work now or with whom you have worked in the past. This does not have to be the person you liked least well, but should be the person with whom you had the most difficulty getting a job done; the one individual with whom you could work least well.

Describe this person on the scale that follows by placing an "X" in the appropriate space. Look at the words at both ends of the line before you mark your "X." *There are no right or wrong answers.* Work rapidly: your first answer is likely to be the best. Do not omit any items, and mark each item only once.

Now describe the person with whom you can work least well.

Scoring

	8	7	6	5	4	3	2	1		
Pleasant	_	_	_	_	_	_	_	_	Unpleasant	_
Friendly	_	_	_	_	_	_	_	_	Unfriendly	_
	1	2	3	4	5	6	7	8		
Rejecting	_	_	_	_	_	_	_	_	Accepting	_
Tense	_	_	_	_	_	_	_	_	Relaxed	_
Distant	_	_	_	_	_	_	_	_	Close	_
Cold	_	_	_	_	_	_	_	_	Warm	_
	8	7	6	5	4	3	2	1		
Supportive	_	_	_	_	_	_	_	_	Hostile	_
	1	2	3	4	5	6	7	8		
Boring	_	_	_	_	_	_	_	_	Interesting	_
Quarrelsome	_	_	_	_	_	_	_	_	Harmonious	_
Gloomy	_	_	_	_	_	_	_	_	Cheerful	_
	8	7	6	5	4	3	2	1		
Open	_	_	_	_	_	_	_	_	Guarded	_
	1	2	3	4	5	6	7	8		
Backbiting	_	_	_	_	_	_	_	_	Loyal	_
Untrustworthy	_	_	_	_	_	_	_	_	Trustworthy	_
	8	7	6	5	4	3	2	1		
Considerate	_	_	_	_	_	_	_	_	Inconsiderate	_
	1	2	3	4	5	6	7	8		
Nasty	_	_	_	_	_	_	_	_	Nice	_
	8	7	6	5	4	3	2	1		
Agreeable	_	_	_	_	_	_	_	_	Disagreeable	_
	1	2	3	4	5	6	7	8		
Insincere	_	_	_	_	_	_	_	_	Sincere	_
	8	7	6	5	4	3	2	1		
Kind	_	_	_	_	_	_	_	_	Unkind	_
									Total	_

Scoring and Interpretation: To calculate your score, add the numbers in the right column; write the total at the bottom of the page. If you scored 64 or higher, you are a high LPC leader, meaning that you are relations motivated. If you scored 57 or lower, you are a low LPC leader, meaning that you are task motivated. A score of 58 to 63 places you in the intermediate range, making you a socioindependent leader.

Source: Adapted from Fred E. Fiedler, Martin M. Chemers, and Linda Mahar, *Improving Leadership Effectiveness*, p. 7. Copyright © 1976. Reprinted by permission of John Wiley & Sons, Inc.

Step Three: Based on what you know about the company or organization (you may need to visit several times to observe or interview members of the organization in order to answer the questions in this step of the analysis accurately), circle the appropriate number next to each question. Once completed, total the scores in each section.

ANALYZING THE SITUATION

A. *Designated Leader–Member Relations*	*Poor*				*Good*
1. There is a friendly atmosphere.	1	2	3	4	5
2. There is a fair amount of good-humored joking between the leader and members.	1	2	3	4	5
3. Conversation between the leader and group members is easy and relaxed.	1	2	3	4	5
4. Members feel as if the leader is interested in them as individuals.	1	2	3	4	5
5. Members feel as if the leader is open and accessible.	1	2	3	4	5
6. The leader believes that he or she has a good relationship with members	1	2	3	4	5

B. *Task Structure*	*Low*				*High*
1. There are written company/organization policies.	1	2	3	4	5
2. There are written job descriptions for all positions.	1	2	3	4	5
3. Annual goal-setting is routinely done.	1	2	3	4	5
4. There is a formal evaluation procedure.	1	2	3	4	5
5. Routine functions are performed in a fairly standard manner throughout the organization.	1	2	3	4	5
6. Members are clear about what is expected from them.	1	2	3	4	5

C. *Position Power*	*Weak*				*Strong*
1. The leader has the authority to make hiring decisions.	1	2	3	4	5
2. The leader can promote or significantly affect member promotions.	1	2	3	4	5
3. The leader evaluates member performance.	1	2	3	4	5
4. The leader is expected to discipline problem behaviors.	1	2	3	4	5
5. The leader can fire or significantly affect an employee's termination.	1	2	3	4	5
6. The leader can affect employee salary increases.	1	2	3	4	5

Answer Key

A score of 18 or above in each of the sections (Leader–Member Relations, Task Structure, and Position Power) equates to:

Good leader–member relations
High task structure
Strong position power

CHAPTER 10

Leadership in the Twenty-First Century

LEADERSHIP MOMENT

You have recently been elected to your first term on the local school board. Over the past several years, discontent has been growing about the students' declining test scores. This has been a concern of yours as well, since two of your children attend schools where there has been a particularly sharp decline. Although most schools within the district have been experiencing difficulty, one school, Smith Elementary, in the most affluent section of town, has been thriving. Not only are test scores on the rise at Smith, but, not coincidentally, each year this school is granted a larger portion of the overall budget and parents compete to have their children placed at Smith. Morale has plummeted at the other district schools, whose staff members feel that they are being asked to do more with less money and fewer staff.

The State Board of Education has threatened to dramatically reduce funding unless your district's overall test scores rise. In response, a proposal has been made that all students must take math and reading exams at the end of each year before advancing to the next grade. Widely supported, the proposal is being hailed by other school board members as the solution to the declining test score issue. You are not so sure that this is the case. At this week's board meeting you must take a position on this issue.

1. *What would you do?*
2. *What factors will play a role in your decision?*

In the midst of the heyday of the industrial approach to leadership, the seeds of a new paradigm of leadership were being planted. Several scholars broke with mainstream thinking about leadership and began to describe it in radically different ways. As we saw in previous chapters, the industrial view of leadership:

- Saw leadership as the property of an individual
- Considered leadership primarily in the context of formal groups or organizations
- Equated concepts of management and leadership

However, the reality of leadership as experienced by many did not always fit these circumstances. Leadership occurred outside of formal organizations and was sometimes practiced by those other than designated leaders. As Kuhn (1970) taught us, no paradigm can explain all of the facts of a particular phenomenon. Several authors began to explore the aspects of leadership not captured in the old story of leadership. Their ideas served as a bridge from the industrial to the postindustrial perspectives of leadership (Figure 10–1). We turn now to three of these transition theories to examine their assumptions about leadership.

THE GENESIS OF A NEW PARADIGM: SERVANT LEADERSHIP

In his work *The Leader as Servant* (1970), Robert Greenleaf (see Appendix II for a summary of Greenleaf's *The Power of Servant Leadership*, 1998) made a radical departure from the industrial paradigm of the leader as an all-knowing, all-powerful hero. Instead, he proposed that "the great leader is seen as servant first" (p. 2). Greenleaf's conclusion was based on the changes he saw emerging in U.S. society at the time, namely, the questioning of power and authority and the emergence of cooperation and support as more productive ways for people to relate to one another. Greenleaf explains:

> A new moral principle is emerging which holds that the only authority deserving one's allegiance is that which is freely and knowingly granted by the led to the leader in response to, and in proportion to, the clearly evident servant stature of the leader. Those who choose to follow this principle will not casually accept the authority of existing institutions. Rather, they will freely respond only to individuals who are chosen as leaders because they are proven and trusted as servants. To the extent that this principle prevails in the future, the only truly viable institutions will be those that are predominantly servant-led. (p. 4)

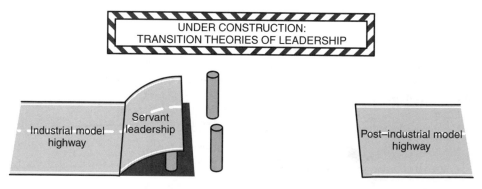

Figure 10–1   Under Construction: Transition Theories of Leadership

Greenleaf (1970) fleshed out this notion of **servant leadership** by stressing that the servant leader is servant first. The servant leader takes care to ensure that other people's greatest needs are being met and that those people, while being served by the leader, "become healthier, wiser, freer, more autonomous, more likely themselves to become servants" (p. 7). According to Greenleaf, servant leaders:

- Listen first so they may understand a situation
- Develop their intuition and the ability to "foresee the unforeseeable" (p. 14)
- Lead by persuasion, forging change by "convincement rather than coercion" (p. 21)
- Conceptualize the reforms they seek and lift others to see the possibilities also
- Empower by creating opportunities and alternatives for those being served

Servant leaders possess the self-awareness to recognize that their own healing is the motivation for leadership. They also grasp that the connection between the servant leader and the led is "the understanding that the search for wholeness is something they share." And finally, as a change agent, the servant leader recognizes that the first step to changing the world is changing oneself

The image of servant leader contrasts with the industrial paradigm of the leader as a power wielding authority figure. Here we see the leader as one whose first responsibility is to consider the needs of others and to create conditions where the led can become leaders themselves. To illustrate the idea of the leader as servant, Greenleaf tells the story of John Woolman, an American Quaker who almost single-handedly rid the Society of Friends (Quakers) of slaves. What Greenleaf particularly remarks on is the method that Woolman used to bring about this change—gentle, yet clear and persistent persuasion. Greenleaf elaborates:

> Although John Woolman was not a strong man physically, he accomplished his mission by journeys up and down the East Coast by foot or horseback visiting slaveholders— over a period of many years. The approach was not to censure the slaveholders in a way that drew their animosity. Rather, the burden of his approach was to raise questions: What does the owning of slaves do to you as a moral person? What kind of an institution are you binding over to your children? Man by man, inch by inch, by persistently returning and revisiting and pressing his gentle argument over a period of thirty years, the scourge of slavery was eliminated from this Society, the first religious group in America formally to denounce and forbid slavery among its members. (p. 21)

John Woolman was a man with a personal conviction that led him to seek change in his organization. He achieved his objective through what Greenleaf calls convincement rather than coercion. In the process, he made his Quaker brothers and sisters leaders in their own right. This is the essence of servant leadership.

In today's world, a well-known example of servant leadership is Mother Teresa. During her lifetime, she achieved leadership status through serving and advocating for the poor in India and across the world.

MOTHER TERESA: SAINT OF THE GUTTERS

Mother Teresa was immersed in projects for helping the poor of India and of all of the world until her death in 1997 at age 87. Through her service to the ill and destitute, she proclaimed her message that the poor must be loved because a loving God created them.

As founder of the Missionaries of Charity, Mother Teresa started rescuing the poor people who were literally dying in the streets of Calcutta. Writer Dominique LaPierre remembers first seeing her washing the wounds of a dying man . . .

So emaciated that he looked like a living skeleton. His flesh seemed to have melted down, leaving only skin over his bones.

Mother Teresa was gently speaking to him in Bengali. I will never forget the eyes of this wretched, dying man. His suffering, staring look progressively changed to an expression of surprise, and then, of peace, the peace of someone who suddenly feels he is loved.

Sensing my presence behind her, the nun turned around. I suddenly felt terribly awkward to have interrupted a dialogue which I could feel was unique. I introduced myself.

Mother Teresa called a young European volunteer who was passing by with a wash-basin in his hands.

"Love him," she told him, "Love him with all your strength."

She . . . invited me to follow her toward the small waiting room that separated the men's and women's wards.

There was a table and a bench, and on the wall a poster which said: "The worst misery is not hunger, not leprosy, but the feeling to be unwanted, rejected, abandoned by everyone."

These words summarize the universality of Mother Teresa's work.

Detractors who accuse her of not providing any real medical treatment to the destitute people who are brought to her homes, and whom she is the only one to rescue, should know that half of them are able to leave her "dying homes" on their feet after a few days, having regained dignity and enough strength, thanks to the loving care received.

Mother Teresa believed that the poor are not just the millions who are starving, but also the millions of excluded, lonely, untouchable, or homeless people. These people most needed the human touch of things like love, justice, hope, and dignity.

She said, "The most terrible disease that can ever strike a human being is to have no one near him to be loved. Without a heart full of love, without generous hands, it is impossible to cure a man suffering of loneliness."

She told reporters in England: "I have walked at night in your streets. I have entered your homes. I have found in them more poverty than in India. I have found the poverty of the soul, the lack of love."

LaPierre said,

Each time I return with my wife to Calcutta to visit the dispensaries and the schools I support with the royalties from my book, *The City of Joy,* we never fail to attend

Mother Teresa's 5:45 A.M. Mass in her convent headquarters, set in the very heart of the teeming megalopolis.

As sole decoration on the walls of the large room that serves as a chapel in the daytime and as a dormitory for the novices at night, there is a simple crucifix with the inscription that says, "I thirst."

... What an emotion to rediscover around her all these dark-skinned Indian novices who tomorrow will join their Japanese, European, Australian and American sisters in some 500 orphanages, leprosy homes and rescue centers in more than 100 countries on the five continents.

The order of the Missionaries of Charity cannot accept all the postulants knocking at the door of its novitiates: today it has more than 5,000 sisters, 500 consecrated brothers and more than 4 million lay co-workers.

In 1979, she won the Nobel Peace Prize. Some complain that Mother Teresa could use her charisma and fame to attack the roots of poverty, but she said: "Fortunately there are in this world people who fight for justice and human rights, who struggle to change the structures. The daily contact of our sisters is with people who do not even have a scrap of bread to feed themselves.

"Our mission is to consider the problem on an individual rather than a collective basis. Our concern is for one person, not a multitude. We are looking for the human being with whom Christ identified himself when he said, 'I was hungry and you fed me.'"

LaPierre said,

If this uncommon woman has succeeded in developing so quickly in the whole world the congregation she founded in 1950, it is thanks to an exceptional reunion of gifts and remarkable qualities, among them a faith to lift mountains and a leadership that may sometimes appear tyrannical, an indomitable will to rely for everything only on divine Providence, an exceptional charisma which has conquered the public as well as the media and those who govern the world, an innate gift for organization and a rare capacity to adapt to all situations and face all problems.

For sure, so many qualities represent many handicaps to surmount for the woman who will succeed her. Let's hope the day will come as late as possible and let's quell our fears for the future.

As Mother Teresa has so often said: "The work is not mine but God's. I am only a small pencil in His hand."

From Dominique LaPierre, "Mother Teresa Is Still Offering a Hand at 84," *The Cleveland Plain Dealer*, Dec. 19, 1994.

TRANSFORMATIONAL LEADERSHIP

James MacGregor Burns extended the debate about what comprises leadership by conceptualizing it as occurring in two forms, transactional and transformational. He arrived at this conclusion through analysis of the leadership functions of such political figures as Mahatma Gandhi, Franklin Roosevelt (profiled in Chapter 6 on political science), and Mao Tse-tung (profiled in Chapter 7 on military science). In prefacing his work, Burns (1999) noted that the concept of leadership in this century had "dissolved into small and discrete meanings" (p. 2). In seeking to generalize about the leadership process across time and cultures, he wanted to establish a school of leadership where none existed. In addition, Burns also desired to unite the previously unconnected roles of leader and follower. These, then, became the foundational assumptions that underscored his perspectives of leadership (Figure 10–2).

According to Burns, **transactional leadership** is a barter, an exchange of wants between leader and follower. The transactional leader satisfies followers' needs by entering into a relationship of mutual dependence in which the contributions of both sides are recognized and rewarded. The transactional leader helps followers achieve their goals; thus, we follow the transactional leader because it is obvious to us that it is in our own best interests to do so (Kellerman, 1983). The image of leadership as transaction has assumptions in common with the industrial paradigm of leadership.

Transformational leadership, by contrast, goes beyond the notion of exchange. Burns (1979) proposed that transformational leadership includes two essential elements—it is relational, and it deals with producing real change. He explains: "Transformational leadership occurs when one or more persons engage with others in such a way that leaders and followers raise one another to higher levels of motivation and morality" (p. 20). This approach is a commingling of their needs and aspirations and goals in a common enterprise. The purpose of this engagement with followers, Burns tells us, is to bring about change; in fact, in his estimation, the ultimate test of practical leadership is the realization of intended, actual change in people's lives, attitudes, behaviors, and in their institutions. Transformational leadership has a moral dimension as well, because those engaged in it "can be lifted into their better selves" (p. 462). This articulation of the moral dimension sharply distinguishes transformational leadership from the views of leadership promoted by management scientists.

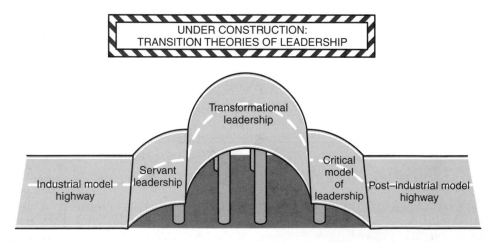

Figure 10–2   Under Construction: Transition Theories of Leadership

Mahatma Gandhi, in particular, epitomized Burns's ideal of the transformational leader. Gandhi's leadership was *causative* in that the nonviolent and egalitarian values he espoused changed people and institutions in India. His leadership was *morally purposeful,* because his objective was to win individual liberty for his countrymen and women by freeing them from the oppression of British rule. His leadership was *elevating* in that he raised his followers to higher moral ground by engaging them in nonviolent activities to achieve social justice. In so doing, Gandhi asked for sacrifices from his followers rather than merely promising them goods and favors.

Burns's seminal work enlightened us to see that leadership is about transformation. It is a relationship between leaders and followers in which both are elevated to more principled levels of judgment. It is about leaders and followers engaged in a change process. It is about power "to" rather than power "over." Burns and Greenleaf's ideas began to transform our notions of leadership.

RACHEL CARSON: WRITER, SCIENTIST, CRUSADER

When Rachel Carson journeyed to a summer job at Woods Hole Oceanographic Institute in Cape Cod, it was the first time she had even seen the ocean. The sea had captivated her interest for years, however, even as a young girl on a farm north of Pittsburgh. She had studied diligently enough to win a scholarship in marine zoology at Johns Hopkins University in Baltimore. She earned her M.S. in 1932.

She was repeatedly warned to pursue some other field: women did not become scientists in the first half of the twentieth century. And if they insisted on getting their degrees, there would be no jobs for them. Nevertheless, Carson persisted, fueled in part by her overwhelming passion for the natural world and by her mother's support. She later recounted how much it meant to her when FDR appointed the first woman in the history of the United States to a cabinet position. (Frances Perkins became FDR's secretary of labor.) To top it off, Eleanor Roosevelt was becoming a national figure.

She found a job that combined her loves of language and science through writing scripts for the weekly radio show "Romance Under the Waters." The sea became her touchstone as she began to explain in graceful, nontechnical terms much of what scientists knew about the ocean and its life.

Carson went on to write several books about the natural world, including *The Sea Around Us*, *Under the Sea Wind*, and *The Edge of the Sea*. In between caring for her mother and raising children of relatives who had died, she wrote a moving book, *A Sense of Wonder,* to help young people appreciate the natural world.

A much-awarded and highly praised writer, she retired to her cottage off the coast of Maine. She could easily have lived a contented life producing more of the same type of writings. However, she took a gamble and began to research not the beauties of nature, but the spoilers of nature. Her landmark 1962 book, *Silent Spring,* charged that rampant use of pesticides was devastating the environment, killing birds and other animals, and potentially affecting humans as well. Further, she charged that government scientists had known of the damage from the chemicals but had been prevented from speaking out.

Ironically, shortly before the book was published, she was diagnosed with breast cancer. At the time scientists were just beginning to uncover links between environmental influences and diseases such as cancer.

It's hard to appreciate the commotion the publication of *Silent Spring* unleashed. Many scientific associations, including the American Medical Association, attacked the book, and much of the media went after Carson personally. *Time* magazine called the book "an emotional and inaccurate outburst." The chemical industry spent large sums of money ridiculing her arguments in print. Some suggested she was a communist.

Upset at the unfairness of these attacks, the normally shy woman agreed to a nationally televised interview with Eric Sevareid on CBS on April 3, 1963. Her soft-spoken, articulate remarks convinced millions of viewers and swung public opinion to her side. Legislation passed the next year that tightened requirements for chemical companies.

More significantly, however, Rachel Carson had helped people understand the ramifications of tampering with the environment. As her comments on television showed, she was able to convey the bigger picture: "We still talk in terms of conquest. We still haven't become mature enough to think of ourselves as only a tiny part of a vast and incredible universe. Man's attitude toward nature is today critically important simply because we have now acquired a fateful power to alter and destroy nature. But man is a part of nature, and his war against nature is inevitably a war against himself."

She won many honors and awards for her efforts. Upon receiving the Audubon Medal (the first woman to be so honored), she asserted that "Conservation is a cause that has no end. There is no point at which we will say 'our work is finished.'"

Carson succumbed to cancer just over one year after her remarkable television appearance. She had become well known and greatly admired for her courage and dedication. She acknowledged her real reward, however, in this passage written shortly before her death: "It is good to know that I shall live on even in the minds of many who do not know me and largely through association with things that are beautiful and lovely."

A CRITICAL MODEL OF LEADERSHIP

William Foster (1986) and other critical theorists (e.g., Smyth, 1989) honed in on the concept of leadership as transformation by examining the content of the change that the leadership process might produce. They specified that leadership should address social reconstruction: "Leadership is and must be socially critical, it does not reside in an individual but in the relationship between individuals, and it is oriented towards social vision and change, not simply, or only, organizational goals" (p. 46).

Transformational leaders and followers may be mutually pursuing a vision of greatness, but the critical question becomes "whose vision is it?" In the critical perspective, for transformational leadership to actually transform, it must prompt those engaged in the process to question the assumptions on which their vision is based.

Thus, **critical transformational leadership** requires reflection and analysis: it asks on whose behalf we use our power and makes a place for all voices and arguments to be heard regardless of race, class, and gender (Quantz, Rogers & Dantley, 1991). The critical model of leadership focuses on changing the human condition, and as such, its type of leadership can spring from anywhere. It is not confined to the organizational hierarchy. In this view, leadership is a political and courageous act to empower followers to become leaders themselves.

And finally, Foster (1989) asserts that critical transformational leadership is not "a special or unique occurrence, one that is found only in certain grand moments of human history. Rather, it happens in everyday events, when commonplace leaders exert some effect on their situations" (p. 52).

A good example of leadership from the critical perspective is the work of Brazilian educator Paulo Freire. Rejecting the standard educational pedagogy that helped maintain the social systems oppressing Brazilian peasants, he developed teaching methods he called "liberation education." First Freire taught the peasants to critique the system that kept them in economic slavery and then he taught them about the possibility of reforming that system so their voices would be heard and their needs recognized equally with the wealthier citizens in the society (Freire, 1970). His leadership empowered his followers to initiate change on their own behalf.

LEADERSHIP SKILLS FOR THE TWENTY-FIRST CENTURY

Several common themes emerge from an analysis of this chapter's three perspectives on leadership (servant, transformational, and critical models).

1. Leadership is a relationship, as opposed to the property of an individual.

It is conducted with leaders and followers, and followers are essential parts of the equation. The role of the leader is to serve followers and to empower them to become leaders themselves.

2. Leadership entails change.

Both leaders and followers experience change, originating within themselves and then emanating outward to the community. Leadership requires critical reflection and analysis in order to determine whether the vision of change being pursued is inclusive or whether it excludes or diminishes some members of the community.

3. Leadership can be done by anyone, not only those who are designated as leaders.

Alternative perspectives on leadership gained credence because they more fully captured some aspects of our experience with leadership than did the conventional view. Because the alternative perspectives raised questions that could not be addressed by the industrial paradigm of leadership, they prompted the search for a new paradigm of leadership for the twenty-first century.

THE POSTINDUSTRIAL PARADIGM OF LEADERSHIP

In his 1991 book, *Leadership for the Twenty-First Century,* Joseph Rost offered a new definition of leadership that he quite boldly proclaimed as the postindustrial paradigm of leadership. One does not pronounce a new paradigm without substantial evidence of its need. And so it was with Rost. He built a convincing argument for why the industrial paradigm of leadership is no longer adequate to explain both the realities of leadership we experience and the kind of leadership we need in a twenty-first century world.

What are the realities that prompt us to establish a new paradigm of leadership? U.S. culture is in the midst of a major shift in the ways that we make sense of our world. The globalization of the economy, the rapid and continual change resulting from new technologies, the information explosion, and the increasing diversity of our population create a reality that is messy and ambiguous rather than orderly and predictable (Rogers & Ballard, 1995). As a result, we are moving away from a **mechanistic world view** in which objectivity, control, and linear causality are supreme to a **relational approach,** a world view that recognizes the more contextual, holistic, complex, and relational aspects of the natural world in which we function (Zohar, 1997; Wheatley, 1992; Kuh, Whitt & Shedd, 1987).

Among the consequences of the shift from a mechanistic worldview are the changes in organizational structures and cultures that have been the hallmark of the past 15 years (Rogers & Ballard, 1995; Peters, 1992). Table 10–1 contrasts the culture of the bureaucratic/mechanistic forms of organization with emerging ad hoc models of organization. The latter are rapidly gaining credibility because they more effectively respond to the kind of environmental turbulence that marks our current reality.

TABLE 10–1   **Organizational Culture Transformations**

Old Culture (disappearing bureaucracy)	New Culture (emerging adhocracy)
hierarchy, specialization	transient units
division of labor	reorganization
slow to change	fast moving
roles sharply defined	roles flexible and temporary
chain of command	fluid, participative roles and structures
self-interested outlook	social responsibility is central to success
stable, predictable environment	accelerating change and need for innovation
vertical power	horizontal power, relationships
communication slow, only as needed	communication fast and lateral
simple problem solving	complex problem solving
staff/line distinctions	team approach
emphasis on efficiency	emphasis on people

Source: Adapted from P. Harris. Innovating with high achievers. *Training & Development Journal,* 34, 10 (1980), 45–50.

Recent research and practice suggest that conventional models of organization are not as suited to understanding events and actions in uncertain, dynamic times; thus, organizations are transforming themselves in order to better respond to change. A key activity of the modern organization is to continuously learn and to master new knowledge in order to innovate, solve problems, and maintain productivity. The quality movement of the 1980s and 1990s is a manifestation of the move away from machine-like forms of organization and management to more team-centered, collaborative approaches.

In a similar vein, Rost (1991) debunks the industrial paradigm of leadership because of its grounding in a mechanistic world view. He argues that the industrial paradigm of leadership is industrial because it takes a bureaucratic view of organizations; it has an individualistic focus because it asserts that only great leaders practice leadership; it is dominated by a goal achievement sense of purpose; it promotes a self-interested outlook on life; it accepts a male model of behavior and power (known as leadership style); it articulates utilitarian and materialistic ethical perspectives; it is grounded in rational, linear, and quantitative assumptions about how the world works, and it asserts a managerial perspective as to what makes organizations tick. Although these characteristics may have been appropriate for a world that was more stable, they are not as relevant in a time of rapid change. In the context of our increasingly complex and ambiguous world, Rost extends the work of Burns, Greenleaf, and Foster and offers a postindustrial paradigm of leadership for our consideration.

Rost's definition—"Leadership is an influence relationship among leaders and their collaborators who intend **real changes** that reflect their mutual purposes" (1991, p. 7)—includes four essential elements of leadership.

1. *The relationship is based on influence rather than positional authority.*
   Noncoercive persuasion is used to influence people in the leadership relationship. The influence is multidirectional, coming from all members, rather than only top down. People are free to agree or disagree and to choose to stay in or leave the relationship.

2. *Leaders and their collaborators practice leadership.*
   The word *collaborators* instead of followers is favored because it more closely fits the values of this perspective. The interactions of leaders and their collaborators comprise the essence of leadership, not the individual behaviors of the leader. In a leadership relationship, collaborators are active rather than passive. Leaders are those who at a particular moment commit more of their resources (i.e., their expertise, their passion, their political savvy) to influence the process.

3. *Collaborators and their leaders intend real change.*
   Rost notes that "*Intend* means that the leaders and their collaborators do not have to produce changes to practice leadership, only intend them and then act on that intention" (p. 7). Thus, the very act of initiating a change movement marks the time when leadership occurs, in contrast to the industrial paradigm that leadership happens when any goal has been achieved. *Real* connotes that

the changes are substantive attempts to transform people's attitudes, behaviors, and values.

4. ***The changes that the leaders and their collaborators pursue reflect their mutual purposes.***
   The changes represent what *both* leaders and collaborators desire in a shared enterprise, rather than merely accomplishing the wishes of the leader.

Several important implications are embedded in this definition of leadership. Collaborators choose the leaders with whom they wish to affiliate, and they may or may not be people who hold authority over them. Thus, leadership is not confined to those in power in the organizational hierarchy. Leaders and collaborators often change places in the ebb and flow of the leadership process. A number of leadership relationships may be present in any organization, and the leaders in one relationship may be collaborators in another.

Leadership is episodic, a stream of activities that occur when people intend a specific and real change for their organization or group. One is not a leader all of the time, but rather, when one chooses to exert the most influence on the change process. Rost (1991) elaborates: "Leadership is people bonding together to institute a change in a group, organization, or society. Leadership is a group of activists who want to implement a reformist agenda. Leadership is a band of leaders and collaborators who envision a better future and go after it" (p. 6).

When first introduced to Rost's conceptualization of postindustrial leadership, we may find it difficult to get a fix on just what it entails. Conditioned by our industrial paradigm lenses to view leadership in a particular way, much like the blind men and the elephant in the Indian tale, we have difficulty seeing beyond our own narrow perspective. In particular, we have been so enmeshed in viewing leadership and management as one and the same that untangling these concepts becomes difficult. Similarly, we have problems conceiving of leadership as not grounded in positional authority, hence not naturally accruing to those managers at the top levels of the hierarchy. Yet in order to separate leadership from management, these distinctions are important.

Rost's work challenges us to clearly distinguish between these two concepts. In the industrial paradigm, leadership has been understood as good management, even though it was implied that a manager was somehow less effective than a leader. The industrial paradigm confers much more desirability to being considered a leader than a manager, a perspective captured in the oft-quoted words of Bennis and Nanus (1985): "Managers do things right; leaders do the right thing." While managers are pedestrian, leaders are visionary.

In the postindustrial paradigm, the two concepts are defined as distinct activities. One is not better than the other; they are simply different—and equally important—processes in a postindustrial world. Rost (1991) envisions the two roles playing out in formal organizations in this way:

> Leaders and collaborators are the people involved in a leadership relationship.... Managers and subordinates are the people involved in managerial relationships.... The two

sets of words are not synonymous. Leaders are not the same as managers. Collaborators are not the same as subordinates. Managers may be leaders but if they are leaders, they are involved in a relationship different from management. Subordinates may be collaborators, but if they are collaborators they are involved in a relationship different than management. Leaders need not be managers to be leaders. Collaborators need not be subordinates to be collaborators. (p. 150)

Rost asserts that the way in which influence is exercised is an important distinction between leadership and management. In his view, leadership is a relationship in which only noncoercive influence behaviors are acceptable, rather than one wherein all legitimate behaviors (including authority and other forms of coercion) are acceptable.

Some Additional Postindustrial Models of Leadership

Just as Rost specifically offered a new definition of leadership and labeled it the postindustrial paradigm, other scholars have also proposed new views of leadership in the face of the dramatic changes occurring in Western culture as we enter the new millennium. For example, Bensimon and Neumann (1993) draw from their own research, their analysis of others' research, and their own experiences in organizations to describe the ideal leader in the future. They conclude that the age of the heroic, solo leader is over. Collaborative leadership, they insist, is necessary to respond to the information-rich and complex environment of the twenty-first century. One mind can comprehend only so much; we need the combination of many minds to understand and solve complex problems. As Bensimon and Neumann see it:

> The ideal leader will be someone who knows how to find and bring together diverse minds—minds that reflect variety in their points of view, in their thinking processes and in their unique capacities as well as unique limitations. . . . Moreover, as the world grows more complex. . . it is likely that we will stop thinking of leadership as the property or quality of just one person. We will begin to think of it in its collective form: leadership as occurring among and through a group of people who think and act together. (p. 12)

In a study of college presidents and their administrative teams, Bensimon and Neumann found that the team builders who encouraged their teams to think in diverse rather than similar ways and to engage in a variety of tasks rather than following a strict division of labor were more likely to be associated with effective leadership. The authors conclude that the ability to build and maintain diverse, "thinking" teams is a critical skill for twenty-first century leadership.

Similarly, Margaret Wheatley (1992) advances the new paradigm of leadership in her work, which compares leadership and the new sciences of quantum and chaos theories. She notes, as have others, that the conventional (industrial) perspectives of organizations and leadership are heavily grounded in the principles of Newtonian physics, specifically, the belief in objectivity, linear causality, and control. These influences produce an emphasis on structure and parts, as well as on "our desire to control a reality that is slippery and evasive" (p. 25). In particular, the belief that we can control nature and thus organizations and people makes the Newtonian frame so seductive, and also so difficult to relinquish. However, Wheatley argues that the new sciences offer a much more realistic perspective on organizational reality and a better foundation for leadership in a new world.

In quantum physics she finds the grounding for participatory leadership: "...the quantum realm speaks emphatically to the role of participation, even to its impact on creating reality" (p. 143). She asks, if the universe is participatory, how can we fail to embrace this in our organizations and our leadership practices?

The participatory nature of reality has also focused attention on relationships. In her words, "Nothing exists at the subatomic level, or can be observed, without engagement with another energy source" (p. 14). Thus, in the frame of the new science we move from the separateness and objectivity of the industrial view of leadership to recognizing that leadership is always context-bound and that the context of leadership is established by the relationships we value. The lenses of the new science show us that leadership is a relational act.

Danah Zohar (1997) has continued and extended Wheatley's examination of the new science and its implications for leadership. In particular, Zohar argues that the separation of our lives into "public" and "private" realms is a legacy of Newtonian science. For example, in our public or work life, we are asked to engage our mental/intellectual abilities. We reserve our emotional and spiritual capacities for our private life with family and friends. Framing our world holistically (as we do in the new science), where everything is connected to everything else, we begin to recognize that it is an illusion to think that we bring only our intellectual self to our work in organizations. The recognition of the unbroken wholeness of our universe, and thus the drive to create connected, holistic organizations, compels leaders to take account of people's emotional and spiritual dimensions as well as the mental. As a result, there is a burgeoning interest in understanding and developing emotional intelligence (Goleman, 1998), as well as in nurturing the spiritual dimension of leaders and collaborators (Zohar, 2000; Mitroff & Denton, 1999). An emphasis for twenty-first century leaders is to create environments that call on and nurture all dimensions of the self—mental, emotional, and spiritual.

Writing from the Center for Creative Leadership, Drath and Palus (1994) offer yet another take on postindustrial leadership. They suggest that leadership is "meaning-making in a community of practice," and they contrast this definition with the conventional view in which leaders use dominance or influence to get followers to do what the individual leader wants. The Drath and Palus view of leadership is grounded in **constructivism,** which asserts that reality is a socially constructed phenomenon known only through our perception of it; that is, we use our own perceptual filters to make sense of what we experience. This meaning-making can be achieved individually or with others (socially). We are driven to make sense of things because meaning-making is an important human activity. It is, in fact, the way we come to understand ourselves and our world.

From this constructivist base, Drath and Palus propose that leadership accrues to those who can frame the experiences of those engaged in a shared activity in such a way that helps the group make sense of its actions. Leadership is the process of providing frameworks by which members of a community make sense of what they are doing, why they are doing it, and what they have learned from it.

> Meaning-making happens through such processes as identifying vision and mission, framing problems, setting goals, arguing and engaging in dialogue, theory building and testing, storytelling, and the making of contracts and agreements.... From an individual perspective, it is not so much that a person is first a leader and then creates meaning; it's more that, in making meaning a person comes to be called a leader.... It is the process of participating in making meaning in a collective sense that makes leaders out of people. (pp. 10–11)

Here again, we see that leadership is a relational process in which everyone in a community is engaged. The question for the leader, then, becomes not how to get individuals to do what needs to be done, but rather, how to create communities in which everyone, even those on the margins, can make important contributions. Bensimon and Neumann (1993) hold strikingly similar views with Drath and Palus about the purpose of leadership as meaning-making. They, too, define leadership as the shared construction of meaning.

> Leadership requires skill in the creation of meaning that is authentic to one's self and to one's community. It also requires the uncovering of meaning that is already embedded in others' minds, helping them to see what they already know, believe and value, and encouraging them to make new meaning. In this way, leadership generates leadership. (p. xv)

Rost, Bensimon and Neumann, Wheatley, and Drath and Palus are among the pioneers in defining new images of leadership. No doubt, as we move into the twenty-first century, the postindustrial paradigm of leadership will continue to be refined, modified, and elaborated on. Although still in its infant stages, with much work to be done before postindustrial leadership is widely accepted and fully embedded in our theory and practice, this leadership paradigm offers one clear theme: the age of the individual leader-hero is gone. As we look to the new millennium, leadership must be understood as a relationship, a collaborative process, a community of believers pursuing a transformational cause.

AARON FEUERSTEIN: THE MIRACLE AT MALDEN MILLS

It was nearly 11 P.M. when he heard the news. Aaron Feuerstein, CEO of Malden Mills of Lawrence, Massachusetts, had been celebrating his seventieth birthday on December 11, 1995, with family and friends when he heard about the six-alarm fire that was ravaging his plant.

Most employees were certain that this was the end of Malden Mills, best known as the primary source of the fleece material used by L.L. Bean and Patagonia to make jackets and pullovers. Said union representative Paul Coorey in a 1997 *Life* interview, "We were ready to hear that it was over."

Employee Jim Gillett added in a 1998 article in *George* magazine, "He was 70 years old and was going to get a big insurance settlement. Why would he want to run the risk of trying to rebuild?"

Coorey and Gillett had good reason to expect dire news. Not only was the plant totally destroyed, but for years relocation overseas had seemed the best plan to increase profitability and lower the labor costs of the 90-year-old family business. It was unfathomable to expect that Feuerstein, who had already kept the plant in the Lawrence area longer than most had anticipated, would do anything but take the $300 million in insurance money and close the plant.

But as the smoke was still simmering at the plant, Feuerstein stood in front of his 3,000 employees on December 14 and made a startling announcement. Not only was the plant going to rebuild in Lawrence, but he promised that all 3,000 employees would receive their full December paychecks plus a $275 Christmas bonus.

In January he announced that all employees would be paid an additional month's wages and benefits. In February, he made good on this pledge for a third month. By March, most employees had returned to full-time work. By midsummer, this figure was at 85 percent, leaving approximately 400 jobless. Feuerstein did not forget these displaced employees, extending their health benefits, helping them find new employment, and guaranteeing all their old jobs back when a new plant opened in 1997. By September 1997, all but 70 employees were back to work at Malden Mills. During the rebuilding process, he opened a training center where employees could work to improve their math, language, and computer skills in anticipation of opening a new plant.

An Orthodox Jew, Feuerstein leads through a combination of strong religious beliefs, particularly helping others in times of crisis, and hard-nosed business acumen. Said Feuerstein in a *Parade* interview in 1996, "Hillel (the great Hebrew scholar) said, 'In a situation where there is no righteous person, try to be a righteous person.'"

Some call Feuerstein a visionary, some call him a fool for "wasting" millions in pay and benefits to employees while significant portions of the mill were closed. Said Feuerstein in a 1997 *Life* story, "Other CEOs feel I'm sort of a stupid guy who doesn't know what to do with his money. But treating the workers fairly is good for the shareholder. I consider our workers an asset, not a cuttable expense. . . . When you do the right thing, you'll probably end up more profitable than if you did wrong."

Said Coorey, "He's unique, this company is unique. What he did here has put food on the tables of Merrimack Valley families for years and years."

SUMMARY

The story of leadership from the postindustrial perspective is quite different from the stories we have told until now. For the greater part of this century we have conceived of the leader as a person apart, whose purpose was to provide us with a vision to follow and with answers for our uncertainties. The postindustrial world does not offer us such simple solutions. In a time of rapid and complex change, it is unrealistic to expect one person to be the expert who solves all our problems. We need a different kind of leadership for a new world.

This chapter chronicles the evolution of the postindustrial paradigm of leadership. Several models of leadership served as precursors to the new paradigm, specifically servant leadership, transformational leadership, and the critical model of leadership. These models broke with the industrial paradigm view in several major ways: by describing leadership as a relationship versus the property of an individual, by defining leadership as a change process, and by recognizing that leadership is not confined to those who hold positional authority, but rather, is something that can be performed by anyone.

These transitional theories influenced the thinking of leadership scholars and led Joseph Rost (1991) to propose a definition of leadership that he labeled the postindustrial paradigm. Rost explained: "Leadership is an influence relationship among leaders and collaborators who intend real change that reflects their mutual purposes" (p. 7). The postindustrial perspectives envision leadership as a process done by both leaders and collaborators; a process of bringing diverse minds together in a collaborative effort to enact some kind of real change; a process through which people make meaning of their experience; and a process separate from management

CREATE YOUR OWN THEORY

Are you ready to be a twenty-first-century leader? Do you see yourself as a servant leader, a transformational leader, a collaborative leader…or perhaps some combination of the above? Do you believe in a relational approach or would you do better in a more mechanistic setting? These are but some of the questions we encourage you to ponder as you continue to develop your own theory on leadership. This chapter has presented a number of the most modern perspectives on leadership, but the perspective that matters most is your own.

Now let's revisit our opening Leadership Moment. How would a servant leader approach this situation? A critical transformational leader? If you were the new school board member, how would you proceed? Would your approach be reflective of the models put forth in this chapter? If so, in what way?

KEY TERMS

servant leadership
transactional leadership
transformational leadership
critical transformational leadership
mechanistic world view

relational approach
real change
collaborative leadership
constructivism

QUESTIONS FOR DISCUSSION AND REVIEW

1. What are the characteristics of servant leaders, according to Greenleaf? Why does he believe that servant-led institutions are most successful?

2. What are some of the primary lessons to be gleaned from John Woolman's crusade to eradicate slavery within the Society of Friends? Who are other examples of servant leaders?

3. Contrast transactional leadership with transformational leadership.

4. What are some of the core aspects of the critical model of leadership?

5. What are some of the common themes among servant, transformational, and critical models of leadership?

6. What are some of the societal and historical factors that have triggered movement away from the industrial paradigm and a mechanistic view of leadership?

7. What are Rost's four essential elements of leadership? Do you agree with his assessment? Why or why not?

8. What are some of the distinctions Rost makes between leaders and managers?

9. Think of your own experience doing leadership or your observations of leaders. Which characteristics of postindustrial leadership have you implemented yourself or seen implemented by others? What was the result? From these experiences and observations, what do you think it takes to successfully engage in leadership as a collaborative process?

10. Which elements of postindustrial leadership do you already practice? Which do you think would be most difficult for you to learn and why? Which aspects do you find most useful, and which aspects are the least useful?

11. Do you agree that the age of the individual leader is over? Why or why not?

12. Do you think that it is important to separate leadership and management and describe them as different processes? What do you see as the differences between the two?

EXERCISES

Exercise 10–1   Understanding Transition Theories

In his book *Imaginization,* Gareth Morgan (1993) graphically illustrates that the commonly used team metaphor for leadership is shaded with very different meanings for different individuals. The use of the team metaphor is helpful as we attempt to understand the differences between the industrial paradigm of leadership and the servant/leader and transformational theories of Greenleaf and Burns. Using a sports metaphor, please give an example of a sport (hockey, basketball, football, rowing, soccer, baseball, swimming, lacrosse, golf, bowling, horse racing, etc.) that illustrates leadership as defined in the industrial paradigm, the servant-leader model (Greenleaf), and the transformational leadership model of Burns.

SPORTS METAPHORS

INDUSTRIAL PARADIGM	SERVANT/LEADER MODEL	TRANSFORMATIONAL LEADERSHIP
1. Sport:	1. Sport:	1. Sport:
2. This is a good example because:	2. This is a good example because:	2. This is a good example because:
3. In this sport, the leader plays what role?	3. In this sport, the leader plays what role?	3. In this sport, the leader plays what role?
4. Could this leader play this sport so that it would fit into the other two categories?	4. Could this leader play this sport so that it would fit into the other two categories?	4. Could this leader play this sport so that it would fit into the other two categories?
5. How?	5. How?	5. How?

Exercise 10–2   Understanding the Organizational Culture Transformations

Step One: Identify three examples of bureaucratic/mechanistic forms of organizations (old culture) and three examples of the emerging ad hoc models of organizations (new culture). These examples can be drawn from business, industry, politics, government, volunteer, or service organizations.

Bureaucratic/Mechanistic Organizations (Old Cultures)	**Ad Hoc Organizations (New Cultures)**
1.	1.
2.	2.
3.	3.

Step Two: Answer the following questions about the examples you have given.

1. What are the major differences between the two types of organizations? Be specific.
2. Will the new ad hoc organization be as successful over the next 25 years as the older bureaucratic/mechanistic organizations were for the past 25 years? Why or why not?
3. Which type of organization would you be most comfortable working in?
4. Which is easier to lead?
5. Do they require the same types of leaders?

Exercise 10–3   Understanding Differences Between the Industrial Model and Rost's Postindustrial Model of Leadership

Directions: Part One: Fill in the chart highlighting the differences between Rost's postindustrial model and the industrial model of leadership by placing choices A–L in either the "Industrial Model" or "Rost's Postindustrial Model" column.

A.   This has a bureaucratic view of organizations.

B.   Relationships are based on influence rather than positional authority.

C.   Collaborators and leaders intend real change.

D.   Model is grounded in rational, linear, and quantitative assumptions.

E.   *Leadership* and *management* are often used interchangeably.

F.   Leadership is dominated by goal achievement sense of purpose.

G.   Leaders and their collaborators *do* leadership.

H.   A leader's vision, style, objectives, and personal characteristics determine desired outcomes.

I.   This has flexible, multidirectional, ad hoc view of organization.

J.   Leadership and management are two distinct and equally important processes.

K.   Changes that leaders and their collaborators pursue must reflect their mutual purposes.

L.   Model has an individualistic focus—only great leaders do leadership.

INDUSTRIAL MODEL	ROST'S POSTINDUSTRIAL MODEL
1.	1.
2.	2.
3.	3.
4.	4.
5.	5.
6.	6.

Directions: Part Two: Arrange the six descriptive phrases for each model in a "point–counterpoint format," so that the descriptive phrase under the Industrial Model is balanced on the Postindustrial side of the chart with its opposite.

INDUSTRIAL MODEL	ROST'S POSTINDUSTRIAL MODEL
1.	1.
2.	2.
3.	3.
4.	4.
5.	5.
6.	6.

CHAPTER 11

Practicing Leadership: It's Your Turn

"We use journey as a metaphor for how we come to understand leadership over the centuries."

"Leadership is a personal journey."

*T*hese quotes from the book's opening chapter help end it as well. You have effectively ended this portion of your leadership journey by completing this course of study. What does it all mean? What have you really learned? What are the "take aways" those ideas that make sense as you attempt to answer the ultimate final exam for this journey: What is Leadership?

We suggest that you attempt to answer that complicated question by completing the exercise that follows. When finished, you should have a personal leadership road sign that briefly details the most important features of your own leadership theory. Remember, as you attempt to describe the various leadership components, this text begins and ends with practicing leadership. Therefore, answer or complete the segments as you intend to practice leadership in the real world.

Table 11–1 provides a road map of where we have been and an atlas of destinations visited, or authors, models, and theories studied.

TABLE 11–1 The Leadership Journey

Destinations	Concepts to Remember
Getting Started	"Leadership is one of the most observed and least understood phenomena on earth."
	Our basic assumptions:
	1. Where we are in our understanding of leadership is a function of where we have been.
	2. There is no one formula for leadership.
	3. Leadership is not differentiated by setting.
	4. Our understanding of leadership requires the vantage point of multiple perspectives.

(continued)

TABLE 11–1   The Leadership Journey (*Continued*)

Destinations	Concepts to Remember
	5. Studying leadership across a range of human differences is the only way to approach the subject in the twenty-first century.
	6. Leadership can best be understood through metaphors and described indirectly through paradigms.
	7. Leadership is a verb. It is what you "do," not only how you think.
Psychology	The nature or nurture distinction is a myth. All of us are a *combination* of our genetics and our experiences; our personalities are shaped by each.
	Effective leaders understand the dynamics of personality differences and know how to motivate others to achieve their potential.
Management, Quality, and Team Building	Although the effects of management were felt more than 200 years ago during the Industrial Revolution as factories developed, it is only in this century that its impact has been systematically studied. Taylor, Fayol, and Weber were the forefathers of the burgeoning classical approach to management.
	Although the words are frequently used interchangeably, *management* and *leadership* are not the same thing. A person can be skilled as a leader or manager or both—or neither.
	Management is often described by Mintzberg's 10 primary roles or Yukl's fundamental processes.
	Although classical management theory stated that there is only one best way to resolve an issue, today there is widespread agreement with the contingency theory model (House and Fiedler).
	The quality movement gained widespread popularity in Japan after World War II as the country's businesses tried to rebuild.
	Deming (perhaps the best-known of the "quality gurus") developed control charts and a 14-point quality plan.
	Juran published the *Quality Control Handbook*, which many people still consider the quality bible, and created a 10-point quality improvement model. In addition, he emphasized his trilogy: quality planning, quality control, and quality improvements.
Communication	Communication is a transactional process. Both the sender and the receiver of a communication filter what they hear and see into their own personal sets and the success of a given communication is based in large part on the degree to which sender and receiver are aware of and understand these sets.

(continued)

TABLE 11–1   The Leadership Journey (*Continued*)

Destinations	Concepts to Remember
	Communication is multifaceted. It can come in verbal form or it can be nonverbal. It can come through formal channels or it can come via the grapevine. One must be aware of the source and context of a particular communication if one is to interpret this communication as it was intended.
	Among the factors that can lead to communication breakdowns are differing frames of reference, selective perception, semantic problems, filtering, constraints on time, and communication overload.
	Charismatic leadership involves a relationship between a leader and the persons being led in which the leader is believed to possess inspirational charismatic qualities. Charismatic leaders are capable of introducing quantum change, sometimes for the better and sometimes for the worse (Adolf Hitler was a charismatic leader).
Cultural Anthropology	Cultural anthropology is the study of the development of human cultures. Culture is the totality of societal relationships between variables like words, behaviors, and physical symbols and the meaning that we attach to them.
	Cultures can and do change. Culture exists in a constant state of change because the relationship between what is taught and what is learned is not absolute. What is taught is translated through an individual's cultural lens.
	Leaders who are culturally flexible can build rapport with people who hold different assumptions, values/beliefs, and behaviors.
	There are several definitions of culture, each with its own implications for leaders. Among the common adjectives used to describe culture is that it is topical, historical, behavioral, normative, functional, mental, structural or symbolic. Every individual views culture through his or her own lens.
Political Science and Presidential Leadership	Power is something used by many people for many purposes. Among these are to obtain influence. Seven common tactics for obtaining influence are reason, friendliness, sanctions, bargaining, higher authority, assertiveness, and coalition-building.
	The five sources of power are *expert power* (based on knowledge or competence), *referent power* (based on relationship and personal "drawing power"), *legitimate power* (bestowed by formal organization), *reward power* (the ability to offer and withhold types of incentives), and *coercive power* (the ability to force someone to comply through threat of physical, psychological, or emotional consequences).

(continued)

TABLE 11–1   The Leadership Journey (*Continued*)

Destinations	Concepts to Remember
	Another way to view power is to distinguish between personal and positional power. Positional power is derived from one's place in an organization while personal power is derived from an individual's personal attributes.
	The presidency of the United States is the most powerful position in the world. The modern-day president's powers are at once defined by the parameters put forth by the Constitutional Convention and evolution and expansion of this position since that time. FDR can be considered the first "modern president." Among his legacies is the shift of power toward the president and away from Congress.
Military Science	Persons with military backgrounds abound in all segments of corporate, university, and private life and the lessons of military leadership are instructive well beyond the military setting.
	The 14 core leadership traits within the U.S. military model include: dependability, bearing, courage, decisiveness, endurance, enthusiasm, initiative, integrity, judgment, justice, knowledge, tact, unselfishness, and loyalty. Many military students believe that, of all these traits, integrity is the most important.
	The 11 core leadership principles of the U.S. military are know yourself and seek self-improvement, be technically proficient, develop a sense of responsibility among your subordinates, make sound and timely decisions, lead by example, keep your people informed and look out for their welfare, keep your people informed, seek and take responsibility for your actions, make sure that assigned tasks are understood, supervised, and accomplished, train your people as a team, and employ your unit in accordance with its capabilities. Leading by example is the most important leadership principle of all.
Practicing Leadership in a Multicultural Society	"Our scarcest resource is globally literate leaders." Multicultural leadership allows you to respond to diverse cultures by increasing your insights into each population's needs and worldview.
	Diversity is best viewed as a kaleidoscope, encompassing many layers of who we are as individuals and as members of society.
	What are the characteristics of multicultural leaders? Great multicultural leaders have the ability to generate social capital across cultures, demonstrate multicultural literacy (defined as the skills, insights, and attitudes that allow one to continuously learn from diverse individuals and places), and are skilled in creating and sustaining a rich teaching environment.

(continued)

TABLE 11-1   The Leadership Journey (*Continued*)

Destinations	Concepts to Remember
	The Platinum Rule: "Do unto others as they would like for you to do unto them."
Modern Leadership Theories	Gardner and Bennis detail the functions, competencies, and attributes of leaders.
	Behavioral theories assume that leader behaviors, rather than personality characteristics, exert the most influence on followers.
	Although the Ohio State and University of Michigan studies vary, both centered on two aspects of a manager: concern for people and concern for performance. Most individuals seem predisposed to favor one concern over the other.
Leadership in the Twenty-first Century	James Rost has constructed what he terms the *post-industrial* model of leadership—the kind of leadership, he asserts, that will be absolutely necessary in the twenty-first century.
	There are four essential elements of practicing leadership as envisioned by Rost:
	1. The leader-collaborator relationship is based on influence rather than positional authority.
	2. Leaders and their collaborators practice leadership together.
	3. Collaborators and their leaders intend real change.
	4. The changes that leaders and their collaborators pursue reflect their mutual purposes.
Appendix I	Remnants of the Greek portrait of a leader: decisive, physical prowess; a warrior's guile; and protection of followers are still very widely held even today.
	Plato's notion that leaders possessed inborn traits is echoed by much of the modern literature.
	Machiavelli argued that a leader's primary task was to subordinate simply being "good" for other more attractive ends (power, order, stability, skill at calculation, manipulation, and seeming to possess virtuous qualities). Successful princes (leaders) did not hesitate to take what they desired by force.

Figures 11–1 and 11–2, in conjunction with Exercise 11–1, ask that you describe where and how you intend to practice leadership in your own life.

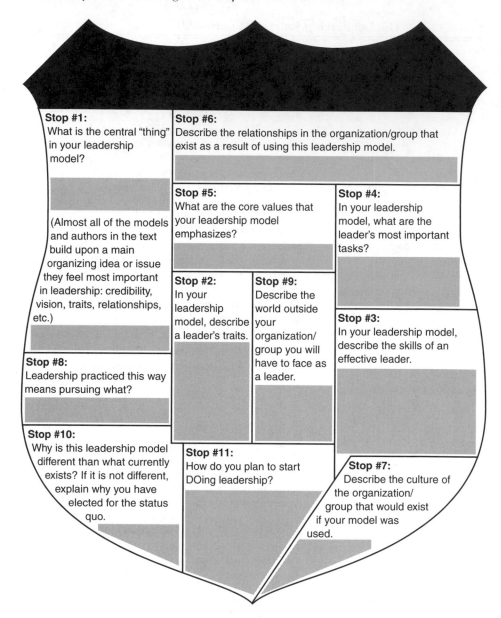

Stop #1:
What is the central "thing" in your leadership model?

(Almost all of the models and authors in the text build upon a main organizing idea or issue they feel most important in leadership: credibility, vision, traits, relationships, etc.)

Stop #8:
Leadership practiced this way means pursuing what?

Stop #10:
Why is this leadership model different than what currently exists? If it is not different, explain why you have elected for the status quo.

Stop #6:
Describe the relationships in the organization/group that exist as a result of using this leadership model.

Stop #5:
What are the core values that your leadership model emphasizes?

Stop #2:
In your leadership model, describe a leader's traits.

Stop #9:
Describe the world outside your organization/group you will have to face as a leader.

Stop #11:
How do you plan to start DOing leadership?

Stop #4:
In your leadership model, what are the leader's most important tasks?

Stop #3:
In your leadership model, describe the skills of an effective leader.

Stop #7:
Describe the culture of the organization/group that would exist if your model was used.

Figure 11–1   **What is leadership and how do I intend to practice it in a business/professional/organizational setting?**

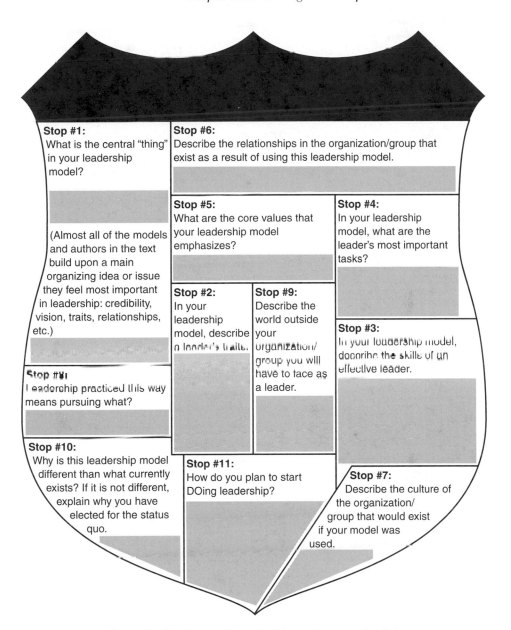

Stop #1:
What is the central "thing" in your leadership model?

(Almost all of the models and authors in the text build upon a main organizing idea or issue they feel most important in leadership: credibility, vision, traits, relationships, etc.)

Stop #8:
Leadership practiced this way means pursuing what?

Stop #10:
Why is this leadership model different than what currently exists? If it is not different, explain why you have elected for the status quo.

Stop #6:
Describe the relationships in the organization/group that exist as a result of using this leadership model.

Stop #5:
What are the core values that your leadership model emphasizes?

Stop #2:
In your leadership model, describe a leader's traits.

Stop #9:
Describe the world outside your organization/group you will have to face as a leader.

Stop #11:
How do you plan to start DOing leadership?

Stop #4:
In your leadership model, what are the leader's most important tasks?

Stop #3:
In your leadership model, describe the skills of an effective leader.

Stop #7:
Describe the culture of the organization/group that would exist if your model was used.

Figure 11–2   What is leadership and how do I intend to practice it in my personal/social life?

EXERCISE

Exercise 11–1   What Is Leadership?: Key for Figures 11–1 and 11–2

What is leadership? How do I "do" leadership in my everyday life at work, home, and play? How do I intend to practice it in a business/professional/organizational setting and in my personal/social life?

Stop #1: What is the central thing in your leadership model? (Almost all the models and authors studied in the text build on a main organizing idea or issue they feel most important in leadership credibility, vision, traits, relationships, etc.)

Stop #2: In your leadership model, describe a leader's traits.

Stop #3: Using your leadership model, describe the skills of an effective leader.

Stop #4: In your leadership model, what are a leader's most important tasks?

Stop #5: What are the *core values* that your leadership model emphasizes?

Stop #6: Describe the relationships in the organizational group that exist as a result of using this leadership model.

Stop #7: Describe the culture of the organization/group that would exist if your model were used.

Stop #8: Leadership practiced this way means pursuing what?

Stop #9: Describe the world outside your organization/group that you will have to face as a leader.

Stop #10: Why is this leadership model different from what currently exists? If it is not different, explain why you have elected for the status quo.

Stop #11: How do you plan to start practicing leadership?

How We Got Here: Premodern Thoughts on Leadership

The conception of leadership, especially as defined by the current text, is intimately connected with the evolution of business organizations that do not originate far back in history. Chandler (1977), in fact, sees the rise of a professional class of business leaders as a nineteenth-century phenomenon.

The Greeks of the classical age had no shortage of great leaders, and they even made the matter of leadership an explicit issue for detailed inquiry, but they were specifically addressing military, moral, and political leadership. The profile of human excellence that emerges from these inquiries is useful for determining what the ideal leadership characteristics are in the abstract, whether they manifest on the battlefield, in daily life, or in the corporate board room.

Our proposal is to look at how leadership is treated in the moral and political sense, since that is a paradigm case of leadership that can be detected in philosophical works as old as the discipline itself. From these studies we will attempt to extract the abstract qualities that make a person an effective leader. Indeed, we shall title these sections to reflect the primary attributes that the thinker argued are central to effective leadership.

THE GREEKS: THE LEADER AS HARMONIZER AND TEACHER

Leadership became an issue in Greece first and foremost in the military sense with the *Iliad* of Homer. That document, set against the epic struggle of the Trojan War, provides many personifications of how leadership was understood in a society presided over by a warrior nobility. The warrior was different from the farmer because he served a different function. What is more, one can perform this function well or poorly. To perform one's function well, one must cultivate the appropriate *arete;* that is, the appropriate virtue or excellence that enables the possessor to perform well. Homer's multiple characters provide a dimension of the warrior's excellence. As Werner Jaeger (1965) writes, "The ideal of decisive action and physical prowess belongs to Ajax, cunning and warrior's guile to Odysseus, the unity of both of these qualities, as well as the possession of many other attributes belonging to the ideal warrior, are found in Achilles."

Yet, by the time of the Classical Age of Athens several centuries later, life had changed significantly from that of the Homeric heroes. No longer a warrior society, the Athens of Pericles was an accomplished economic power with a bustling sea-borne foreign trade. What's more, aristocracy had given way to democracy, empowering many more people from many different social classes. To these people, the heroes of the *Iliad* led lives very unlike their own. Thus, this ideal of leadership needed to be supplemented.

This was the Athens of Socrates (470–399 B.C.). As a philosopher, Socrates' pupil Plato made the problems of morality and politics central. In his treatment of the ideal city, the subject of the **ideal leader** becomes a dominant issue.

Plato's *Republic*: Ideal Leader in the Ideal City

In the multilayered dialogue of the *Republic*, **Plato** engaged a wide range of issues central to the moral and political life of human beings. His treatment in the *Republic* of justice, politics, morality, and education, as well as the more speculative issues of the nature of knowledge and reality, provide an excellent summary statement of Plato's thought at that point in his life.

Before presenting the ideal city presided over by ideal rulers, Plato articulated a portrait of the political status quo. What emerges is a vision of a cynical society that has turned its back on traditional religious values and replaced them with a thor-ough-going relativism based on the primacy of power and self-interest.

The fundamental premise is that it is human nature to be self-interested. People are motivated by the desire to expand their power over other people and over desir-able objects—wealth, influence, position, and so on. The population can be divided into those who are weak and those who are strong. The strong take their opportuni-ties as they arise, while the weak are reluctant to do so. Laws are fabricated restraints placed on human desire and are created in the attempt to introduce some degree of order into this chaotic situation. Since laws run contrary to human desire, in that laws serve as obstacles to human will, they are selectively obeyed: the strong will obey the law only when they must—when the fear of being caught and punished is real. When such a threat is not present, the strong will break the law and thus satisfy their desires.

Assuming a self-interested human nature, coupled with the conviction that there are no absolute meanings to core value conceptions, the leader is that individual who is cunning enough to dupe others into entrusting him or her with power. As the shepherd, the leader appears to have the best interests—the comfort and security—of the flock at heart. In reality, and unbeknownst to the flock, the leader's real con-cerns are to advance his or her own interests at the people's expense.

Thus, the qualities of the ideal leader in this view are strength, cunning, and the ability to cultivate a believable façade. Such leaders manipulate the public for their own advantage. The public believes that their leaders love them and genuinely want their safety, security, and happiness. Yet, in the end this ruler desires nothing differ-ent than the shepherd, and the public is like so many unknowing sheep.

This is the position that **Socrates** must refute. In the course of his construction of the ideal city, we find that the exceptional few who will be its leaders are distinguished by certain talents that are then refined by a specially tailored education, with the result being a cultivation of wisdom.

It is clear that in Plato's opinion, not everybody is suited for this leadership role. Potential rulers are chosen from the population because they possess certain inborn traits and because of the lessons they have learned from experience. Consequently, Plato selected those who love unchanging truth, hate untruth, are moderate with money, are neither petty nor mean, do not fear death, and have a good memory. This is the philosophical nature that serves as the basis for the true leader's character. On their own, these characteristics do not guarantee a good leader; rather, they are the starting points for cultivating the quality of leadership.

The proper education can refine these qualities to the point where the excellence of wisdom emerges. Such truth is found only in the realm of abstract thought, which requires the development and exercise of the highest intellectual capacities found in the human mind. The educational curriculum relies on mathematics and philosophy, which orient the mind toward the abstract, the universal, the unchanging; in short, the Truth. These abstract ideas, called **Forms,** are the carriers of universal and immutable truth.

The ultimate Form for Plato, however, was the Form of the Good. Knowledge of the Good is the most abstract and difficult knowledge to master. It is so complex that in a dialogue, Socrates admitted to his friends that he himself was incapable of providing a ready definition of this Form.

Yet so much hangs in the balance. Without knowledge of the Good, the rest of our knowledge will come to little. Our deliberate actions will be foiled.

Thus, the ideal city constructed by Plato is an intellectual aristocracy, governed by the elite who, in contemplating the Good, have acquired the virtue of wisdom. Wisdom is viewed as the ability to make sound judgments, not about particular matters, but rather "about the city as a whole and the betterment of its relations with itself and other states." The men and women who possess this wisdom will translate their abstract knowledge of the Good into concrete practices: good laws, good public policy, a coherent and excellent program of education, all to the benefit of those who live in the city.

Socrates meant to illustrate that the truly wise ruler leads in order that those who are led can develop their potential as human beings and thereby prosper. In one metaphor, the ruler is compared to the physician, who alone among all people is permitted to administer harsh medicines to sick patients to effect a cure. The physician is permitted to do this because it is only the physician who possesses the special knowledge required to administer such drugs. The leader must likewise attend to the benefit of the led. This daunting task may require that the ruler does things that, like medicine, result in short-term pain. The ultimate goal, however, is the same as that of the physician: the well-being of those to whom the leader attends.

Plato depicted the leader as harmonizer of people, as the improver of those whom he or she leads, and as an individual of rare intellectual qualities.

THOMAS AQUINAS: THE LEADER AS PROVIDER OF RESOURCES AND GUIDE TO OTHERS

Conspicuous on the intellectual scene of the thirteenth century was **Thomas Aquinas** (1225–1274, A.C.E.). Christianity had become the official religion of the late Roman Empire, and thus was also an intellectual focal point for the world that had succeeded the Roman era. Early Christian authors, such as St. Augustine (354–430, A.C.E.), had developed philosophies incorporating Platonic ideas within the framework of the Christian religion. The result was a rich lineage of Christian Platonism that numbered among its company such figures as Augustine, Anselm, and Bonaventure. Theirs was a hierarchical universe with God standing at the summit. In many ways, the human world was a microcosmic version of the universe, and the traveler in that universe, the human soul, must by its own choices proceed to union with God.

Aquinas drew from this tradition, as well. However, unlike his predecessors, he had to reconcile the Christian and Platonic threads of his thought with the newly recovered works of Aristotle, which had been lost to the Christian West since the emperor Justinian closed the Greek philosophical schools in the sixth century. During this period, the great Arab thinkers of the Middle Ages had studied the works of Aristotle closely. Much of Aristotle was not as compatible with Christian ideas as was Plato. Thomas Aquinas came of age in this period of cultural turmoil, and his great achievement was creating a new Christian philosophy that accommodated the obvious genius of Aristotle.

His writing on politics offers an insight into the qualities to be found in the ideal leader. His ideal monarch has the qualities derived from the divine model. A determinate feature of reality is that there is always a distinction between the part that rules and that which is ruled. Aquinas wrote that

> in all things that are ordained towards one end, one thing is found to rule the rest. So, too, in the individual man, the soul rules the body. Likewise among the members of a body, one, such as the heart or the head, is the principle and moves all the others. Therefore in every multitude there must be some governing power.

Thus, he wrote, "Let the king recognize that such is the office which he undertakes, namely, that he is to be in the kingdom what the soul is in the body, and what God is in the world." In discovering what God does in the universe, one discovers what "it is incumbent upon a king to do."

The king emerges as a teacher of virtue as well as the caretaker of human needs. The effective leader "should have as his principal concern the means by which the multitude subject to him may live well." Cultivation is crucial to living well, and the monarch must undertake this as a primary task. Beyond providing the goods needed for a comfortable life, the king must do what is necessary to cultivate virtue in his subjects. His efforts must lie in the direction of the continual improvement of his subjects. The ideal leader gives his subjects what they need to be as fully human as they can be. The result is the happiness of this world and the divine bliss of the next.

The ideal leader, given Thomas Aquinas's political ideas, assumes the role of teacher, improver, and moral paradigm for the people who are led. By embodying the highest standards of behavior in terms of goodness and nobility, leaders contribute to the improvement of those who look to them for leadership. The overall result is a community that approximates the ideal of a self-sufficient and thriving union of individuals, each of whom enjoys the resources needed to function in an optimally human manner.

MACHIAVELLI'S PRINCE: THE LEADER AS CONTROLLER OF FORTUNE

In sharp contrast to the God-centered, Christian world-view of Thomas Aquinas are the very worldly, realistic, and unflinching views of **Niccolo Machiavelli** (1469–1527), a career diplomat immersed in the political intrigues of the Florence of his day. He wrote *The Prince* during his enforced leisure following the expulsion of the Medici as a summary of what he learned during his years of practical experience. Machiavelli addressed the work to Lorenzo de'Medici to exhort him to unify Italy.

With Machiavelli we pass into a world more familiar to the modern reader. Like ours, his society was commercial, with the primary form of wealth no longer land but money. The powerful were those who engaged in commerce in some manner as merchants, traders, or bankers. Indeed, what he says about the political life of the prince is readily applicable to the uncertain and risky world of commercial affairs.

Machiavelli's name has become synonymous with one who delights in manipulation, without scruples in doing what it takes to achieve an apparent good. Suggestive of calculation, manipulation, and the desire for power, *The Prince* does not disappoint on a cursory first reading. He describes the prince as one who would establish a new principality not by inheritance, but rather through force. The leadership qualities Machiavelli set down figure against this backdrop.

First, Machiavelli was loath to construct any ideal city or ruler who lived solely in the imagination. His gaze was directed purely and without apology at this world. He spoke not about human failings, nor did he lament that humans are not better than they are. Rather than creating utopia, Machiavelli sought to give the future ruler the best possible advice about dealing with friends, enemies, conflict, flatterers, and the ever-changing tides of fortune.

Human beings reveal themselves as less than the image of God. Governed by desire and greed, they take offense at minor injuries, break faith without regret, and switch loyalties with startling speed. The prince, he said, who would be successful in such a world must be a student of military affairs and must comb history for the appropriate role models to emulate:

imitate the fox and the lion, for the lion cannot protect itself from traps, and the fox cannot defend himself from wolves. One must therefore be a fox to recognize traps, and a lion to frighten wolves....Therefore, a prudent ruler ought not to keep faith when by so doing it would be against his interest, and when the reasons which made him bind himself no longer exist. If men were all good, this precept would not be a good one; but as they are bad and would not observe faith with you, so you are not bound to keep faith with them.

Gone is the inclination to view the successful leader as a microcosmic god, as Aquinas had, or as the optimally human philosopher-ruler, as Plato had. Machiavelli asserted that there are times when others must be pampered and times when they must be crushed, times when one must be kind and times when one must be cruel. The prince who learns this will be successful; the prince who insists on being virtuous rather than merely appearing to be so will come to ruin.

In terms of the personal qualities of the prince, Machiavelli was no less cynical in his approach. While Plato spent much time defining the virtues necessary for the proper functioning of human beings and Aquinas stressed the cultivation of virtue among the vital projects the monarch must undertake to lead the people, Machiavelli offered a startling alternative view. In the turbulent world of political power and intrigue, the actual possession of virtues may be less advantageous than vice. Addressing the qualities of mercy, faithfulness, humanity, sincerity, and piety, Machiavelli wrote that it is not necessary for the prince to actually possess these qualities,

> but it is very necessary to seem to have them. I would even be bold to say that to possess them and always observe them is dangerous, but to appear to have them is useful. Thus it is well to seem merciful, faithful, humane, sincere, religious and to be so; but you must have the mind so disposed that when it is needful to be otherwise you may be able to change to the opposite qualities.

Neither Plato nor Aquinas could have put another end above the pursuit of the Good. In stating that the end justified the means, Machiavelli subordinated the Good to some other, more attractive end. This end includes power, order, and stability.

Fortune, what Machiavelli called "the ruler of half our actions," also assumes significance for the leader. He called fortune the chance element in events, and in colorful, sometimes notorious metaphors, likened it to a river raging out of control and a woman who can only be brought under control by the bold and impetuous young man who will conquer her by force. Above all else, he asserted, the effective prince must be able to foresee future contingencies so that he can bring them under control. The successful prince will be able to do this most of the time; nevertheless, even the most successful can't completely control fortune.

With Machiavelli, we experience the beginnings of the passage to modernity. Neither the transcendent values of the ancient world, the religious values of the medieval world, nor the artistic values of the Renaissance worlds are prized here. Leadership, instead, lives within a complicated matrix of greed, faithlessness, power, and chance. The task of the leader is to secure some degree of stability, order, and control in this swirling maelstrom of experience. Even the most effective leaders live precarious existences that are only as secure as their control over the ultimately unforeseeable.

HOBBES AND LOCKE: THE LEADER AS MEDIATOR OF INDIVIDUAL SELF-INTEREST

The seventeenth century was a period of turmoil in England. Along with the international conflicts with the Dutch, the domestic scene saw the scourge of civil war, the execution of the king, the turbulence of Cromwell, and ultimately, the victory of Parliament over the monarch in the Glorious Revolution of 1688–89. During this period of upheaval, England nurtured two of her greatest political theorists, **Thomas Hobbes** (1588–1679) and **John Locke** (1632–1704). The problem of legitimate and effective political leadership stood at the core of their respective philosophies.

Thomas Hobbes

Despite England's insularity, Thomas Hobbes followed the Continent's intellectual developments closely, especially regarding the new science being fashioned by Galileo and Descartes. Hobbes's insight was that human beings likewise emerge as material bodies in motion, with a native desire for power. Human life becomes, then, a ceaseless quest for power, and the pursuit of those things that accrue greater power. He concluded that such a nature will, in the absence of strong laws and governmental authority, convert social life into the war of each against all.

In his most celebrated chapter of *Leviathan*, Hobbes described the natural human condition as one of universal war, a world of perpetual violence and fear in which the life of human beings is "solitary, poore, nasty, brutish, and short." Just as the moving material bodies in nature, he saw human beings in motion in the political world, inevitably colliding over the pursuit of objects that promise to expand power. Without a powerful leader, political society, he said, cannot avoid the cataclysm of civil war.

However, Hobbes offered a solution: the **Laws of Nature,** which reason is able to discover, lay down the precepts that rescue humans from the civil war of their natural condition and pave the way to the peace of civil society. These laws instruct humans to seek peace, to fight with every advantage of war should peace not be possible, and to be content with that amount of liberty that one will allow all others to possess as well. His solution was to create sovereign power by a contractual agreement made by all those who live in society.

Yet, the peace that these laws establish is fragile. Human desire for power, and their willingness to dominate others in its pursuit, is simply too strong.

The primary attributes that the effective leader must possess, according to Hobbes, are strength and the ability to instill sufficient fear to keep the subjects obeying their agreements. Recall that human nature is self-interested, and that in the absence of a strong sovereign there is nothing but chaos.

John Locke

Locke proceeded from a statement of human nature in which humans are capable of reason yet also susceptible to passions. Reason, he said, indicates to all who consider it that all human beings have a right to life, liberty, health, and possessions.

The Law of Nature goes on to counsel respect for each other human being as a locus of reason and these rights. However, humans are not unfailingly rational. Passion encourages some to desire what others possess, and in the absence of organized society and political authority, humans will soon slide into a state of war. Passion will incline some to violate others' rights to life, liberty, and possessions. The legislative power is the primary function of governmental leadership, which he defined as the power "which has a right to direct how the force of the commonwealth shall be employed for preserving the community and the members of it." The executive power that carries out the laws must reside somewhere else and is "visibly subordinate and accountable" to the law-making function of government.

For Locke, fundamental decisions about policy should be made at a broadly based level with much participation. The executive leader acts on the decisions thus made and carries them out in the interest of the community. Failure to do this effectively results in the recall of the executive power.

Both Hobbes and Locke envisioned leadership in terms of keeping peace among the members of society, although the difficulty of doing this varies. Hobbes paints a more cynical picture in which the desire for power is so fundamental and overpowering that the leader must resort to fear as the primary mechanism for leadership. Locke, on the other hand, sees humans in more rational control of their lives, capable of rectifying the disruptions that are sparked by passion. The leader, according to Locke, guarantees that each respects the rights of others and refrains from their violation. Beyond that, leadership remains outside of people's lives, allowing them to pursue their own interests without undue interference.

SUMMARY

In this appendix, we trace the evolution of Western philosophical views of leadership. Beginning with the Greeks, Plato's notions of leaders as harmonizers and teachers are discussed. St. Thomas Aquinas's view that leaders must embody the highest standards of behavior is then presented. In marked contrast are Machiavelli's writings, steeped in the political intrigue of his day. The appendix ends with a discussion of the views of Hobbes and Locke.

KEY TERMS

ideal leader
Plato
Socrates
Forms
Thomas Aquinas

Niccolo Machiavelli
Thomas Hobbes
John Locke
laws of nature

QUESTIONS FOR DISCUSSION AND REVIEW

1. What are some of Plato's views on the nature of human beings and the characteristics of the ideal leader?

2. How did Socrates' conceptualization of a leader differ from that of Plato?
3. How did Thomas Aquinas's work contribute to our understanding of leadership? What characteristics did he equate with the ideal leader?
4. According to Machiavelli, why should leaders imitate foxes and lions?
5. What are the Laws of Nature, and how are they beneficial, according to Hobbes?
6. How do Hobbes and Locke differ in terms of their views on the amount of control people have over their lives?
7. How are the views of each of the individuals presented in this appendix reflective of the culture and historical time period in which they lived?

EXERCISE

Exercise A–1   Summarizing Four Views of Leadership

Directions: For each of the statements below write the name of the philosopher(s) who hold that view:

Philosopher(s)

1 Leaders were:
   A. Princes who establish new principalities by force   A. Machiavelli
   B. An elite intellectual aristocracy   B. Hobbes
   C. Warrior nobility   C.
   D. Ideal monarchs   D.

2. Leaders were leaders because:
   A. They derived their qualities from the divine   A.
      model and functioned as microcosmic gods
   B. They had a different function and because they   B.
      cultivated the appropriate arete
   C. They excelled at calculation, manipulation, and   C.
      were driven by a desire for power.
   D. They possessed certain inborn traits—through   D.
      proper education these qualities were refined
      and excellence of wisdom emerged
3. Leadership qualities included:
   A. *Seeming* to be merciful, faithful, humane, sincere,   A.
      religious, but with the ability to switch to opposite
      qualities if necessary

    B.   A contemplative wisdom and love of truth, being   B.
       moderate with money, and being neither petty
       nor mean

    C.   Decisive action, physical prowess, and cunning,   C.
       with a warrior's guile

    D.   Embodying the highest standards of behavior in terms   D.
       of goodness and nobility

4.   A leader's primary task was to:

    A.   Demonstrate the virtue of wisdom, to make sound   A.
       judgments—good laws, good public policy, and an
       excellent program of education

    B.   Be a teacher of virtue as well as a provider of resources   B.

    C.   Protect society by prowess as a warrior   C.

    D.   Subordinate the good to another, more attractive end   D.
       (power, order, stability)

Answer Key:

1C. Greeks

1D. Aquinas

2A. Aquinas

2B. Greeks

2C. Machiavelli

2D. Hobbes

3A. Machiavelli

3B. Hobbes

3C. Greeks

3D. Aquinas

4A. Hobbes

4B. Aquinas

4C. Greeks

4D. Machiavelli

For additional content concerning Summaries of Popular Leadership Works (Appendix II) and Leader's Bookshelf and References (Appendix III), please visit the Wiley Web site at www.wiley.com/college/shriberg.

INDEX

Page references in bold type indicate persons discussed in a Leadership Profile. Terms beginning with numbers are indexed as if spelled out.